# Culture on drugs

MANCHESTER
1824

Manchester University Press

# Culture on drugs

Narco-cultural studies of high modernity

*Dave Boothroyd*

**Manchester University Press**

Manchester and New York

*distributed exclusively in the USA by Palgrave*

*Published by* Manchester University Press
Oxford Road, Manchester M13 9NR, UK
*and* Room 400, 175 Fifth Avenue, New York, NY 10010, USA
www.manchesteruniversitypress.co.uk

*Distributed exclusively in the USA by*
Palgrave, 175 Fifth Avenue, New York,
NY 10010, USA

*Distributed exclusively in Canada by*
UBC Press, University of British Columbia, 2029 West Mall,
Vancouver, BC, Canada V6T 1Z2

*British Library Cataloguing-in-Publication Data*
A catalogue record for this book is available from the British Library

*Library of Congress Cataloging-in-Publication Data applied for*

ISBN     0 7190 5598 9     *hardback*
EAN      978 0 7190 5598 0
ISBN     0 7190 5599 7     *paperback*
EAN      978 0 7190 5599 7

First published 2006

15  14  13  12  11  10  09  08  07  06          10 9 8 7 6 5 4 3 2 1

Typeset in Minion and Rotis display
by Koinonia, Manchester
Printed in Great Britain
by Bell & Bain Ltd, Glasgow

*For my mother and in memory of my father*

Wisdom: that seems to the rabble to be a kind of flight, an artifice and means for getting oneself out of a dangerous game; but the genuine philosopher – as he seems to *us*, my friends? – lives 'unphilosophically' and 'unwisely', above all *imprudently*... he risks himself constantly, he plays the dangerous game. (Nietzsche, *Beyond Good and Evil*)

# Contents

# Acknowledgements

Many people have contributed to the thinking that I have given expression to in this book. Their encouragement, comments and suggestions have always been welcome, as have their objections and criticisms. Some have helped directly, by reading draft chapters and making suggestions for improvement, or by responding to conference papers which were early explorations of the themes addressed here. Others have helped indirectly, as they will be aware – or not, as the case may be.

They are Terry Andrews, Steffi Boothroyd, Roy Boyne, Paul Brightwell, José Cunha, Tracy Davis, Mary Evans, Gary Hall, Ben Knights, Naomi Landau, Aideen Lucey, Ian MacLachlan, Diane Morgan, Marguerite Nolan, André Noor, Jeremy Gilbert-Rolfe, Nicholas Royle, Janet Sayers, Sean Sayers, Miri Song, Michael Syrotinski, Mick Ward and Joanna Zylinska.

I would also like to thank: the Arts and Humanities Research Board for granting me a Research Leave Scheme sabbatical semester (a long time ago!) during which I was able to complete or draft several of chapters included here, as well as all of my former departmental colleagues at University of Teesside, who assisted me by covering for my absence during a second semester of leave funded by the University, the Centre for Contemporary French Thought at the University of Sussex for affording me a useful opportunity to present the ideas contained in Chapter 7, the British Academy for supporting my participation in conferences in the USA, and the editorial team at Manchester University Press for their dedication and extraordinary patience.

To Gary Hall I owe a special debt of gratitude. His support for this project from its inception to completion has been invaluable to me, as has his advice and his friendship over the years.

Earlier versions of two of the chapters included here appeared as follows: 'Medusa's blood: Derrida's recreational pharmacology and the rhetoric of drugs', *Imprimatur*, vol.1, 1996; 'Deconstruction and drugs', in Nicholas Royle (ed.), *Deconstructions: A User's Guide* (Palgrave, 2000).

# 1    Deposition: drugs in theory

> Drugs cannot be placed securely within the frontiers of traditional disciplines: anthropology, biology, chemistry, politics, medicine, or law, could not solely on the strength of their respective epistemologies, claim to contain or counteract them. While everywhere dealt with, drugs act as a radically nomadic parasite let loose from the will of language... Drugs make us ask what it means to consume anything at all. (Ronell, 1992: 52)

## Experimenting with drugs: or, how to take this book

*Culture on Drugs* comprises a series of experimental readings of a number of texts by writers whose own diverse inquiries into the condition of modernity have found prominence in the annals of twentieth-century philosophy and cultural theory. This resulting cocktail of chapters I pass on to the reader to take as they wish. Together they offer a series of oblique and partial entries principally to the work of Freud, Benjamin, Sartre, Derrida, Foucault and Deleuze, in each case from the perspective of their encounters with drugs or on the basis of where the theme of 'drugs' touches upon their writings.

This book addresses the question of the *difference* of drugs – for instance, the difference drugs make to 'the user'. But it does so without assuming in advance either that the difference they make – namely, to the 'drug taker' – is exhaustively accounted for in the normal sense of 'drugs' and 'drug use' or that the identity of 'the user' ought to be exclusively identified in this way either. It is, as the title suggests, 'culture' which is considered to be *on drugs*. The specific sense of what I mean by this will emerge in due course. Just to provide one quick example in advance: drugs are 'in use' in the very writing of this book. Without them it would not have been called for or have happened. Its existence, too, is therefore owed to them.

*Culture on Drugs* thus regards cultural theory *on drugs* as being inseparable from the cultural theorising *of* drugs. And, like the texts it presents readings of, this book itself belongs to a wider 'drug culture'. In so far as 'drugs' figure in the production of texts – either as their direct object of consideration, or as a theme, or, let it be said, as an imbibed spur to thinking and theorising on the part of any author (as indeed is the case in relation to several of the central texts examined here) – then all involved, including the reader, are drawn into a relationship of proximity to drugs, in one form or another and are subject variously to their effects. These 'drug effects' are manifest in many forms and are discernible across the body of culture in general, in the subjective movements of expressed thought, and in the objective consequences of culture's being on drugs in the first place – something reflected in all the cultural products and events, and the social and political practices engendered or orchestrated by them. The principal focus here, however, will be on the place of drugs in the form of culture we call 'cultural theorising'.

The strategy I have adopted in this book involves tracing the effects of drugs across a range of theoretical writings. One of the side effects of this is that it can be read as providing something of an alternative introduction to cultural theory to the more orthodox synopsising discussions of great *oeuvres* and 'big ideas' that are available. At the very least I would want to challenge the very notion that bodies of thought are the kind of systematic totalities they are often represented as, as well as the idea that they can be agreeably reduced to palatable mouthfuls. My preference is to make a meal of the minor detail and to pursue a singular theme. What does this mean? In sympathy with what William Burroughs says of his title *Naked Lunch*: 'It means exactly what the words say: NAKED lunch – a frozen moment when everyone sees what is on the end of every fork' (1993: 7). What I offer here is indeed a 'naked lunch' at the table of recent philosophical and cultural theory, and it is drugs which are on the menu. In fact this book's entire menu is made up of a collection of critical *hors d'oeuvres*: the 'drugs' theme is what enables me to focus in detail on a wide range of titbits of modern theory at a single sitting without succumbing to the reductionist imperative of other kinds of 'introduction to theory' books. It might fairly be said that each of these chapters wilfully reduces its scope to the exorbitant, some would say perverse, detail – the point where drugs come into the picture. But, I contend, it is by paying attention to the largely unremarked details of the 'drugs' embedded in the bigger theory pictures painted by those modern theorists whose work is approached here that some of their most general features can be seen to pivot decisively around encounters with drugs – either substantively or as a theme.

## Narcoanalysis, pharmacography and cultural studies

In what way can cultural theory be considered an experiment, or, specifically, an experiment with drugs? Each chapter of this book provides a possible answer to this question articulated in the context of a different set of theoretical concerns and interests – after which it will be clear that there could be countless others, too. I call the performance of this experimental approach to the conjunction of drugs *and* theory *narcoanalysis*.[1] Narcoanalysis – the critical approach to culture from the perspective of its articulation with and by drugs – I want to suggest, has no obvious limitations to its zone of application. I hope this work will render the field wide open. I have adopted the term having first come across it in Avital Ronell's *Crack Wars* (1992), during the course of which she presents meditations on the relationship between philosophy, literature and addiction in the context of a reading of Flaubert's *Madame Bovary*. I have adapted and deployed the strategy of 'narcotics-centred' critique here to my own ends, in order to reveal how decisive elements of modern cultural theory and philosophy can be illuminated on the basis of the theme and the effects of drugs. Of course, various species of what could be called 'narco-cultural studies' have been around for some time, if one understands the term to refer to all investigations of culture from the point of view of its articulations with drugs, that is. The precise character of the contribution made here to the field narco-cultural studies as I understand this, and its difference from all other forms of writing on drugs, is thus ultimately a matter of the readings undertaken. There are, however, various attendant complexities and definitional contestations relating to the terms 'culture' and 'cultural study' which must be addressed at the outset in view of the many other 'pharmacographies' in circulation.

Anyone embarking on an investigation of the 'drugs and culture' conjunction is faced with a wide range of pharmacographies, to give a collective name to the whole spectrum of genres and styles of writing about drugs. (The term 'pharmacographies' was coined by David Lenson in his own contribution to the field, *On Drugs* (1995).) To get the full measure of this diversity it would perhaps be necessary to calculate the product of all the senses of the two terms 'drugs' and 'culture', and lay out the result encyclopaedic form. No doubt the rich history of pharmacography itself warrants a dedicated study, too – a work which would simultaneously constitute an extension to the very series it would be delineating. This is not the place to embark on such a supplementary task. Nevertheless, in order to indicate the scope and novelty of my project, it is perhaps useful to reflect briefly on the extraordinarily diverse range of cultural pharmacographies (as distinct from scientific and medical pharmacographies, which, though belonging ultimately to 'culture', are not of direct concern here) which comprise the field of narco-cultural studies, and to identify the specific nature of each of their respective interests in drugs.

If, for the sake of simplicity, one thinks of cultural studies as being concerned with 'culture' in terms of the three analytical dimensions of culture as 'way of life', as 'process' (historical, political, social, economic and so on) and as 'creativity' (usually understood in terms of artistic and conceptual creativity typical of the arts and philosophy), then the articulations of culture with drugs can at least provisionally be mapped in relation to three specific styles of cultural pharmacography.

Pharmacographies which are concerned with connections between drugs and 'ways of life' are ostensibly anthropological in character. Amongst them I would count classics such as Louis Lewin's *Phantastica, Narcotic and Stimulating Drugs*, first published in 1924 (Lewin 1964), Thomas Szasz's *Ceremonial Chemistry* (1974) and more recent works of traditional pharmacoanthropology such as Richard Rudgley's *The Alchemy of Culture: Intoxicants in Society* (1993) and Goodman, Lovejoy and Sherratt's collection *Consuming Habits* (1995). These are works which address the drugs–culture relation in ancient and modern societies, describing how tribal practices and religious belief, as well as trade, customs and cultural production, form the cultural contexts of the material and symbolic consumption of drugs. Modern social, political and economic histories of drugs which adopt essentially comparable socio-anthropological approaches to drugs and culture include, for example, Richard Davenport-Hines's *The Pursuit of Oblivion* (2001) and Martin Booth's *Opium: A History* (1996). Even though these latter two studies are notably also concerned with the political economy of drugs as well as with their literary, critical and aesthetic articulations within modern culture, and hence with human artistic creativity, they too are conceived firmly within the *anthropological paradigm*. They do not in any sense attempt to 'use drugs' (in the sense of move outward from 'drugs' as a subject matter) to develop a critique of that epistemic paradigm, nor do they attempt to identify the role drugs may have played in securing (or for that matter loosening) its modern historical and conceptual normativity.

Some of the seminal texts of British cultural studies, written from a predominantly sociological perspective, such as Jock Young's *The

*Drugtakers* (1971) and Paul Willis's *Profane Culture* (1978), along with various texts collected in Hall and Jefferson's (eds) *Resistance Through Rituals* (1976), as well as other Birmingham-School-style analyses of the youth, subculture, drugs and society nexus such as Dick Hebdige's *Subculture and the Meaning of Style* (1979), are works which understand a specific set of contemporary sociologically defined cultural phenomena partly on the basis of their articulations with drugs and drug culture. For instance, drugs are explored in such studies in terms of their incorporation into cultural formations of 'resistance' to the hegemony of the dominant, or 'parental', culture. As drugs are as ubiquitous to modern culture as they were to ancient and premodern cultures, just about any aspect of that culture is, at least in principle, approachable from the point of view of its various articulations with or by drugs, or on the basis of the drugs theme. This is not to claim that these works of British cultural studies ought primarily to be seen as *de facto* and *de jure* 'narco-cultural studies'; nor that to approach any cultural phenomenon on the basis of drugs is necessarily the most cogent and productive to take: just that somewhere along the line the conjunction of drugs and culture is likely to arise in a relevant and specific way in relation to the enquiry's agenda. To illustrate my point here, let me just briefly suggest a number of familiar cultural phenomena, or potential themes of contemporary cultural study, in relation to which an exploration of the link between such phenomena and drugs is likely to be seen as relevant or pertinent. These might be, for instance, popular music, hedonism, sport, sexuality, school life, prostitution, violence, colonialism and empire, mental health, international terrorism, lifestyle, fertility, bio-technology and prosthetics, gender reassignment, twentieth-century art and literature, commercial art and advertising and so on. Clearly, all of these things could be approached on the basis of their connectedness to drugs: they are all figure in the web of connections which make up the fabric of contemporary culture – and in ways I shall for sake of brevity assume are fairly obvious. In common parlance, talk of the 'ubiquity of drugs' in culture expresses the set of connections between drugs and an array of cultural phenomena such as these and directs us to how drugs at least *may* be viewed as entering into every aspect of social and cultural life, blurring the boundaries of what we call Culture (in general) and 'drug culture'.

Within the tradition of British cultural studies – which understands itself primarily as a form of social and political critique – the cultural scenes of such things as youth culture, popular music and crime especially, have been and still are the most obvious kinds of cultural phenomena which call for attention to be paid to their articulations with (above all, illicit) drugs and drug use and abuse. Such studies, I suggest, illustrate extremely well how cultural formations, practices, habits and events can be viewed in terms of their articulation by drugs, and how theoretical investigations and representations of a specific element of culture such as 'drug use' and a range of cultural phenomena and forms co-articulate one another. Work in this tradition contributed greatly to the critical displacement of the rhetoric of 'deviance' in the sociological representation of drug use in favour of a more sophisticated critical thinking which regards drug culture as expressive of social meaning. Viewing culture as the web of interconnections between phenomena is precisely what enables cultural studies to challenge conventional associative mappings of drug culture, allowing novel and unexpected approaches to social, cultural, political, economic issues and their definition and analysis. This style of cultural studies was emblematic of the work which emerged out of the Birmingham School in its heyday: work which typically undertook to revaluate the culturally 'marginal' (of which drug use is just one form) and to reinscribe it at the centre of the inquiry. Furthermore, it enabled certain cultural formations (of youth culture and drugs, for example) to be theoretically conceptualised as dynamic processes expressing such things as 'identity', 'social power' and 'cultural capital', relating them to forms of 'resistance' and 'stylised consumption'.

Such essentially sociological cultural studies typically places great emphasis on the ethnography of group and individual life in specific places and times. It is therefore not surprising that it frequently exhibits a preoccupation with such things as youth culture, ethnicity, gender, labour and consumption. I contend, however, that the scope of narco-cultural studies is clearly not limited to what are perhaps the most obvious (in the sense of the most visible, immediate or 'everyday') domains of cultural 'drug effects': the wider effects engendered by drugs are discernible right across the surfaces of culture and society at large. They are evident also in entirely other registers and in other dimensions of culture; they are traceable, for instance, in relation to the various phenomena of globalisation, such as capital flows, human rights, development, trade and technology (drugs can even be considered *as* a form of technology). If it is possible and meaningful to theorise the double articulation of social worlds and drugs, which it surely is, then is it not equally possible to do so in relation to such things as these? (Illicit trade is in any case parasitic on licit trade, for example in the way smuggling exploits the infrastructure of the official global import/export business, and so forth.) In other words, quite irrespective of how the distinction between licit and illicit drugs operates at a given time – which partly determines the specific forms and prevalence of manifestly drug-centred cultural practices – the political economies of drugs and 'drug culture' clearly exist in parallel with one another.

It is because drug-articulated features of culture function in parallel with a kind of global narco-economy that the system of culture as a whole can simultaneously facilitate and deny the free production and flow of drugs, licit and illicit, medicinal and narcotic, throughout the world. I suggest that specific formations of culture – and not merely economic systems and legislative regimes – have allowed narcotics to effectively become an alternative global currency in the global black economy whilst denying medicinal drugs to vast sections of the world's population. Unquestionably, drugs have attained in late modernity an extraordinary role on the geopolitical stage, and are associated with an almost limitless range of narco-cultural phenomena. So conceived, cultural 'drug effects' range from the commercial production of drug detection kits for worried parents and head teachers to the napalming of Bolivian coca plantations by covert military agencies; they give a specific character to the latest 'summer of love' and they are the ultimate hope of defence against the next pandemic and so on. This is a for ever evolving state of affairs, and the schematic examples I have just given are only intended to indicate of how a critical narco-cultural studies could be productively extended to a multitude of cultural micro-contexts as well as to cultural phenomena discernible on the geo-political scale. Is there any aspect of culture and society that is not in some way affected by drugs? By the official and unofficial trade in medicines as well as narcotics, and by drugs policies governing these? By the 'war on (illicit) drugs' or the 'war over the distribution of (medicinal) drugs'? Perhaps not. But the description of 'culture on drugs' as a comprehensive totality is not in any case the aim of this volume nor is it the style of the narco-cultural studies it presents: the aim here is merely to explore further that reflexive dimension of culture called 'theory' on the basis of connections with 'drugs'.

The detailed social and political history of drugs presented in studies such as those of Davenport-Hines (2001) and Booth (1996) in fact provide us with a striking image of the diverse, if not limitless, cultural scope of drugs. Whilst neither of these studies embarks upon cultural critique as such, they none the less effectively reveal the interconnection of social, economic and political phenomena pertaining to drug use, the drug as commodity, the drug trade and the historical development of modern culture in general. For instance, whether one considers British ambivalence to the Chinese opium trade in the nineteenth century in historical detail, or the literary critical significance of opium in nineteenth-century literature, opium's cultural reach can be seen to be extensive and to cut across the abstractly analytic division of culture into its several 'dimensions'. In either case, opium is revealed as a determining immanent feature within a historically delimitable cultural context. And its cultural reach today (partly due to the modern technologies of agriculture and drug synthesis) is not diminished but rather extended: the phenomena opiates give rise to and 'organise' in contemporary culture may differ, but their *power* is no less evident in contexts as diverse as the everyday life of Afghani peasants, the 'heroin chic' fashion scene, through to the countless appearances of heroin in cinematic art. (See chapter 8.)

## Narco-literary studies

One of the most obvious places to look for the textual traces of drugs in culture is in the full range of modern literature: in the novel and in poetry, but also in popular literary forms such as newspapers, magazines and samizdat publications, and especially, today, internet publishing. There is, unquestionably, a rich cultural vein to be mined in the field of modern 'drug literature', from De Quincey and Coleridge through Cocteau, Burroughs, Kerouac, Huxley, Lowry and Ginsberg to Hunter S. Thompson, right up to contemporary writers such as Irvine Welsh, Will Self, Elizabeth Wurtzel and Niall Griffiths. The literary arts, along with other forms of art, give expression to the drugs and culture conjunction, collectively providing insightful accounts of the place of drugs in the modern *Weltanshauung*. The creative outputs of many major and minor figures in modern culture constitute evidence of the direct or indirect 'effects' of drugs as an integral feature of modern culture. Those individual works and *oeuvres* making explicit reference to drugs, or artists and authors bearing individual drug-fiend reputations, are only the most clearly signposted. But precisely because psychoactive substances, licit and illicit, are ubiquitous to modern life, one would surely expect the general cultural effects of drugs to be diversely distributed and retraceable in the creative process and the creative act itself, just as much as they are in everyday life, if not indeed more so. After all, the concept of creativity applies to both domains of culture. Whatever set of questions is posed in the context of modern drug culture, and whatever claims the analysis of such traces might lead to (for instance, about the relationship between the biographical details of drug use and the artistic product, or say concerning the sources of 'inspiration' or literary and visual style), the drug connection is, in such an approach to the aesthetic dimension of culture, at least readily acknowledged as a matter of legitimate contention and a feature of cultural production.[2] Alcoholism, nicotinism and other addictions and compulsions; psychedelic distortions and alienations; amphetamine-fuelled wakefulness and so forth, are never merely the *represented*. These all belong to the *materiality* of the cultural.

The literary aspects of 'culture on drugs', in particular, have been explored recently by scholars of comparative literature such as Marcus Boon in *The Road to Excess: A History of Writers on Drugs* (2002), David Lenson in *On Drugs* (1995) and Sadie Plant in *Writing on Drugs* (1999). There are a great many other accounts available in various edited collections of essays on literature and addiction. There are also numerous literary biographies and autobiographies of infamous artistic drug takers, anthologies and edited drug literature 'readers' which in their different and distinctive ways raise awareness of the tradition of modernity, to use a phrase of Ronell's, as 'narcotic modernity'. The popular arts and media, too, in their relation to the multiple worlds of drugs, reflect collectively how modern life variously incorporates drugs into its structures of self-organisation and governance. They often reflect how modern life is unsettled by its relationship to drugs: drugs are 'life-savers' but also used as instruments of execution or euthanasia; drugs are associated with the death drive and with the hedonistic pursuit of pleasure; drugs threaten the stability of social order whilst also being a source of hope as a technological solution to human ills of modern life and the hope for 'better living through chemistry'. The primary sources for narco-literary studies (and, I suggest, for a possible, yet to be defined, narco-media studies) of this kind would simply be too extensive to list and could never be exhausted precisely because there is not, never has been, nor could there be, a drug-free culture: for culture is manifestly a form of being 'on drugs'. We are destined live with the ups and downs of the drug culture we inhabit (and with the consequences of supposing that uppers and downers themselves might help us along in various ways). Once the decision to focus on drug references in literature is made, for instance, one finds they almost coincide with the entire history of literature itself. One could start, say, with the lotus eaters in Homer and trace the meanings and roles attached to drugs in culture in general through their appearances in the literature of many cultures and ages. The briefest examination of a cross-section of modern media culture – film, television, the internet – will immediately reveal that the colonisation of culture by drugs continues apace: new means of imaging them and imagining them have come into being, new ways of buying and selling them have arisen and information on techniques and recipes for their manufacture has been increasingly 'democratised'. Popular culture as much as 'high art' is replete with drug references, with many everyday experiences being indirectly shaped by cultural cues whose origins are linked, however indirectly, to one or another form of drug culture: everyone talks about getting their 'fix', even if it is only in reference to their morning cup of tea, and when they nip out for the milk it might be purchased to the accompaniment of dance beats that emerged out of Ecstasy culture and are now colonising the space of supermarket shopping.

Once one makes the strategic *decision* for 'drugs' *and* cultural theory (as a theme), then the details of this relation can begin to be explored: such is the work of the coming chapters. It should now be clear that the full range of pharmacographies available reflects the simple fact noted by Lenson, that 'if legal drugs are thrown in with the others, then there is no difference whatever between the phrase "drug culture" and the word "culture" *tout court*' (1995: 15). *Culture on Drugs* is testimony to how the reflexive culture we call cultural theory is no exception to this rule.

### Rethinking 'drugs': towards a post-anthropological perspective

In the anthropological tradition within which traditional anthropological studies and critical cultural studies operate, it has long been recognised that ideas about drugs, as much as the uses that have been made of them, have been decisive in the formation of specific cultures through the ages. Pharmaco-anthropological inquiry, for instance, has shown that, since prehistorical times, plants with what are today known as 'pharmacological' or 'psychoactive' properties have *always* found their way into cultural life. This provides one important sense in which it is legitimate to consider all cultures as 'drug cultures'. Such writing on drugs connects the drug cultures of antiquity to the modern forms of drug culture which arise as a consequence of modern cultural appropriations of drugs. Anthropologically identifiable cultural practices range historically from such things as shamanism, religion and ritual through to clubbing, chilling out, getting wrecked, shooting up and so on. In turn modern drug practices can be shown to be underwritten by social, political and economic conditions of a historically determinate nature. Historical narratives of the commodification of drugs and the drugs trade in modern times (such as those given by Booth (1996); Davenport-Hines (2001); Schivelbusch (1992)) provide accounts of the conditions which make specific cultural appropriations of drugs in various social settings as well as their roles in artistic and intellectual creativity, possible. Though British cultural studies produced its analyses of drugs and culture in relation to *sociologically* described cultural formations of everyday life and understood its general project as a political undertaking quite different in character to the traditional expansion of bodies of disciplinary knowledge, the disciplines of the social sciences, arts and humanities are none the less its cognates. Consequently, disciplinary pharmacographies of various kinds do overlap within narco-cultural studies. Each contribution to this field discloses an essential aspect of the reciprocity of the drugs–culture relation. Indeed, each style of writing about drugs and each writer effectively bear testimony to the fact that, as Derrida says: 'there is not any *single* world of drugs' (Derrida, 1995: 237).

Whilst bringing into view the extensive dissemination of drugs throughout culture – in ritual, literature and art, leisure and street life, medicine, trade and so on – and accounting for *what drugs are culturally*, such discourses have, however, also already adopted and taken for granted conventional conceptual definitions of drugs. Sherratt, for instance, deliberately avoids the use of the word 'drug', preferring to speak of 'psychoactive substances' (Goodman, Lovejoy and Sherratt: x–xi). This serves both to make explicit the specific 'effects' of the particular 'psychoactive substances' his study is interested in and to avoid the often highly contentious way in which some psychoactive substances are conventionally identified as 'drugs' whilst others are not. Whenever this substitution of 'psychoactive substances' for 'drugs' is made, however, it reiterates and privileges a certain conventional conceptualisation of 'psychoactivity', as if *it* were free of a comparable determinacy with respect to the understandings of 'drugs' and 'drug culture' it engenders. To make such a move is, in effect, to write *as if one's own discourse were free of the cultural effects of drugs*. It is to write as if it were possible to stand outside drug culture in general; as if a drug-free discourse of drugs were possible. I contend, precisely, here and throughout *Culture on Drugs*, that this is impossible and that, in the final analysis, one would have to refer all such pharmaco-anthropologies to a critique of their underlying transcendentalist assumptions.

Similarly, when considering the relation between that bit of culture we call 'theory' and 'drugs', it must be acknowledged that theory is itself nothing other than a part of 'culture on drugs'. As there is no meta-discourse of drug culture, one must, so to speak, allow drugs to do the talking: as Ronell says, one has to acknowledge that drugs are 'a radically nomadic parasite let loose from the will of language' (1992: 52). The nature of the experiment with drugs undertaken here is to attempt to follow drugs through elements of cultural theory. By examining several examples of theories of such things as consciousness, the mind/body relation, alienation, selfhood, language, the image and virtuality, the nature/culture dyad and everyday life, focusing on those points at which these theories reflexively incorporate drugs into their schemas, one can begin to get a sense of cultural theory's own double articulation with drugs. Drugs, in several senses, thus take thinking to its limit; and in these chapters I direct my attention to points at which the cultural effect of drugs is evident in conceptual thinking and in the determination of theoretical 'decisions' themselves – such as Freud's decision between psychology and neurochemistry (chapter 4), or Benjamin's decision for the method of 'dialectical imaging' (chapter 5). These narco-analytical readings of theoretical texts are possible only because they bear the trace of drugs within them. It is my aim to extend the range of narco-cultural studies to various points where critical thinking and drugs come into contact with each other.

In recognising cultural theory to be a part of drug culture and a form of 'culture on drugs', this book does not thereby amount to a philosophy of drugs or a cultural theory of drugs *per se*. Far from it. Rather, it is premised on the idea that *drugs can be known only on the basis of their singular effects*. The book is not concerned, therefore, with the historical determinations of the distinction between licit and the illicit drugs, nor with the arguments for or against the drawing of the boundary between the two and their sanctioning in national and international laws. Obviously, the access to and availability of specific drugs is always historically and culturally determined, and these determinants always have a bearing on both the actual cultural roles they assume (be these medicinal, recreational, political or otherwise), and on the meanings they acquire in any particular time and place (as scourge of humanity, panacea, wonder-drug, social lubricant, happy pills, mother's little helper, toxin, drowsy drops, energisers and so on). Even ideas of what may or may not be regarded as a 'drug' in the first place are ultimately subject to culturally specific epistemologies, taxonomies, conceptual frameworks and so forth. However, rather than starting out from such 'problems' as those concerning the identification, definition, authorisation and certification of 'drugs', from cultural-historical, socio-critical or conceptual points of view, I propose to take my lead simply from their individual – and more or less 'marginal' – appearances and effects in the *corpus* of theory. In other words, instead of being concerned with the 'entity' or 'substance' or what can properly be called 'a drug', or seek the essence of 'drugs', I approach 'drugs' in these chapters on the basis of the *differences they make* to the thinking expressed in each case, the evidence for which is ultimately *textual*.

Before the reader jumps to the conclusion that my interest here is simply in what cultural theorists and philosophers think when they in one way or another experience and reflect on experiences of such things as intoxication, 'altered states' or 'being high', let me point out that the significance of the biographical detail (either of personal experience *or* of personal abstinence) ought not to be assumed in advance. As noted already, the range of drug effects within culture is not considered to be restricted either to 'actual' drug taking or to the subjective effects of 'actual' drugs on individual users. Anyone who simply knows what psychedelic imagery is and feels they can relate to such cultural ephemera as the advertisers' gag 'you've been tangoed' or 'marmalade, I like marmalade' (Pink Floyd, 'Alan's Psychedelic Breakfast') consciously or unconsciously has been affected by drugs (culture). Likewise, anyone who has gazed in amazement at the drawings of Henri Michaux, read any of the drug literature mentioned earlier, watched the films of Kenneth Anger, seen Slava Tsukerman's heroin cult movie *Liquid Sky*, or watched and heard the synaesthetic performances of the The Future Sound of London – amongst countless other possible examples of belonging to drug-influenced culture – has already entered the zone of drug affect. The approach adopted across these chapters is premised on the view that the production of theory, too, does not escape this cultural affectivity of drugs. Belonging to the culture of which it speaks, I suggest, behoves theory to think through the sense in which that culture is and has always been, amongst other ways of conceptualising itself, a 'drug culture'. Theory's various accounts and deployments of concepts such as 'intoxication', 'narcosis', 'dream', 'trance' and 'hallucination', on the one hand, and its understanding of itself in terms of generic opposites to these – 'clear thinking', 'wakefulness', 'sobriety', 'perception' and 'reason' – are subtly and complexly textually inscribed within one another. These distinctions and their operations are approached here, sometimes thematically, at other times indirectly, incidentally and marginally. In the chapters that follow, I focus on texts and contexts which collectively illustrate how theoretical impulses, trajectories and decisions are shaped and directed, at least in part, by an encounter with drugs, illustrating the sense in which 'high modernity' is a form of 'culture on drugs'.

### The nature/culture dyad and drugs as 'cultural substances'

'Drugs' destabilise the modern distinction between nature and culture. This is not, however, a purely abstract, theoretical matter; a blurring of the distinction between nature and culture in the context of an intoxicated reflective consciousness. It also arises in the context of developments in modern scientific investigation and the further discovery of the material world: for example, by the material sciences of chemistry and physics, and especially today, the bio-sciences. Such natural sciences expose to view the limitations of traditional anthropocentrisms, with their central conceptual division of existence into the human and the non-human, simultaneously rendering 'culture' the exclusive mark of the human. Freud, for instance, always suspected that the neurochemical and neurophysiological processes underlying mental and psychological states would one day be discovered – and hence that psychoactive drugs would eventually find their proper place in psychotherapy. Psychoanalysis remains unquestionably a *human* science, and is concerned with what it understands to be *internal* to the human organism (and hence is strictly speaking entirely 'anthropological'). Nevertheless, in the 1895 *Project for a Scientific Psychology*, Freud presents a sophisticated theory of the boundary between the inside and outside of that organism wholly in terms of impersonal chemical and mechanical processes of stimulation and exchange between the human individual and its environment (chapter 4). Somewhat surprisingly, perhaps even zoological inquiry should give us pause for thought on the topic of the relationship between drugs and culture. The drive toward, if perhaps not the pleasure of, intoxication appears not to be alien to some non-human, even non-primate, animals. Reindeer are known to seek out and feast on hallucinogenic mushrooms. Even the humble fruit fly will drink itself into alcoholic oblivion – and, incidentally, become aggressive toward other fruit flies in the process.

That there exists some kind symbiotic relationship between the living organism *per se* and intoxicating drugs, and that this is likely to have played an evolutionary role, predisposing us humans to partake of the substances to which we give the name 'drugs', is a curious and fascinating discovery. A form of receptivity is perhaps logically, in any case evidently, at work in the human brain in order for us to identify and delimit a substance as a 'psychoactive drug' in the first place. For instance, neurochemists understand well the brain's receptivity to the opiate molecule: it is this receptivity, one might say, that has always guaranteed opiates a place in advance, for both good and ill, in the human cultures they have come into contact with (chapter 8). And as modern neuroscience extends its grasp of the underlying processes of the brain and its receptors, the prospect of a new age of designer drugs offering better 'mental health', enhanced memory and intelligence may be around the corner. The technology of drug design and its applications indicates how drugs are cultural materials with the power to push at the supposedly *natural* border between the human and the non-human and secure a part in the *cultural* mutation of anthropocentric modernity toward the post-human.

The two distinctly different pharmacographies of scientific pharmacology and pharmacoanthropology each articulate a specific set of relations between culture and drugs, ranging from the symbolic meanings attached to them in the earliest societies to the broadly medical appropriations in modern times. Taking drugs as a theme and entry point into the cultural theory of modernity, as these chapters will show, gives rise to a whole new range of possibilities. I emphasise that this narcoanalytic approach is not simply based on the metaphorical extension of *psychological* and *physiological* drug effects on individual users or authors to the interpretation of their critical thinking (which would be to reduce such thinking, *ad hominem*, to a set of drug related biographical details). The aim is rather to approach drugs primarily as 'cultural substances'; as cultural materials and as matters of culture. In line with this, in chapter 5 I examine how Benjamin proposes and experiments with what he calls the 'dialectics of intoxication' in the service of critique: for example, in his account of modern life in the city and the revolutionary potential of surrealism. Indeed, each of the chapters of this book shares the common aim of showing how the critical thinking of modernity thinks *through* the effects of drugs (in several senses). In chapter 6, therefore, I look at how the 'problem' of hallucination proves central to the development of the existential phenomenologies of Sartre and Merleau-Ponty and is indicative of the limits of phenomenology as a methodology; and in chapter 7 I follow Foucault's and Deleuze's exchanges on the subject of drugs around the theme of the artistic life of the West and their thinking of the limits of Reason.

Is it meaningful to think of drugs as 'cultural substances' whose power is allied with thought understood as the power of *differentiation* between the same and the other, the one/many, being/nothing, identity/difference, science/culture and so on? Differentiation is the work of thought itself, the work of distinguishing between one thing and another whilst identifying the nature of their connectedness, and cultural theory is the conceptual pulling apart of culture in order to get a clearer view of its connectivity. Bending and distorting the surface of culture, forcing one thing into contact with another is, for instance, how Deleuze understands the 'originality' of thought (chapter 7). To engage in theorisation is to think the 'as if': as if, for instance, one could serially displace–replace one thing by another and make serial conceptual substitutions such that, in the case of *Culture on Drugs*, this one thing 'drugs' can eventually, by means of such a distortion, be connected to this other thing 'theory'. To theorise, I suggest, is to engage in such serial displacements, substitutions and distortions and thereby to trace and to test the connections across culture which make meaning possible. Derridean deconstruction characteristically exploits this movement of language. Of course the value of doing so remains open to question, but an account of how drugs have figured (in) cultural theory can be derived only from a reflexive narco-analysis of those parts where there is evidence that contact between drugs and cultural theory has happened and produced identifiable effects. Such is the undertaking of this project. As will become clear in the following chapters, what it involves is a theorising of drugs which is responsive to the difference they have always already made within culture itself, right up to the point where their mark within culture is traceable in that bit of culture this book is directly addressing and the sphere of inquiry to which it is closest, namely, cultural theory. As the practices of critical thinking and conceptual invention – the trade of the philosopher and cultural theorist – are accomplished through a 'folding' of the surface of culture itself, to use a Deleuzian term,[3] it is perhaps only to be expected that there must be points of contact between cultural theory and 'drugs'.

*Narco-analysis involves the identification of these points of contact and the evaluation of their significance.*

## Drugs expertise and narco-power

While it is true to say that the internal role of drugs in modern cultural theory has received scant thematic attention, it is my contention that a degree of engagement with 'drugs' is discernible virtually anywhere one cares to look. I shall argue the case here for the significance of the often marginal or oblique references to drugs in each of the bits of theory examined. Doing so, I believe, will help to forestall the otherwise complete epistemological closure of modern thinking on drugs around the various dominant and familiar drug knowledges and forms of drugs expertise which collectively give the appearance that every aspect of drugs already has a knowledge and an expertise to attend to it. All such knowledges, after all, are the outcomes of various kinds of experiments, medical and scientific as well as personal. It is, moreover, the broadly 'anthropological experiments' which might otherwise be referred to as the set of all cultural uses to which drugs have ever been put, that ultimately justify Lenson's claim that 'drug culture' is almost equivalent to culture *tout court*. Drugs in religious rituals, in medicine, in everyday recreational intoxications and pursuits of pleasure, are all uses which, in different ways, times and places, have given rise to ideas about what drugs 'are' or 'are for'. My interest in this book is in how they have also been used in modern times in various senses in the context of experiments with critical reflexivity; experiments which extend our understanding of such things as the mind, the body and the self, as well as of the concept, language and communication, the image and perception and 'everyday life'.

Specialist drug knowledges and forms of drugs expertise, such as those of pharmacists, lawyers, drugs educationalists, criminologists, physicians and others, unquestionably provide something of use to the life of society in general. But such official (often state-sponsored) knowledges are all too readily, and sometimes alarmingly, co-opted into social and political systems of oppression, exclusion and criminalisation, and used, as are drugs themselves sometimes – for instance, in psychiatric institutions – to control and regulate the modern subject. This can take the form of withholding and denying access to drugs, just as much as it can of encouraging, even forcing the 'patient' to take them, or alternatively servicing and supplying the subject as a consumer. Whether users get their drugs at chemist shops or coffee shops, from doctors and pharmacists or from dealers or sports coaches, the total system of drugs production, dispensation, acquisition and use reflects a specific distribution of *narco-power*, and access to drugs in modern societies is generally subject to it.

Narco-power is not wielded by the state and its agencies – though these always have an interest in configuring it such that it does indeed serve their interests. Narco-power is rather a productive power, in the sense that Foucault has described, and is evident in the relationship between drugs and 'bodies', both individual and institutional. This is a relationship which obtains ontologically prior to the emergence of societies of control. The modern distinction between legal and illegal drugs – and, fundamentally, the formulation of drug law – is the outcome of the historically specific, *a priori* formations of narco-power: it is, in this sense, 'after the fact' and *reactive* in relation to already widely dispersed drug effects. Narco-power is distributed with respect to drug laws, but it also spans both sides of the law at once. The co-existence of licit global pharmaceutical conglomerates and the illicit industries of narcotic supply does not express a contradiction but rather a consistency within the particular historical formation of narco-power. Antagonisms may arise – for instance, around the bootlegging of licensed drugs which are subject to patents – though so long as there is no competition for specific customer groups (as there is not currently between the state and drug dealers of drugs such as heroin, cocaine, cannabis, LSD or Ecstasy) then official and unofficial systems of drug production and supply rarely come into direct conflict with one another. Contradictions do arise in the context of supposedly principled distinctions between 'good' and 'bad' drugs (some substances most widely acknowledged to be dangerous being available in every corner shop), but in practice all drugs continue along seemingly uninterrupted channels toward the 'bodies' they are destined for. Despite legal, political and economic controls, drugs are still distributed along pathways cut into the surface of culture by desire (that is, for pleasure or well-being) just as much as they are along routes defined by institutionally accredited notions of medical need, for instance. Hence drugs arrive at their destinations generally unhindered by socially and politically orchestrated concerns over potential harm or injustice to their end users. If I am a heroin addict I can get as much of the stuff as I like, I just have to put up with the danger of impurities, dirty needles, the criminality and violence surrounding my habit and the fear of application of the law itself. If I am a citizen of the UK with breast cancer, then, despite the legality of the drugs I need to prolong my life, I may arbitrarily be denied them by a system of distribution according to postcode rather than clinical need. And, sadly, as for the distribution of retrovirals in this age of the AIDS epidemic, it is my country of residence, my insurance status, the conditions of international patents or the whim of ignorant politicians, not to mention the geo-politics of 'denial' in general, which will decide my personal fate. (Of course, private capital and an internet connection can usually override all such local controls.) This is just one possible illustration of how – irrespective of whether we receive the drugs we need or want, or whether we are denied them or are forced into a multitude of strategies aimed at acquiring them, or indeed at refusing to take them – *we are all modern subjects of narco-power.*

In this cultural struggle and contestation over drugs, and in the middle of the controversies which often surround them, it is easy to forget how 'drugs expertise' is always a key part of the constellation of narco-power. It exerts a hold over the meaning of drugs and over ideas about what drugs 'are' and what they 'are for', just as it does over their quality and supply; effectively, over what it is *to know* them. Ultimately, discourses which claim to know drugs and their effects, that set out to identify them and to say what is and what is not a drug, to classify them (according to various taxonomies – legal, pharmaceutical, medical and so forth) and to control them, collectively share in the responsibility for the modern trauma relating to drugs. I am thinking here especially of the personal and social traumas resulting from the circulation of contaminated products, the avoidable criminalisations of drug users, societal dishonesty about the effects of drugs and lack of research which might lead to the alleviation of the suffering produced by all of the above, of policies which force Third World peoples to opt for narco-cash crops, which may then be symbolically destroyed in a phoney 'war on drugs'. We find ourselves in a world in which the *decisions* concerning drugs have already been made. As a consequence, the prevailing constellation of narco-power appears to be natural.[4]

### The oblivion of drugs

The question of how 'drugs' have figured in the thinking of modernity in general is often forgotten. Of the various oblivions some narcotics are associated with (cracking up, blacking out, losing it, going off with the fairies, dreams, trances and so on), this is the one with which this book is most concerned: the oblivion that critical thinking itself has fallen into with respect to the question of drugs. Recognition of this 'oblivion' is an essential precursor to any possible re-opening of the question of drugs and of the fundamental *conceptual decisions* that determine their place in our lives and in society at the end of modernity. I am proposing a rethinking of 'drugs' which is more fundamental than that which is implied by the conventional expression of critical interest in the 'drugs issue' or the 'drugs debate': namely, disputation regarding proscriptions and prescriptions, laws and civil liberties and so on. Although such matters are highly worthy of serious attention and are indeed potentially vital in terms of shifting boundaries and redressing the many injustices resulting from the present system of controls, a refinement of the arguments surrounding drug use and the associated laws is not ultimately a radical enough gesture. In order to recover the question of drugs in a fundamental way, the power of critical discourses such as those of philosophy and cultural theory must be brought to bear on the question of 'how to think drugs' whilst paying heed to the inherent reflexive relation between such thinking and drug culture in all its manifestations.

To some extent, such a cultural retheorisation of drugs and a deeper understanding of the power of drugs is today being forced by technological developments which promise to go 'beyond drugs' as we currently know them. Advances in genetic medicine and the prospect of other new types of biological interventions in human life are already producing new ideas about our relationship to both our bodies and our identities and who or what should have jurisdiction over them. For instance, the possible production of 'ideal' types of human individuals – be these aesthetically or athletically specified, engineered for longevity or maintained through body part replacements (Frankenstein's experiment updated to the age of anti-rejection drugs, transgenics and stem cell technology). Personalised genetic medicine may soon provide idealised 'silver bullet' quasi-drug therapies, modified to suit the individual. By the same token, new biotechnologies, it is mooted, may even come to form the basis for future weapons of selective annihilation for use against some genetically identifiable, and thus genetically susceptible, enemy. Such spectres are already with us and we are inclined to regard them as monstrous. We live in times in which drugs and our relationships to them are fundamentally paradoxical because there is no single *doxa* which is adequate to them; in which the actuality of drugs begins to collide with imagined future 'drug cultures'. Narco-cultural studies is the name I have given to one of a multitude of the possible – and possibly 'monstrous' – futures of cultural studies.[5]

## Drugs and monstrosity

> The future can only be anticipated in the form of an absolute danger. It is that which breaks absolutely with constituted normality and can only be proclaimed, presented, as a sort of monstrosity. (Derrida, 1976: 5)

Some drugs at least are widely considered to be agents of monstrosity, in that they effectuate monstrous distortions of normal perception and cause the user to suffer delusions and hallucinations (as well as fantasised versions of drug-fuelled aberrations, such as the one about cooking the baby in the microwave), or to engage in monstrous 'deviant' behaviours, ranging from acts of violence and destruction to vomiting in public places, noisy exuberances such as laughing, shouting and going crazy to repetitive beats – in short, forms of compromised self-control. Evidently the most monstrous of drugs in the UK at the start of the twenty-first century is alcohol: a new social phenomenon called 'binge-drinking' has hit the night-time streets of many of Britain's major cities. The retiring Chief Commissioner of London's Metropolitan Police Service, Sir John Stevens, commented in 2005 that the two great future tasks facing the service were binge-drinking and international terrorism. To write a book about drugs, to call it 'cultural studies' (albeit sticking the 'narco-' prefix on the much used phrase) while not addressing such pressing and urgent sociological themes, may itself be considered monstrous: monstrous in its apparent disinterest in the 'harsh realities' of the 'drugs scene', 'drugs crime' and 'drugs tragedy'. If there is such a risk of opprobrium (and no doubt there are others too) then I suggest it indicates another dimension of the very theme this book does address: namely, the conterminal monstrosity of 'drug culture', as I have generally sought to redefine it, and abstract thought itself. In other words, I wish to openly acknowledge that there is indeed something *ludicrous* about the project of experimenting with 'drugs' in this way. This is the 'Nietzschean moment' of this narco-cultural studies of high modernity: 'I do not know any other way of associating with great tasks than play' (Nietzsche, 1969: 258).

There is perhaps something monstrous, too, about suggesting that drugs have played a part *in* modern cultural theorising rather than merely that modern cultural theory might have something to say *about* drugs and a role to play in the understanding of how drugs figure in and configure culture. This is, after all, not a proposition that will be justified here on the basis of a grand thesis concerned to prove that there is a symbiotic relationship between drugs and culture, and therefore by a principle of inclusion also between drugs and that bit of culture we call theoretical critique or reflection. Instead, I present a series of *examples*; experimental sample texts, aimed at testing only whether such a grand conclusion would be too outrageous. (This notion of 'exemplarity' as a feature of theorising is discussed directly in chapter 3.) Adorno provided perhaps the truest image of intellectual work when he said that it was like tossing bottled messages into the sea of communication: this implies that every 'message' is always also an experiment in communication – and this book conforms to this condition.

More monstrous yet: imagine for a moment a future in which the concept of the *pharmakon* (drug) has usurped the place of *ousia* (being) in metaphysical thinking, and all thought is articulated according to a drug-centred conceptual matrix. What would it be like to philosophise and to do cultural theory in such a world? One in which ontology has been supplanted by pharmacology and in which all paths lead back to the 'poison/cure' dichotomy and speculation about better dosages and side-effect factors? Instead of praying to a Supreme Being, it might be commonplace to 'take drugs' (whatever that means!) in search of redemption, or in order to feel at home in such a world. Of course, it could be said this (experimental) substitution produces a not dissimilar monstrosity to the one we moderns are already living with: a world in which we self-medicate intermittently with supplements of all kinds – pills, potions, herbs, tobacco and alcohol – and are simultaneously encouraged and lambasted for doing so from all directions by major social and commercial institutions and political authorities. Are we not generally aware of this already as our 'narcotic modernity'? If we are, then this is at least partly because we see it, too, through the eyes of others whose commitment to their premodern idols has yet to fade. Maybe there is indeed a connection between what the retiring Chief Commissioner of Police identified as two distinct phenomena, the two monstrosities in his policeman's eyes, at the start of the new metropolitan, post-9/11, century: binge drinkers and religious extremists, and the wildly imagined war to come between the hedonist infidels and the abstinent martyrs (who, we are told, partly finance their 'war against the West' by means of the illicit drug trade).

## High modernity and high theory

Because drug culture is ubiquitous, popular discourse has become con-taminated with drugs-speak. I have tried to avoid all the obvious gags and puns that could so easily have spilled into my own 'ludicrous' text. None the less, the expression 'high modernity' has been used in the subtitle of this work. To my mind it captures what is common to the selection of texts the book discusses, namely, their highly (modern) reflexive theorising of aspects of modernity, whilst drawing attention fortuitously to the book's interest in rethinking 'high modernity' in terms of its imbrications with 'drugs' and therefore with modern cultural forms of being high. The 'will of language', it seems, sometimes gets its own way, or perhaps even leads the way to thinking: in other words, the conjunction of 'high modernity' and the formations of 'drug culture' is a matter of language as much as it is of anything else and they often simply coincide (see chapters 3 and 7).

'High theory' is an essentially modern form of discursive expres-sion. The term connotes a sense of theory's often alleged disconnection with what is called 'the real world': in its very nature it is thus a form of exorbitance. Not surprisingly, those whose intellectual work is designated (usually controversially) as making a contribution to it do not describe their work as 'high theory'. If the 'high' refers to anything recognisable, it refers to a measure of abstraction in philosophical, social or literary theory, each of which feeds into what is called generally called 'cultural theory'. More often than not, the qualifier 'high' in conjunction with 'theory' is used by detractors of theoretical work, or less aggressively, simply to stress the supposed difference between empirical and theoretical work. Theoretical work is most true to itself and at its most responsible, in my view, when it does *not* respond to the demand so often placed upon it to answer for itself: its business is rather to answer for, or to respond to, whatever calls for abstract thinking, and in relation to which it is always essentially exorbitant.

This exorbitance is not equivalent to transcendence though; it corresponds rather to the encounter with a certain notion of the 'limits' of thought. But 'drugs' are at least a figure of alterity and excess in rela-tion to culture (and therefore cultural theory too). The cultural theory of anything (drugs, for instance) is never wholly independent of that of which it speaks, and my general project has been to deal with drug culture – as defined above – as it finds its expression *in theory*. It is therefore not merely a loose figure of speech to describe cultural theory itself as a form of *being on drugs*. That said, the history of modern theory is not, of course, represented by a series of treatises on drugs. On the contrary, by and large, drugs (as a theme or object of theoretical concern) have been effectively forgotten by it and relegated to a number of specific scientific and cultural pharmacographies. As in the reality of their everyday settings, drugs have been, at one and the same time, both 'forgotten' *and* assigned a 'proper place'. Common sense, for instance, regards pharmacology as their ultimate proper discipline and the pharmacy as their proper place of containment. The question of drugs as a philosophical question – or means of philosophical experimentation – has largely been ignored (though not entirely, as I aim to show). However, the attempt to restrict the availability of drugs as substances in circulation, or to delimit them as objects of legitimatised and conventional forms of drugs expertise and knowledge, has never stopped them becoming known in other senses, nor taking on roles in other contexts. The history of modern culture, which as I have already indicated can easily be delineated in terms of its many articulations with drugs, provides testimony to this. A drug-centred history of modern culture would tend to be a history of their propitious epistemological destinations. On the other hand there is, to use a Derridean term, an overlapping, *destinerrant* history of drugs to be told;[6] one whose details are to be found in all the different appearances of drugs in the cultural history of modernity. This history is 'everywhere' and 'anywhere'; wherever drugs may turn up. It is in the archives of culture as well as in the contemporary life of the arts and society in general. Drugs appear in and affect culture: their presence is felt in literature, art, music, design, fashion, street life, dance culture, cyberspace and so on *ad infinitum* – culture is in part fuelled by drugs and fixes their multiple effects in material forms. To theorise about drugs openly and open-endedly, without prejudice and free of the pressure to produce results that either confirm or reject in one form or another the current polarised politics of drugs, involves the attempt 'to be true to drugs' as agents of differentiation. It is to aim at a conceptual and critical thinking of them *otherwise*. This involves, first and foremost, acknowledging the *undecidability* of 'drugs' and the investigation of their cultural inscriptions:

> If you don't experience some undecidability, then the decision would simply be the application of a programme, the consequence of a premise or of a matrix. So a decision has to go through some sort of impossibility in order for it to be a decision. If we know what to do, if I knew in terms of knowledge what I have to do before the decision, then the decision would not be a decision. (Derrida, 1999: 66)

These experimental, narco-analytical readings of bits of cultural theory can, then, by their own logic, no more tell 'the truth about drugs' than could any other drugs discourse. They do, however, demonstrate the sense in which abstract thought, emerging as it does from the surfaces of a culture, is, in each case, a specific articulation of *culture on drugs*.

## Testing drugs in theory

We clearly have a deeply complex, often contradictory and ambivalent relationship with drugs: as individuals, as a society and as a culture. This is ultimately a consequence of the undecidable nature of the drug as *both* poison and cure (see chapter 2). Drugs seem by their nature, then, to call for 'a measure', a dosage, an authority, an expertise, categorisation and classification; for the imposition of some form of propriety. For any substance anyone consumes or incorporates, who should decide and what should determine the appropriate dose? What should determine whether partaking of particular drugs should be allowed or prohibited, recommended or discouraged? Such questions, if they are ever formu- lated and reflected on without prejudice, are always posed in specific existing cultural circumstances, situations and contexts. They therefore arise against a background mixture of decisions always already taken: for instance, with regard to existing licences to produce and supply drugs and existing drug laws, and on the basis of certain research programmes being funded and others not, and so forth. Everything which is thought about drugs emerges contextually from within the modern narco-cultural formation – the given nexus of connections and associations between modern life and 'drugs', the multitude of drug mythologies, popular beliefs, drug literatures, and other manifestations of drugs. All of these configure the modernity of drugs and the cultural theory of modernity is one form among all the others of *culture on drugs*.

With this in mind, the chapters that follow engage with elements of modern cultural theory drawn from psychoanalysis, critical theory, phenomenology, existentialism, deconstruction and libidinal materi- alism, in so far as they may throw some light on the modernity of drug culture. Any familiarity the reader has with the any or all of the above will I hope be rewarded by these attempts to test for 'connections' between twentieth-century cultural theory and the subject of 'drugs'. To the new student of such theory, these chapters may serve as an introduction – but in an oblique and unorthodox way: in each case the theme of 'drugs' and how drugs have figured in the production of theory is the point of entry. The working hypothesis of this book has been that in order to understand the condition of modernity one has to think through the modernity of culture's relationship to drugs.

I have not sought to privilege either phenomenological or biographical approaches. Nor should the reader suppose that his or her own personal experience (or lack of it) of any of the drugs mentioned by name in due course is an obvious advantage or a disadvantage for understanding, accepting or judging the claims made concerning the role of drugs in the elements of theory considered. The research hypothesis effectively states that, as we all live in a culture on drugs – in a culture awash with medicinal, narcotic and recreational drugs – and as theory emerges reflexively from within this drug culture, there is reason to suppose that the effects of drugs are already at work in all our systems (of thought). Abstinence may be an option on a personal level, but the refusal of 'drugs' in *all* of their various forms – in theory or in practice – can itself be viewed as a form of reaction to them. There is, then, no escaping their multiform effects. It has not been a condition of selection of the theory discussed here that the individual authors referred to might or might not have, hypothetically, proved positive (or negative) for certain substances. Obviously, every one of them would have proved *either* positive *or* negative as far as such a crude testing for the presence or absence of drugs is concerned. However, having made a statement which appears like a disclaimer – that this book is not about cultural theorists who themselves experimented with drugs by actually imbibing them – it is, none the less, true that this condition applies in some cases. Freud's use of cocaine, Benjamin's use of hashish, Sartre's experiment with mescaline and Foucault's experiment with LSD at least are well known. Other figures whose names appear here have been cautious, like the rest of us, about what they revealed about their personal experience lest the information be misunderstood or used against them. As it is my aim throughout to give an account of elements of cultural theory as articulations of drug culture, I leave it to the reader to judge the possible significance of subjective, personal experience of intoxications of one sort or another to the general thesis of *Culture on Drugs* and its claim that theory, as culture in general, is not a drug-free zone.

## Notes

1 This is not, of course, a dictionary definition of the term, whose origins are in the combination of psychotherapy and hypnosis with the assistance of narcotic drugs. I do not in my own use of the term allude to this meaning. I use it rather to name a form of theoretical reflection (of which this volume is an example), which is both centred on 'drugs' as a theme and which acknowledges the role that the materiality of drugs (actual drugs) have played in the production of the ideas it discusses. Also, it should be noted that the terms 'narco-' and 'narcotics' are used to refer to drugs and drug-related phenomena in general. Any pharmacological taxonomy of drugs would distinguish 'narcotics' from 'hallucinogens' or 'stimulants' and so on, but such distinctions made by the science of pharmacology would not in any case correspond to the common use of the term 'narcotics' to refer to illicit as opposed to licit drugs. As I am not concerned here with such classifications – other than to loosen the grip such schemas have over the thinking of 'drugs' in general, the term narco-analysis can ultimately be regarded as a flag of convenience to refer to 'drug-centred critique', examples of which I present in each chapter.

2 Cf. Hayter (1968) and Vice, Campbell and Armstrong (eds) (1994).

3 Cf. Deleuze (1988: 94-123). In chapter 7 here I look in detail at the exchange between Deleuze and Foucault on drugs and at Deleuze's idea that drug effects are a distortion of the surface of culture.

4 Though it is true that, for the most part, modern societies experiment with the specific mixture of prescriptions and proscriptions with respect to leisure and recreational drugs, including addictive substances sometimes not even thought of as 'drugs' (such as tobacco and alcohol) they largely leave 'drugs research', like they do the supply of drugs in general, to the free market and to the big-business and the drug barons of both the official and unofficial 'pharmaceutical industries'. This is done in the wider context of 'managing' the politics of drugs – not only the politics of access, rights, manufacture, patents, distribution etc. but also, even especially, the ideological burden drugs are made to bear. With this comes a very narrow cultural understanding of 'drugs research' and 'drugs experimentation'. There is, of course, a social dimension to the latter and liberal societies can show themselves to be pragmatically progressive and open to new social experimentation within their systems of drugs control (for instance reclassifying drugs to reflect the changing consensus on the 'dangers' they are thought to pose to public health or to redress the negative consequences of their illegality).

5 Cf. Hall (2002: 65-91). I suggest narco-analysis is just one of the possible 'monstrous futures of cultural studies' in Hall's sense of this expression.

6 I am thinking here of Derrida's notion of the indeterminacy of communication, for example, of a letter, once posted by the sender (*destinateur*) into a system of communication which may or may not arrive at an intended

destination – an address or an addressee (*destinataire*). It is 'not that the letter never arrives at its destination, but it belongs to the structure of the letter to be capable, always, of not arriving' (Derrida 1987: 444). Narco-cultural studies, I am saying, is comparably a risky posting.

## 2 Medusa's blood: Derrida's recreational pharmacology and the rhetoric of drugs

'Drugs' is both a word and a concept, even before one adds quotation marks to indicate that one is only mentioning and not using, that one is not buying, selling or ingesting the 'stuff itself' (*la chose même*). (Derrida, 1995: 228)[1]

### The decision on drugs

To remove any possible suspicion at the outset of an interview on drugs, Derrida reassures his reader – who may after all be a member of the Drug Squad – that to speak of drugs is not the same as to be on them or to be on the wrong side of the law on drugs. Just to speak of drugs when not to condemn them is clearly a risky business. On the cultural battlefield of the 'war on drugs', to speak of them at all is always to do so between the poles of being for or against them. Anyone treading the middle ground needs the protective armour of expertise. Not being experts on anything in particular, philosophers are, therefore, exceptionally vulnerable. Dwelling philosophically on the border dividing the licit and illicit and questioning the whole notion of expertise under the cover of disclaiming it for oneself, may be viewed as tantamount to trespass on the Law itself. Derrida, famously, was once arrested on suspicion of trafficking drugs. He was alleged to have been in possession of drugs 'found' in his valise by border police in communist Czechoslovakia – a scenario he later described as being 'directed by the ghost of Kafka'.[2] In the case of Derrida here, however, the important issue is not so much a matter of the presence or absence of drugs as it is one of what I shall call his 'pharmaceutical thinking' – a form of philosophy *on drugs* – and the conceptual authoritarianism which attempts to control drugs and all matters relating to them which it questions.

Before any such philosophising, though, it has to be taken into account that the *decision* on drugs has already been made.

As soon as one utters the word 'drugs', even before any 'addiction', a prescriptive or normative 'diction' is already at work, whether one likes it or not. This 'concept' will never be a purely theoretical or theorisable concept. And if there is never a theorem for drugs, there can never be a scientific competence for them either, one attestable as such and which would not be essentially overdetermined by ethico-political norms. (Derrida, 1995: 228)

There cannot be any 'competence' for drugs able to justify itself without its at the same time issuing prescriptions (and proscriptions); no pharmacist whose competence is not institutionally certified, and therefore no *knowledge* of drugs which is not already underwritten by specific ethico-political concerns. This lack of competence is without exception because no conceptual system can act as its own foundation; we are not faced simply with ignorance or knowledge of drugs. One principal well-spring of western philosophy's attempt to see things in terms of the distinction between ignorance and knowledge (of drugs as much as of anything) is, of course, Plato.

## In Plato's pharmacy

In 'Plato's Pharmacy' (1981b), Derrida re-reads a bit of Plato in a way which is intended to sidestep that metaphysical couple. It centres on the role of the *pharmakon* in Plato's text *Phaedrus*. *Pharmakon*, he tells us, can be translated by 'remedy', 'recipe', 'poison', 'philtre' and 'drug'. And, rather than appealing to any theory of this 'drug', he examines the relationship between philosophy and the *pharmakon, through* philosophy. This is an a sense in accord with the Platonic thinking which says that philosophical reflection is always form of participation in that of which it speaks. Derrida's encounter with drugs does not, then, revolve around *possession* at all – which requires first the delimitation of a concept of 'drugs' – but around their *use*.

His reading revolves around the *pharmakon* in *Phaedrus* and pays particular attention to the *use* made of it by Socrates in the attempt to cure blind ignorance and to establish the soul on its proper course. The 'drug' in Plato's text on this occasion takes the form of the text of speech of Lysias (which is concerned with the ideal love relationship). The prospect of hearing a good speech prepared by Lysias is in this case the *pharmakon* that, at the beginning of the *Phaedrus*, has already drawn Socrates out of the city and hence beyond the boundary of its jurisdiction. The young Phaedrus is the one who here supplies the 'drug'; he brings it along with him to his rendezvous with Socrates, knowing well that a good speech is

Socrates' tipple, but little knowing what the effect will be when it is taken in his company. Socrates first of all expresses his gratitude: 'You seem to have discovered a drug for getting me out ... A hungry animal can be driven by a dangling carrot or bit of green stuff in front of it. I don't doubt you can cart me all round Attica and anywhere else you please' (Derrida, 1981b: 71 citing *Phaedrus*: 230d–e). Socrates looks forward to partaking of the speech, confident that he knows how to use the drug properly and that he is not in danger of succumbing to its rhetoric. To enhance enjoyment of the experience, he proposes lying down and Phaedrus gets the speech out. The ensuing discussion concerns its purity: whether or not it is pure Lysias, and whether or not it possesses the whole truth of the matter at hand.

The dialogue at this point revolves around how the drug is *used*, not merely what it *is*. To repeat the speech having learnt it by heart, as the naive Phaedrus attempts (and fails to do, thus providing him with a reason to read it out aloud), enables Plato to illustrate the form of repetition which is governed by possession and re-presentation of the substance of the speech in the analogue in which it is inscribed (the written scroll Phaedrus had stashed under his cloak – in anticipation of his failure of memory). However, it transpires, this is not the kind of 'drug use' Socrates is interested in engaging in. As Derrida says:

> If a speech could be purely present, unveiled naked, offered up in person in its truth, without detours of a signifier foreign to it, if at the limit an undeferred *logos* were possible, it would not seduce anyone. (Derrida, 1981b: 71 citing Plato's *Phaedrus*: 230d–e)

It would not be able to 'seduce' Socrates out of town. Socrates is seduced out of town not by the prospect of 'words that force one to wait for them under cover of a *solid* object' (Derrida, 1981b: 71), which might be thought to satiate the hunger for 'knowledge', but by the prospect of a *fluid* engagement with Phaedrus, when they partake of the drug together. Mere possession of the drug does not amount to *knowledge*, nor is it the same as *knowing how to use* it and to appreciate its effect, and Phaedrus is in need of guidance on this matter. Although the speech is rather weak, Phaedrus does the whole thing top to bottom and, in possessing it thus, without recourse to any certified dosage, is effectively poisoned by it: he thinks it 'wonderful' and 'a good piece of work', not least because 'it has one merit above all others', namely, that 'no single aspect of the subject worth mentioning has been omitted'. (Plato, 1978: 31, 234b) In the state it has put him in, it is for him the whole truth of the matter. Phaedrus feels that he has seen it all – a delusion caused by the drug. Socrates, however, has seen this youthful euphoria and such excessive consumption before. Paradoxically, high on the speech though Phaedrus is, the pharmacist Socrates is able to administer the very same drug as an antidote; he talks him down from his bedazzled state of being. Socrates himself is clearly not so easily intoxicated. For him the effect of the speech, despite its being 'wonderful' and 'breathtaking', is down not so much to the speech itself as down his partaking of it with Phaedrus: 'It was you who are responsible for this effect on me. I saw how what you were reading put you in a glow; so, believing that you know more about these things than I do, I followed your example and joined in the ecstasy' (Plato, 1978: 31, 234b). The *pharmakon* produces a transformation in both of them and, under the guidance of Socrates, it can be made to work as an aphrodisiac and as a means to the Socratic end – in this case, participation in the Form of Beauty. Simple possession is where the danger of *ab*use arises. Socrates had all along an entirely other form of use in mind: he uses it in the context of his maieutics as and epidural to aid the birth of ideas.

What the *Phaedrus* presents its reader with are models of both good and bad *repetition* of the same speech. Bad repetition occurs where the speech/drug is *possessed* and blindly re-presented, in which case the potency of the substance is confused with its effect. Good repetition occurs where the speech/drug is *used* in the furtherance of dialectic: for this *the drug must be subject to a prescription.*

Somewhere around here Derrida breaks into Plato's pharmacy in search of a 'higher form of the drug' (Ronell, 1992: 64). His entry involves the re-writing of this scene around the idea that the Socratic prescription of the drug is one thing, the drug itself is another. The potential effect of the drug is not fully and completely explored under the prescriptive control of Socrates. Just as Phaedrus' supposition that Lysias' speech exhausted its topic was laughable, Socrates' prescription, too, does not exhaust the possible effects of the drug. Derrida's appropriation of the *pharmakon* in terms of the *undecidability* of 'the drug', is where we are headed and I shall return to that shortly, but before I do that I want to explore further this relation of philosophy to itself as the urge to philosophise; to repeat, to dedecide and redecide traditional meanings, in terms of philosophy's relation to something which may be passable under the sign of 'the drug', and therefore something which would link philosophy to the trope of addiction. This is a link has been explored by Avital Ronell (1992) and I shall take a short detour at this point to consider her findings and make a further, I hope illuminating connection to Jean-Luc Nancy's discussion of the 'decision of existence' (Nancy, 1993: 82–109).

## Addiction and the decision of existence

Ronell examines the role of 'addiction' in Heidegger's account of the existential structure of *Dasein* in her attempt to investigate the kind of existence that could be called 'being-on-drugs', and which in her view 'has everything to do with the bad conscience of our era' – that is, with respect to drugs (Ronell, 1992: 3). She traces the dynamics of addiction in the existential analytic of Care (*Sorge*) in Heidegger's *Being and Time* in an attempt to locate the functioning of addiction in the self-production of culture.[3] She finds that in Heidegger's account of the fundamental structure of *Dasein*, 'addiction' is both distinguished from and yet grouped together with 'wishing' and 'willing', which are key ontic determinations of the ontological projection of *Dasein*. Whilst willing, wishing and addiction all belong to the basic structure of Care, addiction is distinctive in that it is unable to project itself toward any specific future; it is a hankering after something which only ever aims at itself in the present moment, hence 'the fulfilment of a drive such as addiction cannot be truly projected' (Ronell, 1992: 31). To suppose that it is projected towards its next fix, for example, is actually to do nothing more than to describe a condition of wanting something now. Addiction is both ontically and ontologically (to be) trapped in a cycle of repetition – trapped in the time warp of an inauthentic present: addiction is thus always addicted to itself. For this reason addicted *Dasein* is effectively disqualified by Heidegger from figuring in the *passage* of thought from everydayness to authentic thinking. Addiction causes the projection of *Dasein*, as Being-ahead-of-itself (*Sich-vorweg-sein*) to collapse into a 'just-being-alongside' (*Sein-bei*): it is an ontological way of 'going nowhere fast' (Ronell, 1992: 42). Addiction, therefore, always threatens to disrupt the kind of self-projection which opens *Dasein* to its futurity and the thinking of Anxiety (*Angst*) in an ontologically fundamental way. It is therefore interpreted as being a threat to *Dasein*'s authenticity because it threatens to close the phenomenological door to perception in *Being and Time*: 'freedom depends upon *Dasein*'s openness to anxiety which addiction and urge are seen to divert' (Ronell, 1992: 43).

There is, therefore, no genuine ontological structure of addiction for Heidegger, who sees it solely in terms of its corrosive effect on the dynamics of authentic thinking. For Heidegger it is a wholly 'everyday' phenomenon which figures only negatively in thought's attempt to elucidate the fundamental ontology of *Dasein*. For this reason, Ronell concludes, addiction effectively remains *unthought* by Heidegger. It is all the more important, therefore, that this structure is now reconsidered on precisely the ground that it proves to be that which threatens to thwart the progress of the analytic of *Dasein*. So this is Heidegger's *decision* of addiction: it is wholly inauthentic and draws *Dasein* into the circle of going-nowhere. Now, whether or not the Heideggerian decision of addiction as 'bad repetition' is to be accepted (leaving the phenomenon, as it were, to be dealt with by the discourses of psychology and sociology), Ronell is I believe right to identify the primary philosophical significance of Heidegger's thinking of addiction in relation to the analytic of *Dasein* as being that the *drug structure* precedes the materiality of drugs: 'being-on-drugs indicates that a structure is already in place, prior to the production of the materiality we call drugs' (Ronell, 1992: 33).

Turning to Nancy's account of the 'decision of existence' in Heidegger's thought, now, provides an indication of how 'the drug' might be put back into to the life of *Dasein* in a way which does not limit it to its everyday determination as the mere (ontic) object of addiction (or any other form of simple consumption). And, as I shall show in a moment, this has a bearing on Derrida's entry into Plato's pharmacy and the connection it articulates between 'good repetition' and the addictive structure of philosophising.

The decision referred to in Nancy's essay titled 'The Decision of Existence' (1993) refers to *philosophy's decision to philosophise*; to the reflexive impulse of philosophy, which begins according to Heidegger in a 'vague' and 'average' manner in the midst of the everyday and everyday life: 'the roots of the existential analytic' he says 'are ultimately *existentiell*, that is *ontical*'(Nancy, 1993: 84). Nancy refers to this as the 'mundanity of decision'. He points out that the analytic of *Dasein* as the philosophical undertaking at the heart of *Dasein*'s existential project is itself an example of the decision, but it is a mistake to think that it is a de-*cision* which cuts through 'everydayness'; through the 'they say…' (here, for example what 'they' say about drugs in everyday culture at large) to a supposedly deeper level of understanding. This decision is not itself the *founding* decision of *Dasein*:

> The thought of decision is thought *at the limit* of the decision that has already brought it, *existentielly*, into play as thought… By this we mean

to say that decision is not open to, or decided by anything other than, the world of existence itself, to which the existent is thrown, given up and exposed. Decision decides neither in favour nor by virtue of any 'authenticity' whereby the world of existence would be surmounted or transfigured in any way whatsoever. The decision is made... right in ontical experience... Ontical experience takes place *right at the 'they'*. (Nancy, 1993: 87)

The trajectory of this analysis eventually elucidates the idea that it is wrong to think that the Heideggerian analytic of *Dasein* proceeds by peeling away Matrushka-like layers of inauthentic being, passing through stages of sublation (*Aufhebung*). Philosophising never leaves the upper-most surface of the everyday world, whose solidity is not something for philosophy to penetrate, but rather something to interpret. The decision (of philosophy/to philosophise) does not culminate in the accomplishment of transcendence.

Nancy reminds us that any *re-deciding* which philosophical thought undertakes, of 'drugs' or anything else, never leaves the everyday world of the 'they' in which *Dasein* lives. Any attempt to think and articulate a 'higher form of the drug', as Ronell puts it, begins from within a meditation on 'the drug' as it is already thought and experienced. This leads us to the conclusion that *drugs have a role to play in the rethinking of 'drugs'*. Where 'addiction' dominates the everyday thinking of the relation to drugs (as in many everyday contexts it does) then it attributes the power of addiction to the substantive drug itself. Hence we are inclined to think on the everyday level that drugs *cause* addiction. It must be emphasised at this point, however, that Heidegger at least indicates the manner in which addiction is a basic disposition of *Dasein* – indeed this is what gives force to Ronell's notion of addicted *Dasein* as 'being-on-drugs'. But in refusing to incorporate addiction into the analytic of *Dasein* at the *existential* level, Heidegger also abandons the decision of its meaning to the 'they'; to its determination in everyday discourse. In deciding *against* addiction, in the sense described above, Heidegger effectively decides *resolutely for* the modern everyday understanding of the phenomenon of addiction and, therefore, also for the everyday conceptualisation of its object. The decisive modern determination of drug addiction is *toxi-comania* – a disease – and drugs are deemed, therefore, to fall wholly within the domain of the 'appropriate' forms of modern 'drugs expertise' – be that legal, psychiatric or medical and so on. The modern conceptu-alisation of both addiction and drugs and the relation between the two would apparently escape the general Heideggerian *de-struktion* of traditional thinking on account of this blind spot on addiction. By specifically excluding addiction, Heidegger closes down a re-thinking of drugs – because they are, after all, from an everyday point of view, simply what fuels addiction. On the other hand, Heidegger must be given credit for the general de-structuring of the conceptual framework in which addiction and its relation to drugs have been assigned their modern specificity, because the analytic of *Dasein* constitutes a certain opening up also – one which both Derrida and Ronell are able to exploit. 'What is required', says Ronell, 'is a genuine ethics of decision. But this in turn requires a still higher form of the drug' (Ronell, 1992: 64).

Derrida is 'the supplier' Ronell is dealing with when she makes this remark. The compulsion to philosophise in Derrida's text and what draws him into Plato's 'pharmacy' is the habit of returning to the *aporetics of decision*, a way of thinking which results from his own use of the *pharmakon*. The aporetic logic of the unthinkable and unsayable 'beyond the decision' circulates everywhere in Derrida's corpus. His use of this drug, ontically speaking, is 'recreational' rather than 'addictive' because it opens up the possibility of *re-deciding* everything. For Derrida, the *pharmakon* can do more, for example, than Socrates' own decisive use of it suggests: it can be used, for example, to work against itself to effect a return, or repetition, of the moment of *indecision*. The way this deconstruction works is not by peeling away the layers of everyday meaning to reveal the truth of the drug, in the sense of the true meaning or being of the drug, but by exploiting its inherent polysemy and by restoring its *undecidability*. It exploits the drug's own resources for such a re-decision. In this case, it is in the form of Derrida's reading of the *pharmakon* in Plato's *Phaedrus*, but, more generally, it is through 'the decision of each reading' (Derrida, 1981b: 63). Understood as a literary practice, deconstruction can therefore be said to be a form of compulsive return; a kind of addiction to the practice of re-decision as a re-reading of the text. However, as we have just seen, the compulsion which gives rise to it 'precedes it and does not belong to it' itself (Nancy, 1993: 87). The addiction of such deconstructive rereading is to that to which has never been present, in the sense of available to reflection, without being experienced *through* addiction in the first place. This is the addiction to an *alterity*, in whatever form it comes (*advient*) to make its demand upon thinking. Deconstruction does not return thought to a point somehow prior to the 'decision', but it does instruct thought in how the *deciding* of the 'drug decision' (that is, of its normative determinations) is a more fundamental object for thought than any given (*decided*) *concept* of the drug. All of this indicates that there cannot be a decision (a philosophising) on (the nature or concept of) drugs which is not already, as Ronell puts it, a form of 'being-on-drugs'.

If the situation of theoretical reflection is governed by the 'drug structure' Ronell calls being-on-drugs, then there are no doubt many reasons to return to the pharmacy of Plato and the scene of the platonic prescriptions to which western thought inevitably got hooked. Addiction implies that there can be no simple stopping of the habit, not in this case because of the potency of platonism but because platonism and platonic prescriptions point to an addiction older than platonism itself. Derrida's entry into Plato's pharmacy is not a return to the place where the drug *originates* but to the place where it has been *written up* into a number of prescriptions. Exposing the decisionism implicit in the traditional ascendancy of speech of over writing, one strand of Plato's text, at the same time as demonstrating the instability of this decision, is at the centre of Derrida's essay. The strategic *in*-decisionism of deconstruction offers an alternative entry into the theorising of 'drugs' which is not aimed at the linguistic mastery (conceptualisation and representation) of the truth about drugs. Instead, it attempts to deal with drugs in a way which is responsive to the discovery, as Ronell puts it, that 'drugs resist conceptual arrest' (Ronell, 1992: 51).

In *Plato's Pharmacy* Derrida views this pharmaceutical thinking in terms of the entry of thought into *the game* (*paidia*). The reading undertaken marks the entry into, or the opening gambit, but does not aim at *mastery* of the game:[4]

> There is always a surprise in store for... any criticism that might think it had mastered the game, surveyed all the threads at once, deluding itself, too, in wanting to look at the text without touching it, without laying a hand on the 'object' without risking – *which is the only chance of entry into the game*, by getting a few fingers caught – the addition of some new thread. (Derrida, 1981b: 63)

Playing the game, like addiction, might be considered to be a way of 'going nowhere' in the teleological order of things – a suspension of the projection which opens the future – were it not for the ethical dimension of *playing* the game *well*. A *playing well* that would have everything to do with what Ronell refers to as an 'ethics of decision' and links with the attempt to 'think the drug at a higher level'. We need to ask what such a *playing well with drugs* could possibly mean in terms of the everyday world, which Nancy, reading Heidegger, reminds us takes place 'right at the "they"', and which, despite all this hyperbolic reflexivity, thinking never essentially leaves. Or, in plain English, we need to ask how might this change the way we live our relationship to drugs in our culture today.

### Intoxication and dosage: doing drugs well

> There is no system that can hold or take 'drugs' for long. Instituted on the basis of moral or political evaluations, the concept of drugs cannot be comprehended under any independent scientific system. These observations do not mean to imply that a certain type of narcotic supplement has been in the least rejected by metaphysics. To a great degree, it *is all more or less a question of dosage.* (Ronell, 1992: 61, *my emphasis*)

For Socrates the *pharmakon* is a truth drug which works well, but only in the proper dosage: as noted above, he is against the 'blind usage of drugs' (Derrida, 1981b: 72). The philosopher is here identified with the certified pharmacist. Derrida's attempt to attain a still higher form of the drug discovers how Socratic truth is itself but one of the effects of the drug (in the form of Writing). Clearly it will be necessary to experiment with a drug which is not licensed (nor can be licensed) and for which no reliable table of dosages can exist. To get beyond thinking the drug as *substance*, there is no alternative but to *partake* of it. One has to philosophise *on* drugs, which amounts to a kind thoughtful self-administration which avoids cultural submission to drug expertise. The rhetorical attempt to impose *drug-freeness*, which is being obsessively pursued especially in certain quarters of the USA today, is complicit with the squeaky-clean-ness of the objectivist neutral perspective. It aims at something utterly unattainable, because language itself is irreducibly metaphorical, or, to borrow a word Ronell invents, a kind of 'tropium'. This is something Derrida's writing always acknowledges. When Derrida proposes a further substitution: 'Writing is not only a drug, it is a game (*paidia*)' (1995: 234) he is evoking his earlier discussion of the relationship between the drug and play which serves as a *mis-en-scène* to *Plato's Pharmacy*, and proposing a recreational, pharmaceutical alternative to the metaphysical addiction which 'goes nowhere'. For any writing or drug-taking to be of value it must enter the game, it must be 'well-dosed' and not the arbitrary addition of 'any old thing'; not the sterile conformity to '"methodological prudence", the "norms of objectivity" and the "safeguards of knowledge"' (Derrida, 1981b: 62). A good dose neither fuels addiction nor is it (the pretence of) abstemious sobriety. The writing/drug supplement must be 'rigorously prescribed, but by the necessities of the *game* and the logic of *play*' (Derrida, 1981b: 62). Such a being-on-drugs is neither before nor after the decision on drugs, it is simply *on* drugs. The *pharmakon* as either drug or writing aims at a kind of exemplary coincidence of play and pleasure; at *jouissance*.

Any *theorem* of drugs is always late on the scene of the *responsibility* for drugs; responsibility precedes any *system* of drug prohibition and control – and it is a characteristic of every attempted 'deconstruction' (of whatever text or theme) that it directs thought to this ethical dimension. In the modern everyday world, taking drugs *well* is still conceptualised on an essentially platonic basis; something reflected in the fact that 'we do not object to the drug user's pleasure *per se*, but we cannot abide by the fact that this pleasure is taken in an experience without truth' (Derrida, 1995: 236). Derrida's skilful loosening of the concept of *pharmakon* in Plato, however, is precisely a loosening rather than a loss of control. It does not lead to libertarianism, neither with regard to the 'materialities' we call 'drugs' nor with regard to all the writerly inscriptions of drugs. Drugs for Derrida do not present a means of transcendence and deconstruction is not so much concerned with the task of breaking through certain limits as questioning the operation of limits in the first place. It represents, rather, a return to the passage or impasse of the border by aiming at *good repetition*.[5]

## Sacrifice and bad conscience

The 'bad conscience of our era' with regard to drugs comes with the uneasiness of the sacrifice associated with them. The decision on drugs determines the reality of drug culture and selects 'drug victims' (drug addicts and victims of drug crime alike) who are often paraded ceremoniously before the rest of society in the media. At the same time it passes the responsibility for this drama to the drugs themselves. This relationship between drugs and scapegoating can be traced to the conceptualisation of the drug itself. In *The Golden Bough*, for instance, J. G. Frazer records how the sacrifice of human scapegoats (*pharmakoi*) was once employed by the Athenians in order to restore cosmic balance and political legitimacy:

The Athenians regularly maintained a number of degraded and useless beings at public expense; when any calamity, such as a plague drought or famine befell the city, they sacrificed two of these outcasts as scapegoats. (Frazer, 1971: 758)

The use of the *pharmakoi* as a cultural prosthesis appears to have a direct connection with representation of narcotics in general today, as personal, chemical prostheses. In modern times, the role of the sovereign subject is considered to be central to the idea of cultural self-determination and individual freedom, and the use of the personal chemical prosthesis is figured as having its sacrificial victim in the (ab)user himself or herself. This is because drug abuse represents the contamination or falsification of the body of society as a whole. Drug users whose use breaches prescriptive controls (and by definition, all users of illicit drugs) are seen as potential self-sacrificers and a general threat to society at large. The contamination of any part, particularly contamination that circulates in the blood, is deemed the most threatening of all.

Any systematic representation of drugs implies the sacrifice of the drug as *play*. But if, as Derrida insists, there is no escaping 'the sacrificial structure of discourse' (1991b : 112–13), any new thinking of drugs – which invokes the notion of an encounter with drugs beyond 'the system' (of controls and so on) – can also only be formulated in language on the basis of a sacrifice. So, how might such a rethinking of drugs ever come about? Derrida's approach is to propose the controlled decommissioning of the concept of 'drug'. Rendering 'drugs' unthinkable by making 'drugs' a trope of *différance* is the first stage of an always imminent refiguring of the conceptual frame which contains it. The deconstruction of drugs is directed at the *decisions* which have always already been made, concerning them; it is aimed at returning to a point where the 'conceptual' jury on drugs is out (and will always remain out). It involves working within a moment of *in*decision, out of which a new precedent may always be set. It is the committal of thought to experimentation. Such theoretical reflection can promote changes in the law by putting questions to 'the law on drugs' and by shaking the very concept of what a drug *is*; by appealing to the idea that, perhaps even more urgently, we should consider what it is that a drug *does*. And, by demonstrating that the whole debate is already a form of being-on-drugs in the first place, there opens the prospect of exposing how the *decision* has become embedded within drug cultural praxes. Far from knowing 'the truth about drugs', the conventional wisdom and expertise about drugs are revealed to be 'confirmed' only by their own reflection in the everyday life they rule over.

The 'law of sacrifice' requires that a price is always paid in accordance with the specific delimitation of drugs (for example, drug-related crime is the price of drugs being illegal). I am wondering here about the nature of the alternative (understanding of) drugs Derrida's pharmacy dispenses. What does a prescription written according to 'the necessities of the *game* and the logic of *play*' imply with regard to the materiality of 'actual drugs'? The idea of *dosage* is a key to the answer. Firstly, the term 'dosage' as it is ordinarily understood must be provisionally suspended: if 'dosage' is uncoupled from the systems of prescription and proscription and general ethico-political decisionism of tradition, it becomes available for re-decision, and, with that emerges the possibility of a new *measure* for drugs. If 'drugs' could be freed from medico-juridical monopolisers of 'the truth about drugs', then the specific constellation of narco-power – which distributes the drug trade between the official drug marketers of the pharmaceutical industries on the one hand, and the unofficial drug-baron fiefdoms on the other – might shift in an ethically productive way. Secondly, the discourse of drugs and drug taking needs to be freed from the requirement to articulate itself in the language of individual rights, the public/private distinction, and in relation to the given norms and mores of psychic (and most often psychiatric) propriety. A deconstructive approach assists this by holding in abeyance the false alternatives of libertarianism on the one hand and rigid prescriptions and proscriptions on the other, and it proposes allowing, in a sense, for 'drugs' to speak for themselves. Can drugs, whose effects are not merely bodily and psychological but also social and political (as a consequence of their position before the law) be used, *in the right dosage*, to work at their own detoxification; to undo the toxic effect that is always associated with them and given to them by virtue of their figuring in systems of representation?

## Applying drug(ged) theory to the everyday drug(ged) world

What I have done in this chapter so far is to apply Derridean thinking to the subject of drugs and the discourse of drugs. It is a style of 'application' in the form of reflexive philosophising and involves the drawing into the *game of reading*, others such as Plato, Socrates, Heidegger, Nancy, Ronell by proxy or directly, and, so to speak, playing the dope trope. It involves casting the philosophical scene as a substitute drug scene and mapping one onto the other. Deconstruction does and does not allow itself to be easily applied in any ordinary sense. But if 'application' is generally understood to involve forms of intervention in the everyday understanding of cultural matters at large, then this application risks limiting itself to the realm of 'theory'. Nancy's reminder that all thinking ultimately lives in the everyday reminds us also that life's ordinary concerns are not put on hold whilst such theorisation attends to thinking them otherwise. Thinking otherwise needs also to be committed to *re-creation* in the widest possible sense: we need an 'ethics of decision', but we need for this to be practical ethics also. Derridean pharmaceutical thinking is a work needing to be done and redone; to be *repeated* but at the same time to be done *anew*, precisely because it does *not* result in the issuance of directives. What it does do is radically shift the ground of thinking that ultimately aims, in wholly practical terms, to redecide and implement controlling decisions on drugs. In the last section of this chapter I shall sketch some reflections on everyday drug use as they are related to what has been said so far.

It may be the case that deconstructive scepticism translates more readily into political wariness rather than radical policy ideas. Deconstructing 'drugs' leads thinking into the border zone between dictated juridical prohibition and an 'everything is permitted' libertarianism, but to what end? The point is that to decide well at this level requires not blind reliance on expertise, but for expertise to be exposed to a rigorous decommissioning of its entire system of regulation and conceptualisation of drugs, from within which and through which it speaks. This already, and perhaps unavoidably, begins to sound like the preparation of the ground for a new liberalism with regard to drugs. *Dosage* is an appropriate and useful metaphor for the non-dictatorial decision for control. It is dosage, rather than the law proper, which opens up the possibility of a relation to drugs which is ethical rather than dictated by mores. The rejection of certain laws in the ordinary sense is not against 'the law in the ethical sense'.[6] The idea of the good use, or 'good repetition' of drug use, is not exhausted by medical expertise, whose prescriptions aim only at health understood on the basis of the *medical body* and the use of drugs may be measured independently of their medical use. For example use of various psychotropic drugs within Rave culture may or may not be judged to be 'good use' in the lives of those who choose to use it, by, for example, moralists, judges, doctors and indeed by the users, but their use may also be 'measured' in relation to its stimulation of the *dancing body*. Opium may be measured in relation to dreaming, amphetamines in relation to energy, hashish in relation to the imagination, nitrous oxide in relation to laughter, Viagra in relation to sex and so on. The technology of drug design and manufacture today presents the possibility of future drugs used for optimising various species of aesthesiological experience. None of this would preclude general cultural debate about the 'morality' of self-intoxication (for example, in terms of the 'artificiality' of certain pleasures, to recall the reflections on drug use of Baudelaire).

In *The Rhetoric of Drugs*, Derrida acknowledges the necessity of *controlling* substances, but his pharmacology does not preclude a liberal politics of drugs. It seeks, on the contrary to keep open the questioning of the political, the discourse of rights and of the public and private, as well as that of drugs, all of which genuinely present matters for 'experts' to deal with on an everyday basis. On the other hand Derrida seeks to think precisely such notions as these always in relation to the price paid for forcing them to enter systematic discourse as such. The necessity of the 'theorem' with its implicit decisionism and the 'limits of theorising' must be thought together in an experimental the search for new recipes. Without this the thinking of drugs will continue to be controlled by 'experts' and the battleground of drugs and drug culture, upon which so much blood is unnecessarily shed, will be perpetuated. Derrida distances himself emphatically and repeatedly not only from the metaphysics which governs this situation, with its polarity of being for or against drugs, but also from any ethico-political position which ultimately derives from it. He links this kind of assumed authority with the threat posed to civil liberties by the very juridicality of the law itself. The control of drugs and civil liberty is not merely a matter of political resistance narco-power alone, because the political is only a part of the picture. Thomas Szasz puts this less equivocally than Derrida ever would when he says:

> It is impressive testimony to our powers of self-deception that we believe we can expand our civil liberties by opposing threats to it from politicians, while at the same time inviting and embracing threats to it from physicians and psychiatrists. (Szasz, 1974: 21)

Why is the 'deconstruction of drugs' committed to equivocality? It is because libertarianism rests on a simple reversal of the relationship between the law on drugs and a rectification of the substance/effect dichotomy, which according to Szasz is simply perceived the wrong way around:

> We are repelled by the opium habit (for example) not because it is harmful, but the other way around: we regard it as harmful in order to maintain our justification for prohibiting it. (Szasz, 1974: 34)

For Derrida this would constitute a kind of double-blind argument: it is a *pharmakon* whose effect is distorted by a placebo factor. In other words, with this simple inversion of the decision on drugs, the drug user never knows what he or she is getting. It proposes, I suggest, a bad use of drugs precisely because it has absolutely no regard for dosage. The reversal in Derrida's thinking of the drug, quite unlike that of Szasz, aims at incorporating drugs into the activity of rethinking the concepts of 'drugs'. It therefore works toward a displacement of the 'shared axiomatics' of both pro- and anti-drug discourses' (Derrida, 1995: 247).

If Derrida's thinking on drugs could be said to prepare the space for a new thinking of the playful usage of drugs, and to point the way to a new social wisdom on drugs, then it still remains for us to think through the meaning of this in everyday terms. In particular this needs to be done in relation to the themes of sobriety and intoxication and their respective positions in modernity's cultural self-image. It is interesting to find, at the very point where Nancy emphasises the contiguity of the everyday and the ontologically significant in relation to *Dasein*'s 'decision of existence', that one can discern what looks suspiciously like a concession to the policing of excess, when he says:

> Right in the situation, decisiveness 'does not stem from idealistic exactions soaring above existence and its possibilities; it springs from a *sober understanding* of what are basically the factual possibilities of *Dasein*. *Not the intoxication*, the enthusiasm of floating ideals, but the simple fact of existence. (Nancy, 1993: 106 citing Heidegger, 1973: Sect. 62, *my emphasis*)

The phenomena of sobriety and intoxication would be far from irrelevant to any re-thinking of drugs at an everyday level, and I fail to see how this declared preference for sobriety can escape the negative aspects of the decisionism language involves us in. For example, it certainly does not help us interpret the factual possibility of *Dasein* which is, amongst other things and on occasion, to be as a high as a kite. The preference for the 'sobriety' of the everyday is no doubt, in an everyday manner, an aspect of the prejudice of the cultural project which valorises sobriety and reason and demands that they be made to prevail and rule. But privileging the thinking of drugs 'soberly', immediately threatens to close off what might otherwise be regarded as the subjective experience of drugged consciousness – the everyday reality of being on drugs – and the insight such experience might be thought to provide. Derrida, too, as noted, expresses wariness with regard to the way in which, just as religion was once the opium of the masses, drugs easily become the 'religion of the atheist poets' (Derrida, 1995: 240). But what might be the ontologically interpretative standing of such an everyday being-on-drugs experienced as a controlled dose of madness, in comparison to the phenomenology of *angst*, 'thrown-ness' (*Geworfenheit*) and mountain hut repairs, which are at the centre of Heidegger's analytic in *Being and Time*? Someone on amphetamines, cocaine, Prozac or Ecstasy has little in common with the tranquillised *Dasein* which is 'addicted to going nowhere'. The creative output of those atheist poets (and artists) on drugs such as Artaud, Coleridge, Poe, Trakl, Jünger, Lowry, Huxley, Michaux,[7] Warhol, De Kooning – just to start a list which would leave out fewer twentieth-century writers and artists than it would include – points to the profound cultural significance of drugs beyond the usual concerns of the law and medicine. But there is no reason to suppose they have not played a role in the exercise of power by political culture makers, too, democrats and tyrants alike: Victoria, Churchill, Hitler and Kennedy are only some of the better known to have their doctors supply them with drugs to help them cope with the pressures of office.[8] Here we see a clue to perhaps one meaning of Nietzsche's comment that the history of narcotica is 'almost the entire history of our culture' (Nietzsche, 1974: Sect. 86). The 'almost' indicating that it is almost literally true that history is on drugs.[9]

Derrida clearly rejects the role of drugs in any notion of the *passage* to 'the other side', and has in many contexts sought to expose the shared axiomatics mystical and scientific claims to the truth. In *The Rhetoric of Drugs* he emphatically argues that 'a thinking and a politics of "drugs" would involve the displacement of these two ideologies *at once* opposed in their common metaphysics'(Derrida, 1995: 246). Despite Derrida's personal refusal to commit himself to an everyday position on drugs, the deconstructive re-thinking of 'drugs' he proposes is far from apolitical, for it challenges the logic which ties 'drugs' with the cultural practice of scapegoating those who are represented as the 'drug abusers' and 'traffickers'. It shows there is scope for rethinking the decisions that have already been made concerning drugs and hence opens the prospect of a culture which would have different sense of its relation to them.

In ancient times it was said that the Medusa's blood was a *pharmakon*: one drop cured disease but two drops were a deadly poison. With such blood circulating in the body of modern culture, there will always be a need to get the 'dose' just right.

## Notes

1 The 'The Rhetoric of Drugs' interview was first published in the journal *Autremont*, 106 (1989). All references here are to the M. Israel translation (Derrida, 1995).

2 A comment Derrida makes about the occasion in Ken McMullen's film *Ghost Dance* (Looseyard Productions, 1983).

3 Ronell's focus is on Div. I Part VI, esp. Section 41.

4 For an interesting discussion of play as Derrida's 'Hyper-Nietzschean Strategy' see M. Haar, 'The Play of Nietzsche in Derrida', trans. W. McNeil in D. Wood (ed.) (1992: 52–71).

5 Derrida discusses the aporetic logic of borders and limits and their thematic privilege in his work in *Aporias* (1993a). Another discussion, particularly relevant to this chapter, is to be found in the essay 'Before the Law' (1993b), originally published in 1982. Derrida explores there the relationship between 'the law' of a discourse and 'play' as *jouer la loi*. Cf especially 216f. and n. 27.

6 Cf. Derrida and Pierre-Jean LaBarrierès (1986) and the discussion of this expression by J. Llewelyn, 'Responsibility and Undecidability' in D. Wood (ed.) (1992: 72–95).

7 In the following chapter I discuss at length Henri Michaux's *The Major Ordeals of the Mind* (1974).

8 The case of Victoria's use of opium is well known. Not unsurprisingly politicians have a penchant for amphetamines. Szasz provides journalistic evidence of a Kennedy physician supplying 'speed' injections to JFK during the 1961 summit with Khrushchev in Vienna. Cf. Szasz (1974:13).

9 Ronell cites this passage and states that her own work 'settles with this Nietzschean "almost" – the place where *narcotics* articulates a quiver between history and ontology' (Ronell, 1992: 2).

# 3    Deconstruction and drugs – all mixed up

> Nick had a deprecating little laugh that he used for punctuation. Sort of an apology for talking at all in the telepathizing world of the addict ... (W. Burroughs, *Naked Lunch*, p.170)

> 'You're feeling it aren't you?'
> 'Yeah, I am actually.'
> 'It's quite impossible to describe, isn't it?'
> 'Yeah, it is.'  (M. Amis, *Dead Babies*, p.187)

> Sometimes ah think that people become junkies because they subconsciously crave a wee bit of silence. (I. Welsh, *Trainspotting*, p. 7)

> He couldn't tell at first but he was dancing like a maniac... they were all going crazy. (I. Welsh, *Ecstasy*, p. 27)

> No doubt we should have to make some distinction between... drugs, but this distinction is wiped out in the rhetoric of fantasy that is at the root of the interdiction: drugs, it is said, make one lose any sense of true reality. (J. Derrida, *Rhetoric of Drugs*, p. 236)

## Culture and interdiction

Shortcircuiting the exasperating detour of communication, or more generally suspending the proactive expenditure of the will's energy as it works to fuel its own consciousness, is the mark of an urge to a junky-like descent into a silence which few people at some point in their lives wouldn't admit to craving – if not at some point every day. But drugs and their effects are always a matter of the mix, the concoction or recipe, the purity and the impurities, as well as of the 'set and setting', as Timothy Leary and his coterie never tired of saying; and, with street drugs, there is also the matter of all the unknown ingredients, the precipitates of amateur chemistry, or whatever was to hand to give bulk to the stuff as it changed hands on its way to market. It is such contingencies as these which determine whether drugs intoxicate, narcotise, energise, silence, make a person withdrawn and dreamy, talk their head off, suffer genital retraction or an inconsolable erection – or just go plain crazy.

It is widely known and acknowledged that 'recreational' or 'lifestyle' drug use is a pandemic phenomenon and 'addictive' drug use is becoming increasingly widespread in all western societies. As Noel Gallagher of the British rock band Oasis infamously commented, taking (illicit) drugs is for the 'chemical generation' like having a cup of tea, a part of normal daily life. Given the popular deployment of the binary distinctions such as recreation/addiction and the use/abuse within the wider discussion of drugs in society today, it might seem to be obvious that there is an urgent need to challenge such simplistic thinking and that deconstruction is unprecedentedly appropriate for this. Clearly the network of discourses organising the 'drugs debate', and, ultimately, the logistics of the 'war on drugs', too, if only for their crass 'binaryisms', are potential sites of deconstructive interventions of one sort or another. The outcome of this chapter's thematic conjunction of 'deconstruction and drugs' might at least go towards a re-ordering of the controlling distinctions operating in the world(s) of drugs and drug taking. That is, after all, surely what is hinted at in Derrida's remark (cited above) about the 'rhetoric of fantasy' and the 'rational' rejection of the pleasures gained from drugs, which are generally assumed to be enjoyed in the absence of any 'truth'. There is a need at the very least, surely, to remake some governing distinctions.

But even more crucially, 'truth' and 'the truth about drugs' cannot avoid cross-contamination: as the former must somehow contain the latter, they can never be entirely unaffected by each other. Consequently, drugs, as much as anything else about them (their social and political contexts, the 'altered states' they produce, the 'drug scenes' they figure in and so on) play a part in determining the specificity of their own multiple manifestations. The 'truth about drugs' is distributed and presented in a spectrum of well-known and lesser-known drug literatures, ranging from those expressed in terms of 'mental experiences', 'rushes' and 'highs', through pharmaco-anthropological studies of mystical tribal rituals, to textbooks recording the medical and legal classifications of drugs. Such discourses and narratives figure yet more widely in innumerable cultural forms as different from each other as 'great modern literature' and school playground chat. However, when *the* so-called 'truth about drugs' is marshalled to serve as a rhetorical weapon in the armoury of prohibitionism, one can be sure that behind this there lies a degree of conflation and confusion of elements of the many possible drug discourses and narratives. As was pointed out in the last chapter, 'there is not a *single* world of drugs' and the tendency to regard drugs as belonging to an homogenous series is itself, as Derrida says, 'delirious, indeed narcotising' (1995: 237). The trouble is that the 'truth about drugs' is always exactly what it thinks it is not: it is itself a particular kind of discursive cocktail and not at all the drug-free, uncontaminated, sober, pure of heart and mind, objective, legitimate regulator of drugs.

A deconstructive approach to the 'truth about drugs' – the truth authorising *all* current delimitations of drugs – offers the prospect of rethinking our relation to the alterity of drugs, for example, with respect to their prescriptive and normative systems of reference. The question I want to explore further in this chapter is: in what ways might it be possible to exploit drugs to disrupt the many attempts to contain them? Could deconstruction 'take drugs' in order to inaugurate a cultural 'new deal' on drugs, one that would be ethical in so far as it would enable our culture to get along with drugs – whose ubiquity in every sense is never in doubt – *otherwise* than we currently do? Such questions are of course 'theoretical', but they are always directed too, at the possibility of discovering alternative 'drug practices'. Such practices could never simply be derived from a better understanding of drugs in the traditional sense of possessing new knowledge about them. They could emerge only out of a double-science which attempts to think together the theoretical as well as the practical aspects of the modernity of 'being-on-drugs' (Ronell, 1992: 59). It is modernity's 'intersecting cut' between drugs, freedom and what Ronell calls the 'addicted condition' that must be subjected to an 'interminable analysis' (1992: 59).

This chapter will try an experimental mixture of 'drugs' and 'deconstruction' in an attempt to discern the nature of the peculiar relation between them. It will show that the theme of 'drugs' is as useful a way to elucidate the workings of 'deconstruction' as is deconstruction a means of reworking our understanding of drugs and their effects, making each serve as a user's guide to the other. Disciplinary propriety would ordinarily demand that it be made clear at the outset what type of drugs this chapter brings into conjunction with the subject of deconstruction. It would insist on a preliminary compliance with one or another, or several, determinations of the object as such – by means of definitions, taxonomies, systems of classification and so on. But, as the nature of this 'complicity' with supposed drugs expertise (and typologies in general) is precisely a theme here, and because the deconstruction of anything has to begin by means of a partial suspension of the metaphysical conceptual determination of the object in terms of what it *is*, any such demand must also be subject, by the same logic, to a strategic suspension. Such a placing of the object of inquiry – namely the word/concept 'drugs' – under erasure (*sous-rature*) by deconstruction is in anticipation of a new thinking of them eventually emerging.

Thus the initial move of a deconstructive approach to 'drugs' begins with an act of 'abuse' – not of actual drugs, but of their concept: Derrida in fact uses this very metaphor 'abuse' to describe deconstruction itself. Deconstruction is 'an abusive investigation which introduces beforehand what it seeks to find' (Derrida, 1978: 154). This chapter itself is 'abusive' too in that, like all inquiry, it introduces the 'foreign substance of a debate' (Derrida, 1978: 154). Deconstruction is, therefore, no stranger to abuse. It is 'parasitically' abusive in relation to the tradition of western philosophy, and, as is so often the case in relation to discussions of deconstruction, the theme at hand – the 'abuse' in question – is doubled-up in it: deconstruction itself has often been made an object of abuse for the alleged irresponsibility of its 'nihilism'. It has, nonetheless, always recognised the importance, even the necessity, of 'abuse' in another sense: as a tactic in its strategic underminings, loosenings, erosions, subversions and (one might add and add…) its '*et ceteras*'; its chains of substitutions and linguistic gamings without end – all of which are abusive in the conventional sense, from the perspective of orthodoxies, authorities, institutions and so on, which supposedly underwrite the 'truth' about *everything*. But without some sort of 'abuse' somewhere along the line, without some sort of break with regulation and with modernity's decision of the meaning of 'drugs', and the drawing of the line, as if once and for all, between ab/use, regarding propriety in general and with respect to anything in particular (not just drugs in fact), nothing would ever change. Without experimentation, without acting on the urge to excess, without 'aggressions' and 'infidelities', as Derrida says at the same point, in whatever cultural forms these take – and here we are talking not only of philosophical and literary modes of experimentation but of all 'heresies' and even half-formed heretical impulses – there would never have been anything worthy of the name 'culture'. Any culture identifiable on the basis of its *interdictions* only stands to confirm this.

What is abusively introduced beforehand in this chapter is the idea that there is an affinity between deconstruction and drugs. This is, of course, directly remarked in several ways and in several places, more or less explicitly, in Derrida's writings. In particular, as the previous chapter showed, in relation to his discussions of the *pharmakon* in the essay 'Plato's Pharmacy' (Derrida, 1981b); in relation to supplementarity, undecidability, play, repetition, in other words, right at the heart of deconstruction's thinking of *writing* (*écriture*) and textuality. As with the term 'drug', *pharmakon* bears the sense of both 'antidote' and 'poison', but it is (in Plato) as discussed in the previous chapter, a metaphor for writing, too. Derrida's account of the *pharmakon* (in this instance in the form the text of Lysias' speech) as it is in play in the opening scene of *Phaedrus*, undermines the possibility of its representing, or offering up, an 'unveiled' or 'naked' truth (Derrida, 1981b: 71, citing Plato 230d–e). The difference between deconstruction as *writing* and 'drugs' is seen as being reducible, though never quite entirely to zero: 'writing is not only a drug' (Derrida, 1995: 234). By attempting to think the 'drug' *as* 'writing' and vice versa, the concepts of 'drugs' and 'writing' are made to operate in Derrida's text, each in the guise of the other – allowing each to participate in alternative systems of substitutions. They each thereby become available for reinscription; their recuperation by the system which controls them and distinguishes them is *deferred*. In this linguistic play, 'drugs' become approachable in their 'undecidability', as not-yet-decided, not as they are when locked into traditional, orthodox, institutional, normative and prescriptive systems of reference. Playing with drugs, experimenting with them, engaging with them, by means of an 'incessant tropism' (Harvey, 1992: 215) or by other experimental means and in other senses, is what their conjunction with deconstruction makes possible.

The investigation of this chapter is undertaken, then, with a view to the possible refigurings of 'drugs' this conjunction might produce and which subsequently might be seen to bear on their current cultural toxicity and future prospects for cultural detoxification. Undeniably, such a project requires a certain kind of abusive *yes* to drugs 'in advance' of any conclusion that might be arrived at by saying *yes* to deconstruction as the means of getting there.

## Saying 'yes to drugs' and 'yes to deconstruction'

In everyday life and on different cultural plateaux today, countless people are saying yes to both deconstruction and drugs, some of them undoubtedly to both. But what is the significance of these affirmations and what is the nature of the connection between them here? There may be many instances of yea-saying to both deconstruction and drugs, literally in the same head, but in this chapter the real concern is not with what goes on inside heads but with the 'yes' which can be said to the conjunction of 'deconstruction *and* drugs' heading this chapter. It engages in an experimental affirmation of the reciprocal supplementarity of deconstruction and drugs, and seeks to discover whether drugs can serve as an 'ally' in the deconstruction of the rational normality Reason imposes on thinking in general.

What then is the point? To say that deconstruction is 'like a drug'? Yes. That drugs figure in the thinking which attempts to approach the limits of Reason? Yes. To supplement all previous delimitations of 'drugs' with an account of the unthought, or even unthinkable, *pharmakon* of 'drugs', and to find that the values of purity and sobriety are merely rhetorical, antithetical mythologies figuring in a system of oppressions? To see that contamination is a more useful trope for thinking about our 'narcotic modernity', and that the addiction/recreation dichotomy needs greater attention than it has received in other approaches to drugs?... Yes, yes, yes, yes.

> I say the *yes* not the word 'yes', for there can be a *yes* without the word, which is precisely our problem... What is it that is spoken, written, what occurs [*advient*], with *yes*? (Derrida, 1991a: 590)

Derrida's meditation on the *yes* – on the 'before language, in language, but also (the) experience of the plurality of languages' (1991a: 590) – is helpful here. The expression *yes* connects drugs and deconstruction: it marks a correspondence between the *yes* of the drug user (sometimes verbalised) at the point of 'the rush' or onset of the effect of a drug introjected (ingested, inhaled, imbibed and so on) into the body and it is the *yes* of deconstruction's effects with the corpus of metaphysics. Both are an occasion of a certain affirmation and 'coming' (*advient*). This reminds us of two important things: firstly, that experience is (something) more and other than the particular language (*parole*) which expresses it, but also, secondly, that this difference, between these two yesses, is in no way independent of the system of representation which 'feeds-back', determining the understanding of experience itself. In other words, experience is always structured, organised and 'experienced', on the condition of its contamination by the marks of language (*langue*) – of one 'yes' by another 'yes'.

This all really began with a simple observation: both deconstruction and drugs are to be found at work everywhere, changing, in one sense or another, the way that our culture relates to, sees, thinks, perceives and represents *everything*. The bigger theme of *totality and its transgression* is what has prompted this framing of their conjunction. For this to begin to take effect, we must specify the drug/text this chapter is really on. The other ingredient, another text, or *pharmakon*, taken here as a point of focus, is *The Major Ordeals of the Mind* (1974) by the French poet, essayist and artist Henri Michaux.[1] In this work he writes-up an account of his experimental explorations of the limits of human reason through the use of drugs. The first section, entitled 'Disorientations', opens with the following:

> I want to lift the veil from the 'normal', the unrecognised, unsuspected, incredible, enormous normal. The abnormal first acquainted me with it, disclosing to me the prodigious number of operations which the most ordinary of men performs, casually, unconcerned, as routine work, interested only in the outcome and not in the mechanisms, however marvellous, far more wonderful than the ideas he sets such store by, which are often so commonplace, mediocre, unworthy of the matchless instrument that reveals and plies them. I want to lift the veil from the complex mechanisms which make man, first and foremost an operator. (Michaux, 1974: 3)

Michaux finds the psychotropic drugs he uses to 'brilliantly dramatise' these 'operations' which give rise to 'normality'. The work the above-cited paragraph prefaces consists of a series of reports recorded within the drama of his being high, which are interwoven with more sober reflections, footnotes and asides. This text of Michaux will be taken as the *pharmakon* of preference for the experiment with deconstruction and drugs I wish to undertake here, and for several reasons. The descriptions, narratives and comments it presents, parallel in several respects, if only metaphorically (that is, by way of a certain displacement), the effects of deconstruction as it works away at the limits of metaphysics, exposing the instability of its foundations and promoting its auto-destruction. Both deconstruction and these reflections of Michaux, which record, often in a style which mimics empiricism, the struggle of consciousness to retain control of its thinking at the point at which 'thought is short-circuited and left behind' (1974: 139), involve an onslaught on Reason. They each undertake de-systematisations of systems of organisation, both egological and ontological, and approach the institutions Reason and 'good sense' in their various states of ruination. As we shall see, for Michaux, the loosening of control over thinking's grip on 'reality' which the drug (mescaline in this case) facilitates, engenders, most interestingly, an experience with language. From his perspective, this exposes how what is soberly regarded as the grip *on* reality can also be seen as the grip *of* normality. And, it demonstrates that this is something the poet, even if unknowingly, is both sensitive to and driven to contest. For Michaux, it is drugs, rather than any philosophical poetics, which are able to transport thinking to the point, or border, at which the operation and force of the normalising rhetorics orchestrated by Reason can be 'observed'. Drugs are Michaux's means of entry to this scene of destruction and it is from amongst the wreckage of the machinery of normalisation that he articulates his claim to go beyond what 'the metaphysicians' are able to think.

> More than the all too excellent skills of the metaphysicians, it is the dementias, the backwardnesses, the deliriums, the ecstasies and agonies, the breakdowns in mental skills which are really suited to 'reveal' us to ourselves. (Michaux, 1974: 7)

But, despite their shared interest in and distrust of the delimitations of the thinking authorised on the basis of the 'all too excellent skills of the metaphysicians', no one would deny that doing deconstruction and doing drugs, in this sense, are two wholly different things. Their respective relationships to Reason and modern rationality, intrinsic to their approaches to the *abyssal* (whether in terms of 'logic' or 'experience') are as different as Newtonian experiments and bungee-jumping, when used as means of exploring the earth's gravity. And yet, as Derrida acknowledges, drugs or the drugs theme, once taken (up) into the deconstructive frame of reference produces intriguing results:

> [T]he farther we go the more the question of drugs seems inseparable not only from such tremendous questions as 'the concept', 'reason', 'truth', 'memory', 'work', and so forth, but also from the centres of urgency where all these things appear to gather symptomatically… (Derrida, 1995: 248)

The already vast literature around the 'theory of deconstruction', concerning what deconstruction is and what it can do – for example, as a way of reading texts, of re-reading the tradition, of restaging of the ancient question of the relationship between philosophy and literature or reason and madness and so on, is increasingly being extended to a wider array of cultural and political themes.[2] What is often understood as deconstruction's parasitical relation to 'metaphysics' is in fact inversely reflected in its need to be always fuelled by the 'foreign substance of a debate'. And whereas the theme of 'drugs' is normally anchored in the traditional disciplines of economics, criminology, health and addiction studies and so on, deconstruction remains open to the destabilising effects of drugs on 'normality' itself.

For Michaux, though, it is psychotropic drugs themselves which effectuate a breakdown of what he refers to as 'normality'.

> In quite different ways, in many ways, the drug catches out, discovers, unmasks mental operations, injecting consciousness where it had never been, and at the same time dislodging it from places where it had always been: a queer case of drawers that can function only alternately – *some must be closed before others may open.* (Michaux, 1974: 5–6, *my emphasis*)

Deconstruction's engagement with (the theme of) 'drugs' is twofold. Firstly, it calls for the deconstruction of the discursive totalities which frame a 'drug world' in which drugs are made the scapegoat for a series of oppressions – too numerous to mention, but ranging (at the end of a lengthy chain of substitutions concerning, above all, the determination of the drug as 'toxic substance') from the murder of Colombian peasants to the normalisation of the casual violence of the strip-search. As Derrida asks: 'How can one ignore the growing and undelimitable, that is, worldwide power of those super-efficient and properly capitalist phantom states that are the mafia and the drug cartels on every continent?' (Derrida, 1994: 83). This is indicative of the ethico-political dimension of the general deconstruction of drug rhetorics. Secondly, deconstruction presents the further possibility of a transfigurative *opening* and an alternative thinking of the relation to drugs. Having recognised that 'Every phantasmatic organisation, whether collective or individual, is the invention of a drug or rhetoric of drugs' (Derrida, 1995: 247), there emerges the prospect that drugs may be taken *otherwise* – in a sense for which there is as yet no concept, on the basis of a non-authoritarian, deregulated understanding of their many and diverse cultural effects. In other words, the force of dominant drug rhetorics may be countered by the de-rationalising force of a reinscribed notion of drugs. But could there be such a *measure* for drugs, unfettered, for example, by such rhetorics as those of authenticity and inauthenticity, of health and illness, of use and abuse and so on? This is the key question deconstruction enables us to ask in a meaningful way, and this style of questioning is itself a certain sort of 'measure' of its own distantiation from those rhetorics whose authority it intrinsically challenges. Where it might lead is hardly clear, but this possibility is something very real, not just a moment in a *closed* circle of substitutions: it signals more than a return to the same set of alternatives concerning drugs; it signals more than an inversion of traditional, hierarchical, binary evaluations.

These two elements of the deconstructive engagement with drugs, the dismantling of rhetorics and the generative openness to 'semantic' (and ontological) transfiguration, are not distinct; they are certainly not separated in time, and both the drug user and drugs discourse are always, in relation to drugs, in reality caught up in both of these systems which govern our thinking and the discursive practices structuring everyday life (including the practical pursuit of chemo-technological pleasures and escapes). And just as this 'double-science' of deconstruction never *wholly* exceeds metaphysics, the deconstruction *of* drugs can never be *wholly* separated from being high. Both deconstruction and being high encounter one another at the border between them. They do so by means of a of tropic blurring of 'taking drugs' literally and thematically – and of which Michaux's psychotropic experiments are at once an *example* and a *partaking*.

The deconstruction of 'drugs' actually involves action on both of these fronts: it deconstructs the multiple rhetorics of drugs, but at the same time directs thinking to that other, transfigurative, moment in which the deconstructive potency of 'drugs' – taken in any one of their many possible senses – has another kind of effect: *an effect related to their alterity*. Michaux, it is perhaps true, is principally concerned with this latter aspect; with what he refers to as the 'alienating' and 'defamiliarising high' produced for instance by hallucinogens, and in this sense he fails to relate his own drugged discourse to any other rhetorically constructed drug worlds. This is not to suggest that the poet on drugs should particularly concern himself with the politics and law of the 'drugs bust' which could storm in on him at any moment, but rather to acknowledge that in the emphasis his thinking *on drugs* attaches to being high, it remains blind to the conditions of its own rhetorical construction (that is, the rhetorical construction of the discourse of highs, rushes, disorientations and transcendences and so on). Directing thought along a path between between the two is central to Derrida's critique of what he calls the 'shared axiomatics' of prohibitionist anti-drug rhetoric and the libertarianism of 'atheist poets' of intoxication and excess (Derrida, 1995: 240). As he puts it:

> In the end, or in the very long run (for by definition there will never be any absolutely final term), a thinking and a politics of this thing

called 'drugs' would involve the simultaneous displacement of these two opposed ideologies in their common metaphysics. (Derrida, 1995: 246)

The point to note here is that deconstruction can no more disqualify being high, or disregard its potential usefulness with respect to the transfigurative moment of critical thought, than can those who suppose, all too uncritically, that being high is the bearer of its own truth and do not address the complexities, or even see the necessity, of its being called to account.

Deconstruction serves then as a sort of referee whose function it is to remind the players in this metaphysical game of order versus excess of the dangers of being too entrenched in either camp. Derrida seeks to stress that the desire and pursuit, by any means, of the dual perspective of seeing things from the supposed border between them, is also *impossible*, and moreover a characteristic trait of the 'liminal' intellectual, artist or writer, or drug taker.

> In certain always singular circumstances, the recourse to dangerous experimentation with what we call drugs may be guided by the desire to think the alleged boundary from both sides at once... This experience (one to which artists and thinkers occasionally devote themselves, but which is by no means the unique privilege of those who claim or to whom we grant such status), this experience may be sought with or without 'drugs', at least without any 'narcotic', 'classified' as such by the Law. We will always have unclassified or unclassifiable supplements of drugs or narcotics. (Derrida, 1995: 245)

Drugs are thus of no special significance (amongst the set of all possible themes of cultural inquiry) to deconstruction, but deconstruction can assist in the thinking of their *singular* significance. We are therefore 'provoked' by deconstruction to seek in the deconstructive engagement with the drug-text, the *pharmakon*, both its possibilities and its limitations with respect to transgression. 'Dangerous experimentation' with 'drugs' is, to be precise, *figuratively* advocated – to the extent to which anything can be regarded as a 'drug', and therefore any activity as 'drug-taking'. And, it is either meaningless or otherwise inconsequential to be for or against this. Michaux's text has been taken, accordingly, into the body of this chapter as a *pharmakon*.

From Michaux's own perspective, though, it is indeed psychotropic drugs 'themselves' that have a decisive role to play in the experimental deconstruction of 'the normal'. Consequently, he approaches the subject of limits from the perspective of being on drugs in the 'normal' or 'proper' sense of the phrase.

> Not until insidious derangement by a drug had brought this mecha-
> nism to a halt did I at last, quite late in life, realise experimentally so
> vital, almost omnipresent a function, whose incessant action had just
> ceased. (Michaux, 1974: 4)

The 'insidious derangement' Michaux recalls here is achieved, he suggests, by a prosthesis whose role is entirely passive. The drug is a technology for switching off the machinery which keeps normality and normal thinking going. This use of drugs to supplement the totality of the normal results not in a vision of transcendence and another reality, but in a zone of deferral; a kind of reduction or suspension of traditional systems governing what Michaux refers to as 'mental' orientation. On drugs he enters the zone of the *'yes* without the word' with which we began this part of the discussion. At least for moment, he enters what Derrida once referred to as 'the element of the *pharmakon*... the combat zone between philosophy and its other, an element which is in itself, undecidable' (Derrida, 1981b: 157–8). Michaux's affirmation coincides with the rush, or hit, of the *undecided* drug, which is then brought under control by his thinking and naming of it, an 'insidious derangement'; by the act of referring this being high to the ordered arrangement it displaces.

## Rejecting transcendence

By the very necessity of its being *written*, Michaux's account of this experience of the limit whilst on drugs, the zone of deferral and undecidability is never simply a representation of some 'other place'. Despite his enthusiasm and his obvious taste for 'insidious derangement' and the discoveries this allows him, being high is ultimately not an inhabitable territory for the poet who would actually write. Control, come down and being straight evidently have a logical as well as pharmacological relation to writing. The following remark of Derrida is one of many which articulate the same idea in terms of en/closure:

> Even in aggressions and transgressions, we are consorting with a code
> to which metaphysics is tied irreducibly, such that every transgression
> re-encloses us – precisely by giving us a hold on the closure of meta-
> physics – within this closure... One is never installed within transgres-
> sion, one never lives elsewhere. (Derrida, 1981a: 12)

That drugs cannot be a means of transcendence, of passage to an 'else-where', is not only made clear in everything Derrida has said about the *pharmakon*, but is echoed again in his discussion of 'drugs' in the *Rhetoric of Drugs*. To propose that they can be only amounts to a feeble repetition of the *theme* of transcendence: in fact, such thinking takes us back to an unaltered state. Michaux resoundingly rejects the return of normality in any of its many inverted forms, of which transcendence is just one, and he is at pains in a number of his sober reflections to distinguish his own drug-taking experiments from the activities of others; from those whose experiments leave them 'enclosed', in one sense or another.

> Those who have taken a powder with quasi-magical effects and consider themselves quite unfettered, entirely liberated, and out of this world perhaps, are still running on tracks. (Michaux, 1974: 105)

> Those who take drugs in order to surrender themselves to collective release and emotional abandon need not read further. There is nothing here that is meant for them. We do not speak the same language… The observer of psychic experiences has to be 'entrenched' (Michaux, 1974: 156n.2)

'Entrenchment', for Michaux, is a methodological principle of his own narco-analytic experimentation. The 'entrenched' observer is the one is able to straddle the limit between exuberant abandon and systematic recollection. And although, as already noted, Michaux's recollections are clearly caught up in discourse of psychic experiences, he makes use of his being high to anchor his thinking, and in part his writing, within experiences of dissolution, derangement, alienation and psychosis.

The problematics of locating this or any other kind of experiment with drugs in relation to the collective 'knowledges' of drugs and drug taking, on the one hand, and the supposed experience of the 'other side', on the other, creep back in at this point and indicate a further aspect of Michaux's own rejection of transcendence. It is perhaps in the *difference between* his sober self-commentaries and footnotes and the deranged paragraphs to which they are appended; between what *comes* in madness and what *comes* as the thinking of the limit, that the affinity, or 'allegiance', between drugs and (deconstructive) transgression is to be discerned:

> [T]here is one possible way to abort madness… there exists a possibility of transforming the scattering, dissipating, dislocating, devastating, breaking, tearing, dis-coordinating convulsiveness into an ally. (Michaux, 1974: 156)

This 'possibility of transforming' is engendered by the drug.

What it shows is that our understanding of 'taking drugs' ought never to be limited to what 'drug taking' is normally 'taken for' (that is, 'to mean', or, 'to bring about'). Drugs can be taken for many different reasons and in many senses, but what drug taking *is*, as articulated within the nascent deconstructive logic of Michaux's double-writing, is a means for rethinking liminality. He takes drugs to supplement the 'marvellous normal' and because they enable him to 'think the micro-phenomenon... its numerous meshings, its many silent micro-operations of dislocation of alignment, of parallelism, of displacement, of substitution' (1974: 5). In principle, deconstruction could be brought to bear on anything, but in order to convincingly carry out the substitution by which it proceeds – rendering supplementary or 'liminal' the matter at hand – the matter at hand must, so to speak, present itself in a condition of ruinous auto-deconstruction. Deconstruction in the first instance just highlights the liminality of 'drugs': the 'drug' *deconstructs itself* (Derrida, 1995: 274). In other words, drugs could not be made an 'object' of deconstruction if they were not, from the outset, a marker of the rips and tears, resulting from the 'infidelities and aggressions', in the general metaphysical diktat by which Reason attempts to assert its authority over Unreason, madness, intoxication, and so forth.

In taking Michaux's text here as an object of deconstruction, taking it as a *pharmakon*, we expose, in part, the degree to which it is attentive to the 'drugged-up' condition of its production. Approaching a text in deconstruction involves becoming attentive to the manner in which each of the meanings it might be considered to bear is possible only on the basis of what remains unthought within it.

The deconstruction of the modernity of being on drugs is not aimed at reviving or re-establishing an alternative form of 'the normal'. It must therefore, in addition to the deconstruction of drug rhetorics which Derrida indicates, also deal with drugs in such a way as to exploit their (implicit) liminality and what they enable one to observe with respect to the *abyss* – 'if [indeed] the word "observe" applies to an abyss into which one is flung and from which nothing any longer separates you' (Michaux, 1974: 93). In order to figure out further how the *abyssal* in Michaux relates to the chiasmic *sous-rature* of deconstruction, we can must go by way of the *example* which 'drugs' are held in all of this to be.

## Taking drugs, for example ...

What authorises making 'drugs' serve as an example of deconstruction in general and justifies including them in its theoretical project aimed at the deconstruction of 'the greatest totality' (Derrida, 1974: 46)? If deconstruction were a new 'system of thought', for example a 'Derridean system of thought', then the following might, in principle, be all the authorisation required:

> The example itself, as such, overflows its singularity as much as its identity. This is why there are no examples while at the same time there are only examples... The exemplarity of the example is clearly never the exemplarity of the example. We can never be sure of having put an end to this very old children's game in which all the discourses, philosophical or not, which have ever inspired deconstructions, are entangled even by the performative fiction which consists in saying, starting up the game again, 'take precisely this example' (Derrida, 1992a: 15)

But given that such examples, or elements, of deconstruction do not stand as parts to a whole and that they cannot be aggregated into a system as such, deconstruction remains a slippery notion. Slippage rather than control is the name of the theory game deconstruction plays, and we are actually forewarned by Derrida of having to understand deconstruction on the basis of an indefinite series of examples. What we are pursuing here is the way in which the example of 'drugs' and deconstructive theory co-articulate one another. They do so, for example (and this is unavoidable), in relation to the following question: what do drugs or deconstruction contribute to the thinking of the limit? A deconstructive response and elaboration pursues the overlap, as it were, between 'doing drugs' and 'doing deconstruction'. The two overlap in relation to the themes of liminality and drugs as agents of transgression – as this is exemplified in the context of reading Michaux's accounts of his experiments.

Having thus decided to say to say *yes* to the *pharmakon* – to doing deconstruction or to doing drugs, at once as it were – what comes next is:

> Diffuse agitation. Difficulty in thinking. Thinking according to my previous tendency, the point of view I had... The point of view I am led to abandon. I am overwhelmed by a current to the point where my thoughts move with this hyperactive, torrential, rushing 'something' which I feel flowing by... Ideas which, beyond my intervention, no longer control themselves, *aspire to transgression*. (Michaux, 1974: 45)

Deconstruction is the scene of precisely such an aspiration; it oscillates between the thought of transgression and retention of the foothold in metaphysics which anchors its very sanity. The dosage required to balance on the edge of this disintegration (of language and experience) is not subject to any expert prescription, it is entirely to be determined by the experiment itself. Too much and you slip over into the telepathising 'silence' of the uncontrollable gigglers, the mystics or the comatised. Too little and you just do not get off at all.

Examples never succeed in arriving at their destinations, as if, for instance, *différance* were the object of a deduction based on them: they are without any exemplar. The example is thus neither central nor exorbitant. Its non-paradigmatic status in deconstructive thinking must therefore be emphasised. They are always, precisely, *supplementary*, and operate across strategic conjunctions, which are thereby rendered non-hierarchical. This amounts, in effect, to the destruction of the metaphysical understanding of exemplarity itself. The 'deconstruction of metaphysics', proceeds on the basis of a series of examples, such as the chapters comprising this book: narco-analysis comprises a series of singular examples rather than a meta-narrative of a unified method of doing theory. So, once again, there is no suggestion here that 'drugs' are in any sense exceptional, or present us with an exceptional insight into deconstruction. However, the 'singularity' of their relationship to it is what the encounter between Michaux's text and deconstruction reveals something of. It is ultimately this 'logic' which permits the deconstruction *of* drugs, and all attempts to think drugs in relation to their undecidability, rather than because Derrida's own *exemplary* deconstruction of that undecidable drug in *Plato's Pharmacy*, the *pharmakon*, is somehow final, for it expressly is not. It is because the drug will always be apprehended as both antidote *and* poison that it is intrinsically undecidable, liminal and transgressive. And, it is because there are no ultimate exemplars that there are no narcotic means of transcendence either. What deconstruction accomplishes 'positively' is a disruption of the epistemological closure of the drugs theme according to the authority of conventional knowledge and expertise governing the conventional wisdom about drugs.

What is it then that deconstruction itself gets off on? The undecidable *pharmakon* is the 'drug' deconstruction is on, and taking it as a supplement is the means to a possible re-inscription of the cultural 'drugs script' authored by the prevailing, dominant drugs knowledge and expertise which determines the normative relationship to drugs. Taking drugs into to the orbit of deconstruction's 'incessant tropism' is what any deconstruction of totality must do whilst bearing in mind the need for some sort of *measure*. Deconstruction offers such a controlled slippage: it remains wary of the line between an effective and a toxic dose of whatever it is on (or about) at any given time.

Irene Harvey's sober analysis of the question of exemplarity in deconstruction, in which she finds Derrida's writings to foreclose *the question* of exemplarity (Harvey, 1992: 216), retraces this foreclosure. But, by stopping short of the 'intoxicated' extension of deconstruction to its other supposed moment – the opening of thought onto the alterity which exceeds metaphysics – her analysis itself comes to exemplify the characteristic sobriety of rational thought. Rodolphe Gasché, too, has articulated an *ethos* of deconstructive restraint: he is a principal critic of the reception of Derrida's philosophy which, he says, 'more often than not (has been) construed as a license for arbitrary free play in flagrant disregard of all established rules of argumentation, traditional requirements of thought, and ethical standards binding upon the interpretative community' (1987: 3). Even Michaux articulates a similar reserve with respect to the interpretation of drug experiences, as was noted above – but then, most drug takers reach the point where they feel they have had a touch too much!

These expressions of concern with *measure* (rather than propriety) serve to remind us at this point that it is precisely the problem of the *in-between* of sobriety and intoxication that this entire reflection is aimed at. I am in agreement with such expressions of the need for a measure of control, which any responsible deconstructive thinking calls for. I would certainly concur also with Gasché's view that deconstruction is more than the promotion of 'licentious free-play, nihilistic cancelling out of opposites, abolition of hierarchies' (1987: 3) But I have also attempted to show – of necessity by means of a certain exemplarity – that the project of 'grasping' deconstruction 'in all its specificity' (Gasché, 1987: 3) would itself be limited to deconstruction's metaphysical moment. To be hooked on such a project is to be caught up in a circle of bad repetition. And it is a form of bad repetition which is marked, as Avital Ronell has described this, by our 'addicted condition', but also by 'the exposition of our modernity to the incompletion of *jouissance*' (1992: 59). Perhaps more importantly, it must be asked at this point whether the urge to redress the 'incompletion of *jouissance*', which in Ronell's analysis is seen as fuelling the circuit of addicted repetition, has any bearing on the singularity of Michaux's experiments with the hallucinogen mescaline (as opposed, say, to opiates). In parallel, it must also be asked whether a general theory of 'narcotic modernity' would be able to deal with the singularity and specificity of the drug and, therefore, Michaux's text. These questions are too large to deal with here, but let us suppose in any case that the modern experience of the 'incompletion of *jouissance*' is linked directly to the 'addicted condition' and this applies to drugs other than those which are 'addictive' according to psychological and medical discourses.

Do we not find that this 'addicted condition' – or, more generally expressed, the urge to excess – has its counterpart in the holier-than-thou preference for being straight and 'drug free', which is in the final analysis no better nor worse than its arch-enemy, being but an inverted form of the drugged madness, which Michaux, who attempts to *take drugs well*, recognised was, no matter how apparently exotic, still no more than a 'modulation' of *the same*? According to him, being straight and being high both tend to give rise to ideas that being 'made up of similar elements... are capable only of modulations' (Michaux, 1974: 105). The deconstruction of drugs should, therefore, neither remain fixated on the sober moment of providing an alternative *logos* for them – a new 'pharmakology' – nor be averse to the auto-deconstructive possibilities presented by partaking of drugs, as Michaux's usage exemplifies.

## Rewriting the drugs text and taking drugs otherwise

When Derrida expressed the idea of the text in deconstruction by saying that there is no 'outside-text' (*Il n' y a pas de hors-texte*), it was widely suspected that deconstruction was a sophisticated denial of 'experience' and 'the real', and that this was, therefore, a sure sign of its lack of seriousness. Experience was seemingly being rejected in favour of an irreducible discursivity and open-ended textual play. Since then, the relevance of deconstruction as an approach to 'the text', particularly in the literal sense of reading literary, philosophical, historical texts, namely those texts which are materialised in the form of the written word, has found comparably wide acceptance in the academy. However, the truly speculative import and the challenge of Derrida's early provocative remark, which urges the thinking of *everything* as text, still presents a serious affront to common sense as well as to philosophical thought. But then this was, of course, not the least of its aims and consequences. The strategic generalisation of the concept of the text as the 'articulation of differences', was never, as

David Wood has noted, 'opposed to consciousness or experience, [for it] would claim that these themselves would display its primitive structures – differentiation, deferral' (1990: 63). So there never was any *denial* of consciousness, subjectivity, exteriority and the real world. Deconstruction represents the attempt to think from the limit of the inside/outside difference, and in a manner which resists its own immediate reduction to being purely and abstractly a theory of limits, a *liminology*.

> If deconstruction takes place everywhere it takes place where there is something (and is not therefore limited to meaning or to the text in the bookish sense of the word, we still have to think about what is happening in our world, in modernity). (Derrida, 1991c: 274)

The task of such a 'textualisation' is the re-inscription of an exteriority always delimited correlative to (a prior) inscription. Gasché has usefully described inscription as what contextualises rather than engenders (1986: 157–8). Effectively, this means crossing (that is, chiasmically placing under erasure) the difference between constitution and meaning: deconstruction attempts to think, from the limit, of precisely the non-difference of the conceptually polarised 'life-world' and 'the text'. This is not, however, a totalising attempt to think a 'unity', but it does aim at a kind of sublation of the phenomenological into what could be described as post-phenomenological textualisation of difference. It stresses that thinking's 'other side' is the in your face (and off your face) reality of the quotidian – that plane which neither deconstruction nor drugs ever enables anyone to leave.

## Living on the margins of the unforgettable

Like any other deconstructive reading, this one of Michaux's poetical narrative of intoxication has sought to do more than expose the metaphysical presuppositions which lie behind its own production. It was from the outset inspired by Michaux's above-mentioned 'observations', especially in their focus upon the dysfunctional moments in systems of thought, be these conceptual or lived, and I have attempted to use deconstruction to discover the significance of those 'breakdowns' of normality Michaux explores. Whenever and wherever this thought of interruption and alterity finds its expression, it is often associated also with moments of 'delirium', 'agony', 'ecstasy', 'surprise', 'overflowing', none which are ever simply 'figures' but always also moments of 'a life'.

Such 'experiences' of alterity are real enough, as is the destruction of normality Michaux records in his accounts of what he calls his 'ordeals' (*épreuves*). In any case, with what motives would anyone be principally concerned to discredit the claimed insights of intoxication and the experience of the limit it gives rise to, other than as an agent of normalising power? It is more important to recall here that 'deconstruction begins from where we are'; that its beginnings are multiple and that being high is also as much a place to begin as any other. This reading of Michaux has illustrated how a deconstructive approach seeks to avoid, at the very least, the repetition of the metaphysical distinction between intoxication and sobriety and the privileging of the latter at the expense of the former when it comes to understanding 'drugs'. And, it is through such an intertextual, deconstructive engagement with Michaux's drug text that a case can be made, *contra* 'the metaphysicians', for exploding consciousness and raking over the debris of thought as an alternative to the sober activity of traditional philosophy. Taken well, drugs too, it appears, can serve the critique of the conceptual authority of 'the great normal' in general. For Michaux at least, it was in the mind's grievous moments, when 'monstrously excited from the effects of large doses of mescaline', for example, that a trip to the limits of normality occurs as a poetic event, an encounter with language in which the difference between writing and experience is magically unmade.

It is not surprising that moments such as those he records are clearly also expressed in terms of an experience with language. His thinking is overwhelmed at times by an almost Beckettian play of language:

> Words come. Words. Not the words I want. Not properly linked. Not in the right order. Forming only the fragment of the sentence I am searching for, scraps, pieces… Yet I continue to write, to add words blindly aiming at the astonishing phenomenon… *I seem to be writing not in order to get closer to what is to be said, but in order to get away from it.* (Michaux, 1974: 27–31, *my emphasis*)

Does this 'astonishing phenomenon' translate the 'experience of the impossible' so frequently invoked by Derrida as the 'least bad definition of deconstruction' (Derrida, 1992c: 200). Certainly, the arbitrariness of the normality in which the rational mind was at home with itself is exposed on the basis of the *destruction* of its regular order. But Unreason or madness, as such, being made up of its elements, only reflects normality. Deconstruction pushes beyond this truth to recover the sense in which the grievously intoxicated mind is no longer *wholly native* nor yet *wholly alien.*

There is no romanticism, either, in Michaux's trips to the borders of the normal. Owing to his 'difficulties' with language, owing to the ordeal of the 'mental excess' he has to struggle with, he inevitably gets little written down whilst he is high on drugs (Michaux, 1974: 46). What he learns is that in order to write *per se*, he must be a writer of the border. This, too, is a kind of ordeal, one which anyone writing on drugs today must face: such a writer must reject the seductions of both tripped-out mysticism and instrumental reason, evade the police, hide from the psychiatrists, risk being sold poison or placebos and negotiate all other forces of control which strive to determine the meaning of 'drugs' and even prevent her/him from taking drugs (seriously) at all. From his risky, newly found, liminal perspective, Michaux learned of the 'scandalous forced *identity*' he was obliged to readopt on his return – that is when the drugs wore off (Michaux, 1974: 47).

In this case, what goes up comes down elsewhere and somehow altered. The contingency of the 'normal' is now undeniable in a way in which it was not before – prior to the conjunction of deconstruction's tropism conjoined with Michaux's psycho-tropism. Taking drugs (as a theme) has not given rise to nonsense, madness or ranting. A deconstructive approach to drugs exposes the hapless generality of thinking 'drugs' in terms of the false alternatives of *either* panaceas *or* panapathogens, and by means of all the antithetical extensions which stem from these supposed alternatives. This reading has not, emphatically, sought to go along with Michaux's text concerning what drugs 'reveal', as he puts it, of 'ourselves to ourselves', it has sought rather to indicate the bearing of drugs on the delimitation of all known recipes for 'drugs'; it has attempted to use them as a *pharamceutical* prosthesis, in pursuit of an alternative recipe for them, one better suited to a culture 'living on the margins of the Unforgettable' (Michaux, 1974: 170).

## Notes

1 Henri Michaux (1899–1984) extensively experimented with and wrote about his experiences of many psychotropic drugs. In his first book, *Les rêves de la jambe* (1923) he describes his experience with hashish and opium. In *Equador* (1929) and *La nuit remue* (1935) he discussed the effects of ether, and in a series of books in the 1950s he turned his attention to hallucinogens, including mescaline and LSD, which he discusses in *L'infini turbulent* (1957), *Paix dans*

*les brisements* (1959), *Connaisance par les gouffres* (1961) and *Les grandes épreuves de l'esprit* (1966), translated by Richard Howard as *The Major Ordeals of the Mind* (1974). He also produced a vast number of drawings and paintings which express elements of his experiences under the influence of drugs.

2 This represents a significant development beyond the early reception of deconstruction in the disciplines in which it was first extensively taken up, for example in philosophy and literary studies, where emphasis was largely on these disciplines' intra- and inter-disciplinary concerns. Since then, the wider legacy of its radical understanding of the 'text', beyond the disciplinary borders of philosophy and literary theory has been recognised. Of course, Derrida's own writings on democracy, politics, friendship, hospitality, and cosmopolitanism have led the way in this. For a critical discussion of the use of deconstruction within cultural studies see Hall (2002).

## 4    Freud's medicine: from the 'cocaine papers' to 'Irma's Injection'

### Mixing psychoanalysis and psychopharmacology

In an essay titled 'What Good Are Psychoanalysts at a Time of Distress Oblivious to Itself?' the French psychoanalyst and cultural theorist Julia Kristeva provides a succinct and striking image of the modern city and the place of drugs within it:

> I imagine a huge city with houses of glass and steel, reaching the sky, reflecting the sky, itself and you. People cultivate their image, hurried and made up in the extreme, covered in gold, pearls and pure leather. In the streets, on every corner, the filth piles up and drugs accompany the slumber or rage of the outcasts. (Kristeva, 1994: 14)

Modern living is characterised by fetishistic domestic opulence and narcotised psychotic street life: 'the filth piles up', trashiness and trash coincide. This is the element in which psychoanalysis has thrived and continues to thrive as a treatment for the alienating effects of capitalism on the modern subject. She goes on to imagine the role of the psychoanalyst in the quest for psychological survival under such conditions and her role in assisting individuals 'to preserve a life which neutralises the luxury as well as the horror'. But what is to be made of the characterisation of those who – in the absence of guidance from psychoanalysts – variously narcotise their 'slumber' or 'rage' and exist as the city's 'outcasts', barely citizens at all and who signify the threat posed to the city's health by 'drugs' – and whose drug requirements are not served by the city's pharmacists?

This question is all the more pertinent here as Kristeva's essay is, unusually, concerned with relationship between psychoanalysis and psychopharmacology and the modern 'presence' of drugs. Drugs are not only widely deemed responsible for contaminating the city and poisoning the prospects for healthy, modern, psychological interiority, but also held responsible, in so far as they are present, with or without an authorised prescription, in the bloodstream of citizen-patients, for contaminating or interfering with the psychoanalytic process itself. I should make it clear that Kristeva herself is ostensibly concerned in this essay with the drugs prescribed by psychiatrists to patients who may subsequently or simultaneously be referred for forms of psychotherapy, including psychoanalysis. She does not comment on the fact that it is, statistically at least, highly likely that many analysands are also regular or occasional users, abusers or self-medicators, selecting from the full range of licit and illicit drugs in circulation in the modern metropolis, supplied by pharmacists and street dealers alike. Such modern subject-analysands may or may not be telling their analysts whether they are or are not 'drug free' (partly because many analysts will refuse to continue with the analysis unless the drug taking is suspended), but, either way, drugs certainly figure in the psychoanalysis of individuals as well as in the psychoanalytic theorising of modern cultural forms. Such is the ubiquity of 'drug culture' – as already noted

To be more precise: Kristeva's focus is on the medical prescription of psychopharmacological drugs (she discusses the case of a patient prescribed imipramine) and how these figure, and may come in future to figure increasingly, in the analytic process. She acknowledges the short-term benefits of some drug therapies for some patients whilst speaking of the help therapists can give to patients to reduce their psychological dependence on such drugs and their need, as she puts it, to 'lean on chemistry'. Her general view appears to be that psychoanalysis, in any case, ought not to be a closed door to psychopharmacology, but also that, despite the latter's growing sophistication over the last hundred years, it still remains both a much too simple technique and an 'interference' with the psychoanalytic process. This interference needs to be well understood by analysts, she says, because increasingly patients are likely to get 'a mixed treatment' (Kristeva, 1994: 23).

However clinicians might come to understand the nature of 'mixed treatment' and its implications for practice, Kristeva's speculation also goes beyond such pragmatic clinical concerns and raises questions for psychoanalysis as such, about the modern advance of neuroscience towards psychoanalytic territory and the pharmacological management of psychological interiority:

> Two great confrontations await the psychoanalysis of tomorrow… The first is its competition with the neurosciences: 'The cocktail or the word!'… The second is the test to which psychoanalysis is subjected by the desire *not to know*, which converges with the apparent ease offered by pharmacology, and which characterises the negative narcissism… of modern man. (Kristeva, 1994: 16)

This remark clearly acknowledges that competition between psycho-analysis and the neurosciences, in particular neuropharmacology, in the future at least, is something that psychoanalysis will have to consider seriously. Just exactly what it needs now or in the future to consider, however, is not only that there may be drugs whose effects are psychologically more subtle and 'effective' than those available today but that the 'competition' will also stem from the fact that drug therapies are increasingly likely to be seen (falsely and inadequately) as easier solutions to problems that *only* analysis can properly address – such as the desire of patients '*not to know*'; for example, either why they are now well or were previously unwell. Kristeva is suggesting here that this very 'not wanting to know' needs to be recognised as the proper object of psychoanalytic enquiry, and that it is this phenomenon which is approachable exclusively by analysis: it is this which requires psychoanalytic work to be done; a work of thinking and, in a word, 'talk'. Her suggestion amounts to a sort of prediction: whatever the nature and power of the chemistry available, either now or in the future, psychoanalysis will always 'return' in this sense.

> From a logical point of view, the assault by the neurosciences does not destroy psychoanalysis, but invites one to resume and reactualise the Freudian notion of the drive: the hinge between the *soma* and the *psyche*, biology and representation. (Kristeva, 1994: 18)

She proposes rebutting the idea of the idea of 'competition' between psychoanalysis and neuroscience narrowly understood in terms of an either/or, by digging down into the psychoanalytic archive to a point at which Freud (or 'psychoanalysis itself') attempts to theorise the governing modern conceptual divisions around the inside/outside conceptual axis which distinguishes *psycho*logical and *soma*tological phenomena in general. The distinctions between 'biology and representation', between the exogenous and endogenous stimuli and between the organic and the environmental, can all be mapped onto the modern epistemological and ontological distinctions which organise physiological and psychological accounts of the human individual. And Freud's thinking of the notion of the 'drive' (*Trieb*) marks and interrogates these distinctions in a way which recognises above all the aporetic, impossible split between them.

Following Kristeva's suggestion, I shall go back to the work Freud wrote in 1895 and alluded to in his letters of the time to Fliess as his 'Psychology for Neurologists', but which is best known by the title it acquired when posthumously published as *Project for Scientific Psychology* (Freud, 1966, 295–387). In the *Project* Freud attempts to develop a conceptual framework in which it is possible to account for psychological phenomena in terms which are consistent with neurological principles based on a theory of underlying neuropsychological mechanisms, of which the 'drive' is a key example. However, before I consider how Freud attempts to overcome these distinctions on the basis of such theory, I propose to go back further still, to the beginnings of Freud's supposed 'turn' from physiology toward psychology beginning around 1883, and especially to his discovery, investigation and use of the psychoactive stimulant cocaine in the 1880s and 1890s. The argument I shall present here aims to show, on the basis of a reconsideration of Freud's encounter with this drug, that this was not at all a simple turning away from physiology to psychology but an attempt to think the non-difference between them. Having established how cocaine comes to figure in Freud's thinking, I shall then return to the question of how the concept of the 'drive' relates to the 'hinge' between the psyche and the soma, and to Freud's thinking of the chemical interface between them as this is outlined in the *Project*.[1] In this way I aim to show that Freud's thinking from the outset developed on the basis of a certain relation to 'drugs', and that *in a certain sense* psychoanalysis has always borne within it the germ of a 'drugged thinking'.

### Refiguring the 'cocaine episode'

On 2 June 1884 Freud wrote to his fiancée Martha Bernays:

> Woe to you, my princess, when I come. I will kiss you quite red and feed you till you are plump. And if you are forward you shall see who is the stronger, a gentle little girl who doesn't eat enough or a big wild man who has cocaine in his body. (Byck, 1974: 10)

During the period 1883 to 1900, it would not be untrue to say, cocaine entered every facet of Freud's life and work: frequently, it was in his body, in his mind, on his mind as his object of scientific research, and it held, for a short while he dared to think, the key to his imminent professional success as the great (re)discoverer of a 'magical' substance modern European medicine had neglected to exploit. It inspired him to bring the cultural history of coca and reports of its widespread use in South America to a medical audience, and on occasion he all but evangelised about its potential therapeutic value. In various ways, it will become clear in the

course of this chapter, it had a major impact on his thinking and a last-
ing effect on the trajectory of his monumental attempt to understand the
human individual, its relation to its environment, to itself and to others.

Freud's letters tell us that he found cocaine improved his disposition; that it often helped him to write and that he took it successfully
as a remedy for his various ailments – some of which, there are clear
grounds to believe, were probably fuelled as much by the remedy itself
as by anything else. It is fair to say that it invigorated his life and work
intermittently. But this invigoration was itself neither simply physical nor
simply psychological: the impact of cocaine on 'Freud's thought' is not,
despite immediate appearances, reducible to a biographical footnote or a
personal 'episode' either. 'Episode' is the word Ernest Jones, in his *Life of
Freud* (1953) uses to refer to the period of Freud's direct preoccupation
with the drug between 1883 and the publication of the various 'cocaine
papers' during 1884–87.[2] I shall argue that the 'Freud and cocaine' matter
is not so easily bounded either in time or in terms of where the effects of
cocaine began and ended.

In order to illustrate the diverse nature of the 'cocaine effect' on
Freud's ideas, texts and associations, I shall follow the trajectory Freud
takes from the earliest cocaine research itself, through his association and
sharing of ideas with Wilhelm Fliess to the writing of the posthumously
published *Project*, and finally reflect on the traces of cocaine as they
appear in the 'cocaine dreams', especially the one known as 'Irma's Injection'. This was this dream which received Freud's first full dream analysis
in *The Interpretation of Dreams* (1900), the work which is widely considered to mark the beginning of psychoanalysis proper. This particular item
of Freud's self-analysis is closely tied in with what might be described as
the deeper inscription of the 'effect' of cocaine on Freud's thinking and
his intellectual decision, eventually, to 'move on' from cocaine and the
proto-psychopharmacology it had touched upon, into the 'talking cure'.
So I intend to show how in various ways cocaine served at different times
as an object of inquiry, a provocation to Freud's theoretical reflections
and how, in its decisive reappearance in his dreams, it even provided clues
to the workings of the unconscious. It also had a role in the professional
associations that he made and therefore with the kind of ideas he enter-
tained in the course of developing his own. I shall make an argument
here that the 'effect' that cocaine came to have on Freud's theorising up
to and including the birth of psychoanalysis proper must viewed in the
widest possible terms and that this is necessary in order to appreciate the

singular significance and the 'modernity' of the psychopharmacological/ psychoanalytic divide.

In the vast literature of psychoanalysis across the disciplinary spectrum from clinical practice to the study of cultural forms and cultural critique, little attention has been paid to the 'cocaine episode', other than in the contexts of such things as the history of ideas and intellectual biography. It is particularly neglected in relation to its impact on his theorising itself at this time.[3] The reasons for this are probably many. Firstly, it is of course true that Freud's contribution to psychology and his discovery of psychoanalysis together lay the greatest claim on the attention of his students, disciples and critics, rather than his contribution to medical science (which in any case has tended to be regarded by some critics as spurious, and at best rather poor science). The too easy separation between psychoanalysis and medical science, including scientific psychology and neurology, has tended to predominate in twentieth-century assessments of the relation of psychoanalysis to scientific thinking in general – with both discursive systems and intellectual territories concerned to preserve their identities and distinctness. It is precisely such an image of clear-cut difference between these territories that Freud's theorising, influenced by his encounter with and investigation of cocaine, brings into question. Cocaine, I want to argue, effectively directed Freud toward his radical understanding of the problematic nature of the modern distinction between the subjective and the objective in the pursuit of knowledge of the human being, something which he keenly recognised, during the course of his involvement with the drug, was a *necessarily reflexive inquiry*.

To explain how this is so I shall retrace aspects of Freud's intellectual trajectory by retelling the story of Freud's encounter with cocaine, recentring the story on the 'cocaine effect' understood in the wider sense just indicated; from its first appearance in the medical literature he read, to the arrival in the post of his first gram of the stuff from the Merck pharmaceutical company, to the discovery of its affinity with the nose and to its reappearance in his troubled dreams. Finally I shall return to the theme of the hinge between the *psyche* and the *soma*; that zone of interaction and cross-over between 'biology and representation' as Kristeva puts it, or, more generally, nature and culture. My reconstruction of 'the story of cocaine and psychoanalysis' is aimed at disclosing how the cocaine effect inclined Freud to think the non-difference of these, on the way, viewed retrospectively, to psychopathology and psychoanalysis.

### The cocaine research

By the early 1880s the young Freud had already tried his hand at various laboratory jobs working as a junior research scientist mainly in the area of experimental physiology as well as studying brain anatomy. He was anxious to establish a career and reputation for himself and thereby to hasten his marriage to Martha Bernays. Looking around for a research theme that would perhaps enable him to get going on all of these fronts at once, he came to read various reports about cocaine, or to be more precise about the remarkable properties of the coca plant. One influential medical article he came upon was by an army doctor, Theodor Aschenbrandt (1883), who had experimented with coca preparations in the treatment of battle weariness and exhaustion amongst soldiers, who, after taking the drug, were able to perform extraordinary feats of both physical and mental endurance under conditions of extreme hardship. Freud immediately ordered a gram of the alkaloid from the Darmstadt pharmaceutical company Merck and also began researching the history of coca and its use in South American culture. He was also aware that in North America coca extract was added to a variety of 'soft' drinks (such as Coca-Cola) advertised and sold as 'tonics'. He also learned that, in the medical sphere, coca had been used with differing degrees of success for treating addiction to the opiate morphine in a form of what is known today as 'substitution therapy'. He instantly saw an opportunity here to become famous for rediscovering coca and its alkaloid cocaine for European medicine, in which it had gone almost unnoticed – or so he thought. Later, much later, in his *An Autobiographical Study* (1924) he would claim responsibility for having told an ophthalmologist friend of his, Karl Köller, about the easily researchable local anaesthetic properties of cocaine, the discovery of which (by Köller) soon came to revolutionise opthalmological surgery, helping him to make his reputation – somewhat to the professional chagrin of Freud. But Freud was in fact not actually so interested in the straightforwardly physiological effects of cocaine: the bigger prize, he recognised, was in researching the dual effect it had in that it also ameliorated the *disposition* of the patient and promoted a sense of well-being.

In a time-honoured medical tradition, Freud began to experiment with cocaine by trying various doses of it on himself. He passed it on to friends and colleagues to try on themselves and their patients. He even posted little packets of cocaine to members of his family to help cure them of various ailments. He wrote to Martha (2 June 1884) of his successful self-medications with the drug and of his intention to research the subject further: 'I took coca during my last severe depression and it lifted me to the heights in a wonderful fashion. I am now collecting the literature for a song of praise to this magical substance' (Byck, 1974: 10–11). In his enthusiasm, Freud believed that his work on cocaine would make his reputation and secure him many patients – whom he would be able to treat well and who would consequently provide him with further important insights into nervous disorders of one sort or another. The cocaine molecule was to be, he supposed, the key to all of this. And from Freud's first contact with it, it does indeed play a germinal role in the thinking which was to lead, eventually, to his fullyfledged psychoanalytic thought. Initially, cocaine appeared to Freud to be a magical substance that could boost his energies, his relationship and his professional career – which he felt to be stalling – all at once. He saw it as an ideal research topic to which he might dedicate his efforts and one which his own experience of taking the drug told him would provide him with insights into the connection between the physiological and the psychological health and well-being of the patient.

## Experiments with cocaine

In 1884–85 Freud embarked upon a programme of empirical experiments which aimed to demonstrate scientifically the validity of what he had read elsewhere about cocaine's invigorating qualities. He bought two specially designed instruments with which he could measure both the strength of his grip and hence his muscular strength (the dynomometer) and his reaction times (the neuroamoebimeter). The following table shows an example of Freud's recording of the effect of cocaine on the motor energy, or strength, of the muscle group, measured by means of a pressure measuring device, the 'dynamometer for two hands', as published in his paper 'Contribution to the Knowledge of Cocaine' (Byck, 1974: 95–104):

Freud undertook many such tests of muscular strength whilst taking into account his self-observed 'natural' energy levels on different days, taking sets of measurements both with and without the use of cocaine, and his paper includes three similar examples. One of these records in the same fashion his reaction times using the neuroamoebimeter, a device which measured the delay between the sounding of a tone and the subject's switching off of this electrical instrument. He subsequently

**Experiment of November 10, 1884**

| Time | Pressures | Max | Average | Remarks |
|------|-----------|-----|---------|---------|
| 8:00 | 60 | 60 | 60. | tired |
| 10:00 | 73–63–67 | 73 | 67.6 | after rounds |
| — thereupon, a small indeterminate quantity of cocaine | | | | |
| 10:20 | 76–70–76 | 76 | 74 | cheerful |
| 10:30 | 73–70–68 | 73 | 70.3 | — |
| 11:35 | 72–72–74 | 74 | 72.6 | — |
| 12:50 | 74–73–63 | 74 | 70 | — |
| 2:20 | 70–68–69 | 70 | 69 | — |
| 4:00 | 76–74–75 | 76 | 75 | normal condition |
| 6:00 | 67–64–58 | 67 | 63 | after strenuous work |
| 8:30 | 74–64–67 | 74 | 68.3 | somewhat tired |
| — thereupon, 0.10* *cocainum muraticum* (*almost certainly grams, Ed) | | | | |
| 8:43 | 80–73–74 | 80 | 75.6 | ruptus |
| 8:58 | 79–76–71 | 79 | 75.3 | — |
| 9:18 | 77–72–67 | 77 | 72 | buoyant feeling |

drew the following conclusions, which are worth quoting at length here as their formulation highlights the manner in which Freud is beginning to think of the relation between 'disposition', physiology and, though he does not yet mention it, the 'chemical interface' between the two:

> It became clear to me that the above mentioned variation in motor power which does not depend on the time of day is an expression of the general state of well-being; after all, the subjective phenomenon of this state of bodily feeling [*Gemeingefühl* (coenaesthenia)] and mood is to a great extent associated with motor efficiency. I do not consider the cocaine action itself to be a direct one, on the motor-nerve substance or on the muscles – but indirect, effected by an improvement in the general state of well-being... In assessing the standard physical quantities to designate the condition of an individual, preference will be given to those magnitudes which, like temperature, show little individual variation. The motor power of a prominent muscle group should not be rejected to designate various conditions in an individual... A similar, but vaguer, conclusion resulted from the experiments on the influence of cocaine on reaction times. I often noticed that under the influence of cocaine my reaction times were shorter and more uniform than before

taking the drug; but sometimes in a more cheerful and efficient mood, my psychic reactions were just as good. Change in reaction times is then a characteristic of cocaine euphoria to which I have also ascribed an increase in muscular strength. (Byck, 1974: 103–4)

All of this was ostensibly intended to stand as empirical, scientific confirmation of what was widely surmised on the basis of the subjective experience of coca users and cocaine users alike, and the results unquestionably appeared to bear this out. What is of greatest interest here, though, is what Freud says about the relationship between 'cocaine euphoria' and the physiological phenomenon of muscular strength on the one hand, and of mental reaction times on the other: he does not ascribe the cause of improved performance directly to the drug, but rather to the euphoria it produces. A degree of indirection (and subjective relativity) thus remains a part of the experiment: start with low energy or low 'spirits' and the marked effects are found to be stronger – but not always. 'Psychic', or mental, reaction times, unlike strength, are not considered, as they might have been, in terms of the 'speed' or efficiency of a muscle – they are not regarded principally as a physiological or mechanistic matter, at least not at this stage. He is saying that the measurements of strength are dependent on, or mediated by, the state of euphoria – a psychical phenomenon – but also that reaction times, though generally improved by cocaine, can also be matched without it just so long as the starting *mood* is at a high level. In other words *both* mental reaction times and physical strength tend to be improved with cocaine and both are interconnected, or 'united', as a function of euphoria. It might have been expected, given that euphoria is normally regarded as a mental phenomenon, that only mental reaction times should be connected with it. However, Freud unequivocally closes the circle of reasoning here by stating that euphoria can also be 'ascribed to the increase in muscular strength' – it is spoken of as that which gives rise to the increase. Cocaine euphoria is, therefore, found to be both *of the psyche* and *of the soma* and hence experimentally approachable in both its subjective and objective dimensions. There is then something quite remarkable about the cocaine effect in this sense, namely *it makes explicit the psycho-somatic nature of 'well-being'.*

There was, however, just one methodological problem (by conventional standards of scientific reasoning and practice) which appeared to Freud to be inescapable. He was particularly interested at this stage in calibrating the relationship between psychological disposition and physiological response; his subjects, therefore, needed to be as reliable in their reporting of these effects as the instruments were in their measurement of physical strength. And yet, he says, no one he knew to whom he had given cocaine was as 'regular' in their response to a given dose as he himself was:

> I repeatedly carried out on myself, or had carried out, these two series of experiments. I realise that such self-observations have the shortcoming, for the person engaged in conducting them, of claiming two sorts of objectivity for the same thing. I had to proceed in this manner for reasons beyond my control and because none of the subjects at my disposal had such regular reaction to cocaine. (Byck, 1974: 99)

This was an important moment indeed: Freud recognises here that he required a predictable constant, and he came to consider himself to be the only candidate. Clearly troubled though he was by this notion, it none the less appeared to be a methodological necessity and served as a precedent by which he would increasingly come *to regard himself as a laboratory for checking his theses*. He had, in effect, come to regard his own subjectivity as being objectively accessible, and he could therefore allow himself to reason that the cocaine 'effect' apparently lent itself to the realisation of this 'impossibility'.

It could be said that this convinced Freud not to let his thought processes be interrupted by the demands of reason – in other words, the 'hinge' between the psyche and the soma could be scientifically, or transcendentally, explained later – in fact he himself attempts something like this in *The Project* (to which I shall turn shortly). In his *Life of Freud*, Jones clearly tends to see this as a mark of Freud's genius: his ability to focus on 'the singular fact' – for instance his direct experience of the pharmacological alleviation of a depression – and to derive a general truth from that, disregarding irrelevant contra-indicators to what he knew *directly* to be the case (Jones, 1953: 96).[4] And there is something in this beyond Jonesian sycophancy – to the extent to which it is true that Freud was working at the limits of convention in every sense. His mind was racing and it was its very own cocaine-accelerated movements that brought his attention to the urgency of an analysis and analytic method appropriate to the study of psycho-somatic reflexivity, ultimately heading toward a unified understanding of the neuro-psychopathology of the individual.

The therapeutic contra-indicators, beyond the immediate recognition that individual responses to the drug were, as Freud noted, 'irregular', were none the less extremely dramatic: his own attempt to treat his friend and colleague Max von Fleischl for morphinism ended in disaster. Fleischl had become a morphine addict as a consequence of using the drug as a pain killer following the amputation of a finger and Freud, ignoring reports of the dangers of developing a dual addiction, in 1884 prescribed cocaine for Fleischl, who quickly became addicted to it. Fleischl suffered from acute neuralgia, but he was also an experienced intravenous morphine user and was soon administering a gram of cocaine per day to himself by his own preferred method. Freud later explicitly declared that both the dose and the method used were contrary to his suggestion. Fleischl died in 1891, his death arguably hastened by the cocaine abuse. In the interim, other reports of the efficacy and inefficacy of prescribing cocaine in cases of morphinism were discussed in the medical literature and Freud himself had had to endure the opprobrium directed at him by Lewin and Erlenmeyer (Byck, 1974: xxxii), who accused him of having a played a part in popularising and defending the 'third scourge of humanity' (after alcohol and morphine). In Freud's final cocaine paper of 1887, 'Craving and Fear of Cocaine Addiction', he defends again the potential medical value of the drug, mentioning in passing his own use of the drug 'over several months', declaring that it had claimed 'no victim of its own' and that dosage, method of application and the control (or self-control) of the patient in relation to the administration of the treatment were all factors to be taken into consideration. Notably in this paper, he recalls that the successful treatment of female melancholics with mutism had been achieved by means of cocaine injection. Although Freud's cocaine research was effectively to end with the publication of this paper, the effect of cocaine in terms of its impact on his thinking of the relationship between physiological and psychological phenomena was to continue in other forms.

Freud's own use of cocaine as an 'exquisite tonic' had continued during his period of study with Charcot in Paris and, judging by the letters to Martha, it had helped him combat his own 'neurasthenia'. Cocaine had made it disappear as if by a 'stroke of magic' (*mit ein Zauberschlag verschwunden*). He also reports that it countered a certain shyness in social situations (something Breuer had commented on to him) and drove him to be chatty (*zum Reden treibt*) (letter to Martha 2 February 1886, original cited by Von Scheidt, 1973: 398, my translation). So, whatever the consequences of extreme doses, for example, the psychosis and paranoia cocaine could induce in certain individuals – about which Freud had read and even witnessed in the case of Fleischl – for the time being at least, he was going to follow his nose on this.

## From Fliess's nasal reflexology to the nose as the hinge

Cocaine led Freud quite logically, after 1887, into an ever closer association the rhinologist and surgeon Wilhelm Fliess, with whom he had a
long and famous correspondence.[5] Fliess was no ordinary rhinologist: he
was developing a grand theory of 'nasal reflexology' and investigating a
syndrome he came to call the 'nasal reflex neurosis', which manifested
itself in the forms of headache and neuralgic pains widely distributed
in various areas of the body, all of which appeared to be relieved by the
application of cocaine to the nose (Jones, 1953: 319). Needless to say, he
was also an enthusiast for the use of cocaine in connection with nasal
problems. Fliess believed that the nose was the single reflexive centre
through which physiological symptoms and their organic or functional
causes were related to one another, and that this therefore indicated a
possibility of intervention in all manner of ailments by way of the nose:
illness, potentially any kind of illness, could be monitored and acted
upon, by means of nasal surgery. He was later to publish work in which he
claimed to have alleviated birthing pains by means of cocainisation of the
turbinate bone of the nose, and he believed that there was a particularly
strong connection between the nose, the sexual organs and sexual function. As Jones observes, there were clear resemblances between Fliess's
syndrome and Freud's 'actual neurosis', neurasthenia. Freud soon had
his own, to all intents and purposes empirical, reasons for supposing the
nose to be something of a special organ. He suffered over a number of
years from his own nasal problems: he endured both nasal blockages and
discharges, for which Fliess prescribed both cauterisation of the turbinate
bones and the application of cocaine to the mucous membranes.

Freud's regular 'brushing' of his nose with cocaine – which
resulted in his feeling better in every way – no doubt gave him the
singular experience (that is, neither simply subjective nor simply objective, as described above) of how general well-being was connected with
the well-being of the nose. Cocaine had in effect confirmed to Freud that
both he and Fliess were on to something scientifically momentous. At the
same time, his continued 'moderate' use of cocaine (the typical doses in
the experiments above, note, were 0.1g, pharmaceutical quality), to no
apparent ill-effect, nor craving, must have seemed to him like an ongoing
confirmation of its potential therapeutic use, and after all, Fliess was regularly obtaining apparently good results with it. For several years Freud
viewed his own ailments within a Fliessian framework and self-medi-

cated for them, obliging Fliess, as it were in his person, with a running case study. In fact Fliess was to a certain degree a fellow-sufferer and they exchanged with each other details of both their personal symptoms and their unpublished work. There seemed to be plenty of evidence in the cases they dealt with that pointed to the central role of the nose. Freud even passed patients onto Fliess, as this letter of 14 May 1893 records:

> Dear Friend, The bearer of this letter, Mr. F from Budweis suffers from left-sided neuralgiform headaches, is intolerant to alcohol, has pain in the sternum, some dizziness, cannot breathe through the nose when reclining, has a dried-out mouth upon awakening, restless sleep, a suspicious shape to his nose – in brief, I do not doubt that it will be a simple matter for you to free him of his troubles. (Masson, 1985: 47)

The 'suspicious shape of the nose' refers to Fliess's view that certain nose swellings are a sign of masturbatory practices (Masson, 1985: 48n.1). This connection between the nose, masturbation, 'pollutions' (ejaculations during sleep) and neurasthenia was preoccupying Freud around this time and the case evidence for 'crossed-reflexes' – linking the nose, for instance, with the genitals continued to grow. 'It is a shame' he writes to Fliess (15 May 1893) 'that we cannot work on the same cases' (Masson, 1985: 49).

In fact, to a degree they certainly did. Freud himself is a case in point; and over the years they frequently exchanged reports about their own day to day ailments, which were surprisingly similar. These included for Freud mood swings, depressions, migraine, arrhythmia and an infection of nasal membranes resulting in severe discharges of pus – for all of which the application of cocaine still continued to be seen as the best medication. Only Freud's half of the correspondence survives,[6] but during 1893–14 Freud and Fliess continued to discuss the relations between the nose and sexuality, Freud often speaking as if he was in no doubt of the strong connection Fliess had proposed. Everything they discussed was refracted through the Freudian lens of his self-observation and questioning of his own health. Consistent with the degree of his commitment to Fliessian 'nose theory', Freud's own nasal problems, his theorising about sexuality, neurasthenia and the connections between them, and his reflection on the interrelatedness or distinctness of 'organic' and 'neurotic' causes, all began to figure in relation to one another as he attempted to integrate clinical findings, physiological evidence, psycho-logical and metapsychological theory and self-analysis. In an obvious way, in order to avoid severing his psychological theorising from physiological and clinical evidence, he needed to believe in at least the possibility of neuropsychological explanations of the same phenomena.

This was a time when Freud was convinced that masturbation and nocturnal 'pollutions' were a crucial indicator of neurasthenia. He wrote to Fliess asking him: 'Could it not be that organic changes of the nose produce the pollutions and thereby neurasthenia, so that here the latter develops as a product of the nasal reflex noxa?', and tells him 'I hope that you will explain the physiological mechanisms of my clinical findings' (30 May 1893 and 10 July 1893; Masson, 1985: 50–1). And, having reeled off a list of his current cases, he says to Fliess: 'Now imagine what would happen if one were a physician like you, for instance, able to investigate the genitals and the nose simultaneously; the riddle (of their sexual aetiology) should be solved in no time' (29 September 1893; Masson, 1985: 56). And in undated enclosures to Fliess in 1894, entitled 'On the Aetiology and Theory of the Major Neuroses' and 'How Anxiety Originates', he provides an outline how such a genital-nasal theory might look. In these notes he suggests that the neuroses are 'disturbances due to impeded discharge' and says, in the context of a discussion of *coitus inter-ruptus*, that this is 'a physical factor that produces anxiety' (Masson, 1985: 77–8). And, given that there are many cases in which there is evidence of 'an accumulation of physical tension' which is 'the consequence of prevented discharge', anxiety neurosis can be seen to be a 'neurosis of damming up' (Masson, 1985: 79).

Throughout this period Freud's own nasal discharges and block-ages continued periodically to spoil his own health, and in January 1895, in the hope of alleviating his symptoms, he underwent a second direct surgical intervention – a Fliessian nose job – the cauterisation of the turbinate bones at the hands of the master. Fliess, incidentally, was also willing to put his money where his mouth was – or rather just above it. He had had the operation done on his own nose, performed by a colleague of his, Gersuny.[7] In any case, Freud's operation at first seemed to be a great success. Following the operation he wrote to Fliess:

> I must write to you hurriedly about something that astonishes me; otherwise I would be truly ungrateful... I have felt quite unbelievably well, as though everything had been erased... better times I have not known for ten months... (24 January 1895: Masson, 1985: 106–7)

None the less, Freud continued to suffer from periodic discharges of pus from his nose and continued to use cocaine regularly as 'nose medicine' explicitly, to control swelling and pain over several months in 1895. About three months after his operation he wrote to Fliess (20 April 1895): 'Since the last cocainisation three circumstances have continued to coincide: (1) I feel well (2) I am discharging ample amounts of pus (3) I am feeling VERY well' (Masson, 1985: 125). He also hypothesised to Fliess in this letter that there are useful distinctions to be made between local symptoms related to the nose – such as his own – and genuinely distant symptoms, which he suggests to Fliess are possibly to be mapped onto the anatomy of the nasal tissues and the mucous membranes.[8] Freud reminds him at one point (12 June 1895) of his own conjecture that 'the points of entry to the accessory nasal sinuses have a special dignity' – by virtue of their morphological similarity to the female sex organs (Masson, 1985: 131). One such case of suspected neurotic-remote symptoms relating to the nose-genital connection Freud referred to Fliess and Fliess operated on her shortly after he had done Freud.

## From Emma Eckstein's nose to 'Psychology for Neurologists'

Emma Eckstein had presented to Freud suffering from dysmenorrhoea, painful periods and irregular bleeding, which Freud suspected was not 'organic' in origin. Fliess had published work on the 'crossed reflexes' which emphasised the connection between the nose and the sexual organs, (in one paper he claimed to have alleviated pain in childbirth by application of cocaine to the turbinate bone in the nose), and Eckstein was served up to Fliess by Freud as a suitable case for his nasal surgery and as one which would probably provide him with more of the evidence that he urgently needed to prove his theory. As is well known, Eckstein was not to be so lucky; in fact she almost died from haemorrhage and infection following Fliess's neglecting to remove half a metre of gauze from her nose. This near disaster, in which Freud was deeply involved, both clinically and intellectually in terms of his commitment to the theory of the case, deeply affected Freud to the point of his questioning the path of collaboration with Fliess had taken him onto. Although Freud is always reluctant to make any criticism of Fliess's incompetence, he all but disdains from troubling him at first with the news of Eckstein's post-operative crisis: Freud tells him (4 March 1895) to let himself be 'persuaded' to call in Gersuny, who then inserted a drainage tube (Masson, 1985: 113–14). Two days later profuse bleeding reoccurred and Gersuny happened to be unavailable. Consequently Fliess called in another surgeon, Rosanes, who discovered the gauze, but without realising what he was pulling at caused her to have an alarming nasal haemorrhage. Whether her original problem was a nervous disorder or not, she was certainly 'hysterical' now (13 March 1895; Masson, 1985: 120), not to mention the physical discomfort of the 'persistent swelling going up and down like an avalanche' (4 March 1895; Masson, 1985: 113). With the further help of Gersuny, the poor Eckstein then began to make a recovery, bearing no ill will toward any of her doctors (28 March 1895; Masson, 1985: 122).

As if in sympathy, Freud's self-reproach and reflection on the case plunged him into a crisis of his own: he informs Fliess he is suffering from 'motoric insufficiency' and 'fluctuating mood changes' that prevent him from writing. Once again Eckstein began to look dangerously ill: 'The danger that she will run a fever is not far off. I am really very shaken to think that such a mishap could have a risen from an operation that was purported to be harmless' (11 April 1895; Masson, 1985: 124). A couple of weeks later Freud reports to Fliess that Eckstein is finally 'in the clear', and he reassures him that he personally would not hesitate to put himself under his scalpel again for his empyema (blockage of pus). He also mentions that he has been 'miserable' but can write on this occasion because he 'pulled himself out of a miserable attack with cocaine.' (20 and 26 April 1895; Masson, 1985: 126–7).

It is almost as if the instant improvement these nasal applications of cocaine restore Freud's faith in Fliessian gnoseology – to the point of his even suggesting making an appointment for a further cauterisation of his nose. The effect of the cocaine appears to convince him of the nasal origin of his own cardiac symptoms (arrhythmia). And in his letter of 17 June 1895 he reports that he is in fact using 'a lot' of cocaine and smoking cigars again. Though it is not possible to know, it is reasonable to suggest that this cocaine and nicotine double-whammy is in fact the most likely provocation of his ailment, which coincides with a shift in focus in his theorising at the time toward the connection between 'psychic' and 'physiological' well-being. This is then extended further into the major theoretical project he had by now begun, namely the *Project*, which he refers to in his letters to Fliess as his 'Psychology for Neurologists'.

Despite Freud's almost urgently positive outlook, particularly with respect to the activities of Fliess, cocaine's negative effects, about which Freud (to borrow a term from his own future thinking) had been in denial, were beginning (once again) to make him think differently. In other words, he was beginning to develop his own more sophisticated theses about individual nervous disorders and the aetiology of the neuroses, psychoses, symptomatology and so on.

The Eckstein affair had not only shaken Freud 'subjectively' but forced him to reconsider the details of Fliess's understanding of how the nose and remote symptoms were related, and Freud's own nasal problem, in his own view, did not after all fit the Fliessian model that had been the basis of his thinking of the Eckstein case. The Eckstein case had certainly served to indicate the potential for serious damage to the patient of an inadequate theory of the psycho-somatic disorder – and the safety, if not the validity, of surgical intervention on behalf of remote rather than local problems. The riskiness of experimental clinical practice must once again have come to mind for Freud. The professional criticism directed towards him at the time of his cocaine experiments and the misfortune of Fleischl's death were not so far in the past. Fliess too, in the meantime, had been criticised in the *Wiener Klinische Rundshau* for talking complete 'goobledygook' (Masson, 1985: 310n.4). Although Freud had offered Fliess his unequivocal support, that is not to say that he did not have his doubts about the completeness and sophistication of Fliess's theories, or a keen sense of the lacunae in his own. None of this stopped him, however, from sending to Fliess the manuscript of the remarkable theoretical work he began to work on intensively in the months following the Eckstein case in 1895, a work written in a burst of intellectual energy, his nose and head clear, and fuelled, judging by his letters to Fliess, by his regular self-medication with the psycho-somatic medicine that never seemed to let him down – cocaine.

## Freud on the neurochemical/psychological divide

In the *Project* Freud attempts to systematise his psychological and meta-psychological thinking in relation to the neuroscience of his day; for example, in terms of neurone theory, energy storage and cathexis, intensity, processes of excitation, modes of discharge, nerve centres and so forth:

> The intention is to furnish a psychology that shall be a natural science: that is, to represent psychical processes as quantitatively determinate states of specifiable material particles, thus making those processes perspicuous and free from contradiction. Two principal ideas are involved: (1) What distinguishes activity from rest is to be regarded as Q[uantity], subject to the general laws of motion. (2) The neurones are to be taken as material particles. (Freud, 1966, 1: 295)

It is not my intention here to discuss the 'scientific merit' of this work, neither in relation to some contemporary standard of knowledge or scientificity, nor with those of his own day, nor do I seek to question philosophically the mechanistic materialism of his thesis of 'material particles' as such. I refer to the *Project* here principally to indicate at this point that what Kristeva identifies as a contemporary issue for psychoanalysis, namely its relation to the advancing neurosciences, is one which 'returns' from the past of psychoanalysis itself. As Pribam and Gill (1976) point out, the *Project* introduces and suggests neurobiological mechanisms for such major psychoanalytic concepts as the primary and secondary processes, the ego, reality testing, drive and defence – all concepts which are later developed on psychological grounds. And, because it is in the *Project* that Freud elucidates these mechanisms as he nowhere else does, as Strachey at one point says: 'its invisible ghost, haunts the whole series of Freud's theoretical writings to the very end' (Freud, 1966, 1: 290). What I am all along suggesting here is that Freud's 'involvement' with cocaine – in the many senses I have mentioned – from 1883 onwards, including at the time that he worked on the *Project*, plays a decisive role in plotting Freud's theoretical trajectory. And, that if the main body of Freud's 'psychological' thinking bears within it the trace of its 'impossible' split from physiology and its concepts, then the 'two great confrontations' of which Kristeva speaks could in fact be described as the product of a reciprocal haunting, to use her own shorthand, of 'biology and representation' (Kristeva, 1994:18). The understanding of the psycho-somatic 'organism' can never be wholly external or transcendental to it and therefore 'objective' in the classical sense. The self-understanding of the human organism is always derived on the basis of an immanent reflexive exploration of its interiority. Earlier I suggested that Freud's experience of cocaine had provided a form of 'evidence' that the relation between the interiority and exteriority could be approached on the basis of the 'euphoria' it produced, and that this euphoria was neither simply of the psyche nor of the soma. The general effect, as I have identified it, of cocaine on Freud's path from the 'cocaine papers' (1885–87) through to the *Interpretation of Dreams* (1900) – to which I shall shortly turn – might then throw some light on the contemporary return of the issue of the relationship between psychoanalysis and psychopharmacology. I say this because 'chemical stimulation' of the 'hinge' between the psyche and soma makes it explicit and reflexively observable.

Freud's theoretical discourse of 'psychological mechanism' aims to develop a discourse in which it would become possible to explain, in a unifying way, both psychological and neurological phenomena (Pribam and Gill, 1976: 14). The work of the *Project* thus pointed beyond both theories which either postulated that consciousness is a mere appendage to physiological-psychical processes and is therefore of no consequence for actual physical events, and theories for which consciousness is the subjective side of all psychical events and thus inseparable from physiological mental processes. The theory developed here, says Freud, 'lies between these two' (Freud, SE, 1: 311; Pribam and Gill, 1976: 19). The theory of 'psychological mechanism' sought to explain what was known through the observation and clinical experience of psychological phenomena and their manifestations on a basis which was broadly consistent with the neurobiology of the time. The 'mechanism' linking the two, psychological though in one sense Freud most certainly considered it to be, must also be *chemical*: 'a suspicion forces itself upon us that… the endogenous stimuli consist of *chemical products*, of which there may be a considerable number' (Freud, SE, 1: 321; Pribam and Gill, 1976: 44).

### The interface between inside and outside – the neurochemical mechanism of the unconscious

Freud had come to recognise that the interface between the human organism and its environment – between the human body and what is outside it in physical terms – could indeed be considered in terms of chemistry and chemical interaction. This does not amount, however, to a theory of physiological-psychical *equivalence* (as postulated for instance by mind–brain identity theory) or imply the possibility of direct translation between psychological and physiological discourses such that psychological phenomena can be reduced to biological processes. (Pribam and Gill at one point suggest that the *Project* may perhaps serve in this way as a kind of Rosetta Stone for those seeking communication between psychoanalysis and neuroscience.) Nor does Freud conclude that there is at the level of chemistry a *continuum* between the inside and outside of the human organism – such that the border between the human being and its environment could be erased on the basis of a kind of fundamental, materialist landscape of chemical events. Were this to have been his conclusion then the corollary would have been that chemistry is, in the final analysis, the common denominator and psychoanalysis was indeed destined to be in direct competition with psychopharmacology, but he at no point suggests this.

In a move which preserves the distinction between interiority and exteriority, Freud relocates the distinction between endogenous and exogenous stimuli, the interface between the psychological and the physiological, *within* the human organism. In fact, exogenous stimuli acting upon the individual at the level of 'psychological representation' and affecting the individual in the course of ordinary behaviour and experience are considered to interface with the endogenous stimuli at the level of chemistry: a Quantity of external stimulation is translated into Quality – but *not all* of that Quantity is mechanically directed along pathways which result in alterations of consciousness. In other words, there is plenty happening to the individual that does not figure in the register of conscious life at all: there is a *remainder* and that remainder can so to speak have an *unconscious* impact on the organism. Having sorted out a way of explaining why consciousness is not the entirety of the psychic realm but only a function of it, Freud, had in a sense established all the ground he needed – in terms of the question of the underlying connections between neuropathology and psychopathology – to warrant the autonomous progression of psychopathological research. There was in principle no reason at all to suppose that the neurosciences could not catch up one day with any new discoveries made within psychological inquiry.

What is particularly fascinating in Freud's thesis, I suggest, is his thinking of this relationship between representation and biology as being a two-way street. Neuropharmacological substances which could 'interfere' with this moment of 'translation' between representation and neurochemistry could also be regarded as acting *directly* on the mechanisms of representation. This proposes not merely that there is a chemical 'correlate' but that chemicals (psychotropic drugs for instance) have a 'mechanically' direct effect on psychology. The content or form of a psychological state is not itself determined by chemicals, but rather by the state of the psychoneurological system as whole according to the overall distribution of its 'energy'. This solution is remarkably consistent with the insights Freud derives concerning 'cocaine euphoria' at the time of his early experiments with the drug: chemical-mechanical and psychological phenomena had been expressly *indirectly* related to one another through the 'euphoria', which, even then, Freud had considered to be 'as much of the muscles as the mind'. The euphoria was seen neither as a purely neurobiological phenomenon nor as a purely psychological one; nor was it regarded as merely subjective – its objectivity was deemed to be evidenced by its muscular manifestation. The difference between 'interference' and 'activation' of the endogenous stimuli cannot be supported on the basis of an appeal to 'natural' as opposed to 'artificial' processes because the very nature of the human organism is presented in the *Project* as a kind of feedback loop between the inside and outside. Consequently, 'representation', by which we understand, meaning, culture, ordinary life, experience, is always mediated chemically: happiness, depression and other psychological phenomena are manipulable by means of 'sympathetic' neurochemistry. The psychological management and control of the borderline between the inside and outside are what enable the individual to retain his or her autonomy; indeed it is essential to the distinctive humanness, or organismic identity, in an environment which, without such defences, would 'dissolve' it completely.

Later Freud develops his thinking of this borderline in terms of unconscious inner drives responsible for excitations from within, on one side, and conscious defensive mechanisms which control excitations from without, on the other.[9] But this does not imply that drugs which act on this borderline act only on what comes from the outside, and that their 'effects' are exclusively to be found in consciousness, or rather, which are events of the conscious surface. Nor does it mean that neuropharmacologists need explicitly to search for drugs which act on 'inner drives', for the 'two sides' of the border are in a constant process of exchange: this *process* is, so to speak, the borderline between the inside and outside itself. For example, whether Viagra acts on the sex drive or on the vascular system is a moot point: it enables sexual desire to express itself more easily than might otherwise be able to.

The *Project* undoubtedly stands as Freud's most determined attempt to establish the basis on which psychology and neuroscience could be rejoined. But once such a principle had been established, it also served to demonstrate that there was no particular need for them to proceed hand in hand. Even today not only does the biochemical basis of 'mental' disorder remain little understood but clearly, as Kristeva suggests, psychopharmacological therapy always requires supplementary interpretation – psychoanalytic or otherwise – of *what the patient has to say*. Freud's priority became the establishment of psychoanalytic science in its own right, and by 1895 he had that task, too, already in hand. In the final section of this chapter I shall trace the effect of cocaine on the emergence of what could be called Freud's properly psychoanalytic thinking, represented by *The Interpretation of Dreams* (1900).

## Solutions and resolutions: Freud's drug dream – 'Irma's Injection'

Freud tells us that he had the 'specimen dream' of Irma's Injection on 23–4 July 1895 after working on Irma's case history late into the night. The following day in his letter to Fliess he chose to make no mention of what he would later come to regard as the watershed in his thinking deserving of a commemorative plaque on the house on which it had come to him. His daytime intellectual energies at this time were still dedicated to the ideas of the *Project* – a work which he often appears to be writing exclusively *for* Fliess. In his next letter to Fliess (6 August 1895) he says the 'psychological theories' had 'only very laboriously' been arrived at and that he was hoping they were not 'dream gold' (Masson, 1985: 134). Freud's doubts about the coherence and adequacy of the ideas of the *Project* continued in the coming weeks, and despite having the breakthrough that allowed him to finish it, he evidently did not consider that it had been developed to the point of satisfactory completion that warranted publication. None the less, the working through of his ideas on how neurological and psychological explanatory frameworks might translate and complement one another had become sufficiently transparent to him at least for him to feel that they had been taken as far they could be at the time.

Given the long-term and ambivalent role that cocaine – as an agent of interaction between the two conceptual domains of 'biology and representation', or neuroscience and psychology – had played in Freud's life and work between 1883 and 1895, it is not surprising to find its oneiric reworking in his first full dream analysis. The analysis, 'Irma's Injection', represents on many levels the intellectual departure from the theoretical problems of the *Project*, and marks the beginning of the end of the intellectual proximity to Fliess. The interpretation of the Irma dream, amongst many other things, represents both Freud's reworking, and in many respects his setting aside, of the themes of 'drugs' and 'chemistry'. At the same time it stands to confirm the role that they have played up to this point, both in his attempts at theorising and in instances of clinical and experimental practice. This is clearly evident in its various references to drugs and the use of drugs; to the handling of chemical substances, the memory of chemical formulae and the use of syringes and so on – all of which highlight the pharmaco-genealogical root of his emergent psychoanalysis. All of this is revealed as such, as it were for the first time, on the basis of the (psycho) analytic interpretation of the dream itself.

The dream analysis is a turning point in several senses. It is of an *intrinsically reflexive* order: the treatment now takes place in the form of *communication* between doctor and patient, and is no longer viewed as addressing processes taking place solely with the patient. Of course, in so far as Irma's Injection is an element in Freud's self-analysis, he must 'play both parts'. The precedent for this 'methodological necessity', as we have seen, first imposed itself in the course of his psycho-somatic experiments with cocaine. In order for Irma's Injection to function as the decisive stepping stone to psychoanalysis, by providing the key insight into the nature of the dream as the fulfilment of a wish, it must (in both the analysis and in the interpretation of it) be the occasion of a recapitulation of what had led to the dream in a way which is 'acceptable' to the analyst or analysand, namely Freud himself. But the dream is, of course, not only an expression of Freud's wish (which in this case is, he suggests, 'the wish to be innocent of Irma's illness'): it is, in so far as it is about Freud's intellectual conundrums, also about the nature of psychoanalysis itself; it is a dream which provides him with the material by means of which his thinking attains a deeper understanding of, precisely, the psychic mechanism of dreams and their role in the economy of the psyche in general. This particular dream analysis instantiates and inaugurates psychoanalysis itself. It does this merely by virtue of the fact that the dream triggers Freud's leap in understanding about what it means for the dreamer (namely himself) but because it stands as a 'specimen dream' for the psychoanalytic process as such. It is, in other words, an event which becomes transparent to itself in the analysis such that Freud may grasp and illustrate the principle of dream analysis *per se.*

Subjectively, and with great candour, Freud says, the whole dream is a defensive 'plea'; it is about 'professional conscientiousness' and the 'wish to be innocent of Irma's illness'. But whatever the analysis of Irma's Injection is 'about', understanding its (objective) importance for the very idea of analysis itself requires cognisance of its many references to what I have throughout this chapter referred to as the multiple 'effects' of cocaine – all of which, on one level, Freud had reason to be anxious about or to have a troubled conscience about, in both the moral and the intellectual senses. I'll briefly indicate these reference points: (1) Freud's concerns and anxieties relating to the potential misidentification of organic and neurotic disorders (for example Eckstein), but additionally that this represents an inherent, general professional hazard. (2) The potential 'injurious effect of cocaine': he mentions the case of a patient who developed a necrosis of the mucous membrane after following his own example; he mentions the death of his friend Fleischl, which was a consequence of a certain 'thoughtlessness in handling of chemical substances'; he reiterates that injection of cocaine had not been his advice – in the dream analysis 'Irma's pains had been caused by Otto giving her an incautious injection of an unsuitable drug'. He mentions also another actual case in which he had caused a 'severe toxic state' in a patient with what was considered to be a harmless remedy – the sentiment he expresses to Fliess in relation to the Eckstein crisis. (3) 'The chemistry of the sexual processes' and trymethylamin: again a reference to Fliess's theories, and his own thinking of the 'chemistry' of the border between endogenous and exogenous stimuli – this echoes Freud's intellectual concerns about what he later termed the psychoanalytic superstructure and the organic base. (4) The dream analysis demonstrates the autonomy of the 'analysis' it instantiates and the autonomy of such analysis in relation to the kind of medicine and medical practice to which Freud had at least attempted to remain professionally close up to this point. Put in the simplest terms: Freud's dream interpretation represents the attempt to illustrate how the 'resolution' of a dream could provide a 'solution' to a 'problem' – which may be a patient's psychological disorder, but may also be, as it is in the case of Irma's Injection, *the problem of analysis itself*: that is, more precisely, the validity of psychoanalysis. At this point in the development of Freud's thought, as we have seen, this is the problem of the relationship between the psychoanalysis (of the dream) and the kind of analytic thinking that has led Freud all along to struggle with the conceptualisation of the relationship between physiology and psychology.

If the dream is thus pivotal for the emergence of psychoanalysis then it is so because it marks the point at which psychoanalysis gives birth to itself on the basis of the 'resolution' of the physiological/psychological distinction Freud had accomplished in the *Project* and the kind of 'solutions' he had, in the course of his career to date, administered (and self-administered) in clinical practice. Throughout, I have attempted to show, this entire intellectual trajectory was influenced by the multiple and often ambivalent 'effects' connected with cocaine – 'the episode', the drug, his illness and habitual use, his conscience about matters related to it and so forth.

Given the vast critical literature dealing with Irma's Injection, I restrict my discussion here solely to the question posed at the outset of this chapter concerning the connection between psychoanalysis and drugs.

## Derrida on 'Irma's Injection'

Jacques Derrida (1998) has commented on the concept of 'analysis' in psychoanalysis in the context of a discussion of the nature of (his own) 'resistances' to it. He turns to Irma's Injection to examine the manner in which Freud understands the notion of a 'solution' (*Lösung*) – in the sense of its being both the interpretation of the dream and the solution to a 'problem' which it (re-)presents. The 'problem' in relation to Irma's Injection, as I just have noted, is that it is more than just an item of Freud's self-analysis, it concerns psychoanalysis in general.

In the 'Preamble' to the dream, Freud's concern is clearly with his only partially successful treatment of Irma: 'the patient was relieved of her hysterical anxiety but did not lose her somatic symptoms… and I proposed a solution to the patient which she seemed unwilling to accept' (1991: 181). In the dream synopsis Irma is given a 'solution' by Freud's friend Otto in the form of an injection of 'a preparation of propyl, propyls… proprionic acid… trymethylamin', which is accompanied in the dream by the thought that 'injections of that sort should not be made so thoughtlessly… And probably the syringe had not been clean.' In his comment following the dream synopsis, in a paragraph that precedes the analysis as such, Freud says that he 'smiled at the senseless idea of an injection'. Derrida immediately points out that everything in the dream is already, in another sense, already 'concentrated' and 'dissolved' in a 'solution': 'The same word (solution, analytic resolution, *Lösung*) is valid *for the drug* and for the end of the analysis' (Derrida, 1998: 7, *my emphasis*). 'The drug' at this point in Derrida's text is introduced as if it were a synonym for a term used a little later – 'chemical element' and 'chemical analysis', in its characteristic aim to isolate elements, is then referred to later in the essay as a form of analysis which is to be understood in contradistinction to 'deconstruction': 'nothing is more foreign to [deconstruction] than chemistry, that science of simples' (Derrida, 1989: 27). Certainly the references to 'chemistry' here are principally intended to provide a model of a certain species of analysis, but 'the chemical' in question, it must be emphasised, is referred to initially as 'the drug'. This is acutely significant, particularly as the point Derrida is making is that the Freudian 'text' (the dream analysis) is itself to be thought of (on the basis of deconstruction) as a *pharmakon* (see chapter 2). As such the text itself *resists* the kind of chemical style of analysis (knowledge by way of reduction to elements) brought to bear upon it. This is the kind of analysis, Derrida implies, that Freud himself ostensively undertakes in the text 'Dream of Irma's Injection' – and it is exactly the kind of analysis deconstruction resists. It is a style of analysis which, on the basis of Derridean deconstruction (itself intrinsically '*pharmako*-logical'), can be shown never to be final, in the sense of arriving at an elementary truth. Freud's analytical (re)solution is also at the same time a solution to a problem: it 'undoes the symptomatic or etiological knot' (Derrida, 1998: 7). This particular piece of dream analysis belongs to the series of analyses constituting Freud's self-analysis, and it serves to move his understanding of psychoanalysis decisively forward by providing him with *a new understanding of the path to his current undertaking.* It is self-validating and self-serving in this respect, but Derrida will want to insist that it is not thereby resolved in any ultimate sense.

Thinking the 'chemical' in the expression 'chemical analysis' as 'the drug' – as Derrida suggests – makes that analysis auto-deconstruct. The 'drug' resists the kind of 'chemical analysis' as this is traditionally understood: the 'drug' operates in *both* registers – as a 'chemical solution', but also at the level of its figurative representation, namely its appearance in the dream. 'The drug' therefore no more belongs to the scientific discourse of chemistry than it does to any other discourse or form of representation in which it comes to figure. Derrida's point is that no matter how 'convincing' Freud's (or anyone else's) interpretation of this (or any other) dream-text might be, it is not, by virtue of an 'elemental' or 'chemical' analysis, 'true' in any ultimate sense.

Derrida's exploration of his 'resistance' to psychoanalysis takes the form of rejecting the 'chemical' style of analysis – analysis into elements – which Freud deploys in his text 'Dream of Irma's Injection'. Consequently, the drug or text cannot be approached in this way and claimed as an identifiable pillar of a *system of thought* (the status it is widely accorded).[10] Derrida's refusal of this kind of reading may be seen as a manifestation of 'resistance' to psychoanalysis, but what he is actually resisting is its inherent tendency toward a 'chemical' style of analysis. Typically the deconstructive counter-thrust is to turn this approach on its head by insisting on thinking of the text as the drug itself – here in the sense of a text which is shown to be the source of its own 'undoing'. And this 'undoing' occurs in the 'act' of readerly engagement with it.

With characteristic aplomb Derrida demonstrates this aspect of the interpretation by directing his reader to the 'unthinkable', discernible in Freud's text in his reference to the *Nabel* of the dream (the 'umbilicus' or 'omphalus'): the 'one spot in every dream at which it is unplumbable – a navel, as it were, that is its point of contact with the unknown' (Freud 1991: 168n.2). This 'navel' in Freud's analysis of the dream marks

> a reserve of meaning that still awaits us; it concerns rather a night, an absolute unknown that is originarily, congenitally bound or tied (but also itself unbound because ab-solute) to the essence and birth of the dream. (Derrida, 1998: 11)

In other words, any 'solution' involves a certain ab-solute, or something which exceeds the solution. Freud's text bears then what, following Derrida, may be referred to as the 'trace' of alterity: it is a text in which the 'effect' (of the unknowable) has, so to speak, not worn off. And it consequently presents us with the opportunity to contemplate the question of 'resistance' rather than offering a theoretical (that is, 'chemical') style of analysis of its 'true meaning'.

Derrida returns to Irma's Injection to reopen the question of 'resistance' on the basis of Freud's failure to resolve the question of 'resistance' in his own interpretation of the dream. He finds Freud's solution there is to absolve himself (the analyst) of the responsbility for Irma's (the analysand's) resistance to his solution (the analysis) of Irma's symptoms in the dream. In other words, he accepts responsibility for the correctness of the solution but avows responsibility for its acceptance by the patient.

## Freud's resistance to cocaine

Irma's Injection is in many ways the point at which 'drugs', and more specifically what I have here called the 'cocaine effect', are intended to be left behind, namely, at the very point at which psychoanalysis establishes its autonomy. But this is possible only in the form of a reconfirmation of the role that the 'cocaine effect' has played up to this point. Rightly or wrongly (viewed from the clinical perspective) the road to a possible integration of psychopharmacology and psychoanalysis is closed off, so to speak, from the side of psychoanalysis. Or so it might appear and indeed be the case, were it not for the fact that the drug – like the text – has a life of its own: not least because there can be no guarantees of drug-free analysands; not least either because psychopharmacology never really left the stage; not least because cocaine can at any moment reproduce the 'euphoria' which provided an 'original' key insight into the limitation of understanding the human in either purely physiological or purely psychological terms. In view of Derrida's remarks, Freud's 'chemical' analysis of the dream could be described as proffering a resolution of the ambivalence of the 'cocaine effect' and its relation to psychoanalysis as evidenced in the many 'drug elements' of the dream. But it cannot, to follow Derrida's reflections on 'resistance' to elemental analysis, be fully understood, nor is it exhausted, by reducing it to its 'elements'. One could say then that cocaine marks the 'return of the repressed' in the dream: it is the mark of Freud's own resistance in the analysis.

The *Project*, on which Freud was working intensively at the time of the Irma dream, involved working from both sides of the psychosomatic divide at once, providing the approach to the 'chemical' basis of what I referred to above as the mechanism of 'translation' between the endogenous and exogenous stimuli governing the division between interiority and exteriority. Freud pursued this mode of thinking to the point at which he had satisfied himself that his psychological thinking was anchored in a recognisably objective science. And despite the (some commentators would say, notorious) 'untranslatability' of his developed psychoanalytical theses into scientific propositions, he always considered the principle that they could be so translated to have been well established. In later works, his passing references to 'chemistry' indicate that the kind of theoretical description pioneered in the *Project* might have been pursued further, and in parallel with psychological research. In *Sexuality of the Neuroses* (1906), for example, he says of 'sexual processes' and their disturbances that 'it is scarcely possible to avoid picturing these processes as being in the last resort of a chemical nature' and that consequently 'the "neuroses" proper, in spite of their name, may soon have to be excluded from this category' (Freud, 1953: 278–9). And, in the *Introductory Lectures on Psycho-Analysis* (1917), in a reference to the possible existence of 'sexual toxins' and the unknown 'chemistry of sexuality', he expresses the view that 'the theoretical structure of psychoanalysis that we have created is in truth a super-structure, which will one day have to be set upon its organic foundation' (Freud, 1963: 388–9). In *Civilisation and its Discontents* (1929) he emphasises that 'in the last analysis, all suffering is nothing else than sensation; it only exists inso far as we feel it, and we only feel it in consequence of certain ways in which our organism is regulated' (Freud, 1961: 78). One of the most evident forms of 'regulation', and one of the 'crudest, but also the most effective', he says, is 'the chemical one – intoxication'. (He notes that mania is 'a condition similar to intoxication'.) And whilst Freud points to the danger of injury from popular intoxicants, he also positively acknowledges how they have acquired a place in the economics of the libido (1961: 78). The danger arises with the search for 'better conditions of sensibility', but that clearly is not to say that 'intoxicants' (or 'psychotropic medicines') ought to be excluded from that quest.

There is a sense, then, in which Freud's relationship to cocaine made him a pioneer of the theory of 'mixed treatments', even if he and the psychoanalysis which emerged after his *Interpretation of Dreams* have – ever so ambivalently – tended to resist the very idea.

## Notes

1 The word 'hinge' (*brisure*) is used by Kristeva in the passage cited above. I do not know whether she is using it with the section in Derrida's *Grammatology* which bears that word as its title in mind (Derrida, 1976: 65ff.). The significance of the word for Derrida, at that point in his text, is that 'hinge' is a word which expresses both something which joins or articulates something whilst marking the point of a discontinuity. He says there: 'The hinge (*brisure*) marks the impossibility that a sign, the unity of a signifier and a signified, be produced with the plenitude of a present and absolute presence. That is why there is no full speech, however much one might wish to restore it by means or without benefit of psychoanalysis' (69). My discussion here concerning the continuity/discontinuity of Freud's thinking as it moves from neurology and physiology to psychoanalysis, or from somatology to psychology, and the role that cocaine plays in making these joins or breaks, warrants adopting the term 'hinge' in this sense as I proceed here.

2 These are collected and translated in Byck (1974).

3 An exception to this is Jürgen von Scheidt (1973).

4 It should be noted that Jones expresses some ambivalence with regard to whether Freud's genius always served him well: 'His great strength, though sometimes also his great weakness, was the quite extraordinary respect he had for the *singular fact*. This is surely a very rare quality. In scientific work people continually dismiss a single observation when it does not appear to have any connection with other data or general knowledge. Not so Freud (Jones, 1953: 96).

5 Jeffrey Moussaieff Masson (ed. and trans.), *The Complete Letters of Sigmund Freud to Wilhelm Fliess 1887–1904* (Cambridge, MA: Harvard University Press, 1985).

6 Freud claimed to have either lost or destroyed the letters to him from Fliess. For a discussion of his remarks concerning their disappearance see Masson's Introduction (1985: 1–13).

7 Robert Gersuny (1884–1924) was a plastic surgeon who was later to play an important role in the Eckstein case (Masson, 1985: 107n.1). See below.

8 He had in fact two years previously opined that his own nasal symptoms were organic-local rather than neurotic-remote and that 'something organic would be harder to take'.

9 Freud developed his bio-philosophical thinking further, most notably perhaps in *Beyond the Pleasure Principle* (1920). The details of this go beyond the themes of this chapter, but it is worth noting that the text illustrates Freud's unceasing determination to develop an adequate bio-philosophical basis for the principal phenomena of psychoanalytic theory. An excellent discussion of the text from this perspective can be found in Ansell-Pearson (1999: 104–14).

10 Von Scheidt's (1973) reading of Freud on cocaine does precisely this – it remains thoroughly psychoanalytic, interpreting the 'cocaine work' as the clue to understanding Freud's development in supposedly purely psychoanalytic terms. For Von Scheidt, Irma's Injection represents Freud's working through of his Oedipus complex relating it to his theoretical development – euphoria is the feminine aspect, scientific accounting the masculine. This approach to the 'cocaine effect', to use my own term, once again turns it into an 'object' of inquiry and consequently psychoanalysis is effectively rendered a closed system of thought.

# 5    Benjamin's 'curious dialectics of intoxication'

An intoxication comes over the man who walks for long and aimlessly through the streets. With each step, the walk takes on greater momentum; ever weaker grow the temptations of shops, of bistros, of smiling women, ever more irresistible the magnetism of the next street corner, of a distant mass of foliage, of a street name. Then comes hunger. Our man wants nothing to do with the myriad possibilities offered to sate his appetite. Like an ascetic animal, he flits through unknown districts – until utterly exhausted, he stumbles into his room, which receives him coldly and wears a strange air. *Arcades Project* [M 1, 3] (Benjamin, 1999: 417)

## A thinking which is eminently narcotic

For Benjamin the life of the modern subject – of either gender, I suggest he means – is characterised by volatile states of intoxication. 'He' experiences an uncontrollable oscillation between the soporific seductions of what life in the city presents him with and the need to withdraw from the stimulus overload it produces in him. 'The hunger' then begins to rage within, driving him to withdraw in the only way he can think to do. He seeks in his privacy, in his private space, an antidote to that intoxication from which he now flees and doses himself with another drug, 'that most terrible drug – ourselves – which we take in solitude' (Benjamin, 2000: 237). This image of the 'man in the street' at once excited and made paranoid by the cityscape through which he moves is both disturbing and deeply melancholic. Might he not have fled into the company of a friend to help him restore his 'balance'? Or simply have enjoyed the thrill of the street and then been content to withdraw to the quiet safety of his home? Even if were to seek to reduce the 'intoxication' brought on by his walk through the streets it would still constitute a 'narcotic decision' of one sort or another. This is nowhere more evident than in the case of the modern subject as critic or thinker, whose response to modernity cannot escape the fact that all thinking is, says Benjamin, 'eminently narcotic' (Benjamin, 2000: 237).

Benjamin's critique of modernity and modern culture acknowledges the 'narcotic' basis of modern subjective life and considers that this is the key to a genuinely critical relation to culture. The task of the critic is to 'awaken' modernity from the state of cultural narcolepsy into which it has fallen. Benjamin's remarks about intoxication and his reflections on the use of drugs to fuel the processes by which a critique of modernity and its ways of 'seeing' can be developed, are made in a wide range of contexts, often blurring the distinction in his writing between metaphorical narcotic effects and actual narcotic effects.

This chapter will do three things: firstly it will explain the narco-analytic thrust of Benjamin's thinking with reference to several of his well-known texts and explain the idea that a 'theory of narcosis' lies at the heart of Benjaminian critique. I shall briefly explain how this relates to his 'method' and the kinds of cultural 'objects' and phenomena he comments on. Secondly, it will argue that Benjamin's frequent but often seemingly ambivalent remarks about the critical value of intoxication to revolutionary thinking provide a key to understanding his method of 'dialectical images' and its relevance to the study of culture at large. Finally, I shall recontextualise the discussion of his thinking of the juncture between drugs, culture and critique in relation to the apparently eccentric short essay *Hashish in Marseilles* (1979: 215–22) to see how his experiments with drugs bear upon his idea of critical thinking in general.[1]

## Benjamin's narco-analysis of the culture of modernity

Benjamin's contribution to the study of the culture of modernity and the impact of his work on contemporary cultural studies defy any simple assessment in terms of a specific body of knowledge produced or the development of a systematic critical method as such. His legacy is, of course, literally a literary *oeuvre*, but it is one which probes and questions the relationship between literature and its socio-historical contexts as well as the very idea of 'literary representation' itself. At the centre of this *oeuvre* is what is undoubtedly the most famous unwritten book of cultural analysis of the last century, the *Arcades Project*. In this project, begun in 1927, Benjamin planned, replanned and undertook to produce a philosophically informed study of material culture and everyday life. It included material on the most diverse aspects of the 'residues' of nineteenth- and early twentieth-century industrial culture, from the contents of shop windows, photographs, city plans and street-lighting to prostitution, gambling and street life in general. The project, which comprises research notes, plans and fragments of commentary, takes its title from the arcades in Paris, constructed from around 1830 and imitated in several other European capitals and in the USA. (These were the precursors of the familiar department stores and shopping malls of today.) The title appropriately directs attention to those public places, everyday practices and objects which, in their programmatic, literary constellation in Benjamin's work, were to collectively constitute a materialist philosophy of history; a philosophy of history constructed, so to speak, out of material 'residues' of culture itself. This process of collage and constellation, however, was not to be thought of as a kind of 'natural history' of culture; the passage of culture into a literary medium was not intended to be merely a reconstruction or reflection of the *empirical* in a literary form. Indeed, nineteenth-century historical realism, such as that of Ranke (which Nietzsche had on similar grounds so sharply attacked)[2] was referred to by Benjamin as 'the strongest narcotic of the nineteenth century' (1999: [N3, 4], 463), the effects of which his *Arcades Project* was intended to counteract.

The incompleteness of Benjamin's work as a full-blown materialist philosophy of history, and indeed the non-existence of the *Arcades Project* as a finished work, has driven many of his contemporary readers toward the conclusion that its fragmentary nature is itself singularly significant, indeed exemplary of something Benjamin himself could barely have been aware of from his own perspective, namely the nascent stirrings of what has since come to be known as 'postmodernity'. In its eclectic diversity – ranging from philosophical theory through literary critique, and employing a diversity of conventional and unconventional styles and forms of expression (including a stint of popular radio broadcasting)[3] – Benjamin's *oeuvre* may be considered retrospectively as a remarkable record of the collapse of the systematic, universalising thrust of modernity and modern critical thought. It can be seen as illustrative of how the modern prospect and goal of an overarching theory of modernity is an unrealisable, utopian objective. No doubt the contingencies of Benjamin's peripatetic professional life and personal life-story were materially constitutive of its production over the thirteen years during which he worked on it, and were partly responsible for its peculiar trajectory. And, his writerly attempts to constellate those residual elements of modern culture which existed in a state of accelerated dissolution around him, so as to 'dialectically' retell and redeem its history, constitute a valiant but illustrative 'failure' of epic proportions. What Benjamin said in a letter in 1932 to his friend Gerschom Scholem – 'many, or a sizeable number, of my works have been small-scale victories, they are offset by large-scale defeats'[4] – suggests that his work might be regarded as a form of literary accompaniment to the fate of the revolutionary communist politics of his day to which he felt powerfully drawn. However, given that his method and his writings broadly imply a critical refutation of the very idea of mimetic representation, it would be a mistake to conclude so quickly that Benjamin confronts us simply with a 'snapshot' of modernity in disintegration, or that his works constitute a sort of *Vorbild* of postmodernity, and that this is equivalent to their 'teaching' or 'thesis'. Benjamin's work clearly does not merely aim to *represent*, on the basis of new, eclectic and multiple strategies for articulating a postmodern theory of 'culture and society', what had hitherto been unrepresentable. To say this is not to deny, however, that this still burgeoning contemporary genre of social and cultural criticism undoubtedly owes much to his example. In fact, a 'major thesis', in the sense of a singular philosophical perspective of the type that can be straightforwardly represented, embraced and learnt, is nowhere to be found in Benjamin, despite the fact that this was a frequent topic of discussion in his letters to friends and contemporaries. And I am not suggesting that what Benjamin's work demands of its readers today is that they should attempt to reconstruct or compensate for a supposedly underwritten contribution to the systematic philosophy of dialectical thinking. His work can only be seen either as 'positively' postmodern or as 'negatively' lacking as dialectical critique (as Adorno at times suggests) on the basis of a methodological *decision* which is itself 'political' with respect to a given present context, or, NOW. In view of this, it should be considered as taking the form of a projected *futural* redemption of *the present* (of what Benjamin called *Jetztzeit* – literally 'now-time').[5]

Indeed, his notion of *Jetztzeit* serves as a useful terminological point of reference for considering why it is that his remarks are predisposed to attract antithetical readings. Any engagement with Benjamin's thinking which is to amount to more than a form of the critical hermeneutics (aimed at the 'redemption' of meanings) he himself sought to refute must also be an attempt to address its own contemporary concerns – which are of course always more urgent than those of the historian of ideas or 'antiquarian' can ever be, and always political in a more direct sense. (Again, as with Nietzsche's writing, Benjamin's work appears to anticipate the range of possible attempts to dissipate its radical energy by rendering it 'historical' or 'natural'.) But by making the notion of *Jetztzeit* central to his philosophy of time, memory and experience, everything that he says in relation to it lays itself open to the charge of a failure to overcome the mystical or theological mode of thinking said to be evident in such messianism. This failure may be further suspected on the ground of Benjamin's neglect of the material economic and social realities of the present (*Gegenwart*). Adorno, for example, perceived dialectical short-comings in Benjamin's attempt to overcome the distinction between a theological and a materialist conception of 'illumination', and along with that a tendency to either slip back into the realm of theology and redemption through the recovery of the lost meanings of texts, or to fall prey to the seductively uncritical notion of experience itself. Many of Benjamin's readers working in cultural theory and cultural studies today, on the other hand, are much more concerned with his methodological employment of what he called 'dialectical images' and see Benjamin's approach to critique as being profoundly attuned to the shift in the twentieth century from a narrative to a predominantly visual culture.

The 'method' of dialectical images works on the basis of a visual rather than a linear logic and owes more to the techniques of montage than to sequential reasoning (Buck-Morss, 1989: 218). As well as in the *Arcades Project*, this method was most explicitly adopted by Benjamin in his essay 'One Way Street' (2000: 45–104), which comprises short, aphoristic and often personal texts with titles such as 'Gas Station', 'Gloves', 'Mexican Embassy', 'Stand-up Beer Hall', 'Fire Alarm', 'Lost Property Office'. As Richard Wolin has commented, by working in this way Benjamin tends to obliterate traces of 'subjective interference' and consequently the 'excessive abstraction' of theory:

> The overall effect of this procedure on the reader was intended to be one of *shock* by wrenching elements of everyday life from their original contexts and rearranging them in a new constellation, Benjamin hoped to divest them of their familiarity and thereby stir the reader from a state of passivity into an active an critical posture' (Wolin 1982: 124).

This effectively results in an intervention in the process by which consciousness is produced. (Later I will suggest that this has its correlate in a form of a critical 'passivity before the object'.) Indeed, Benjamin's method aims to directly disrupt the processes of consciousness production; of the thinking which arises in relation to cultural forms and whose self-image is one of a rational autonomy floating above its material engagements in culture in general. According to its own logic of presentation, his work could be said to be substantially comprised of such 'dialectical images' which themselves substantively constitute material historical residues of a literary nature. These literary residues demand in turn from the reader, who comes to them in his or her own *Jetztzeit*, a form of engagement which is akin to the processes of Benjamin's own refigurings, gatherings and juxtapositionings of all other such residues of the antecedent material culture he was dealing with. So rather than hermeneutically recouping lost meanings through *repetition*, the critic should aim to *make use of* these elements of culture.

## Baudelaire and the high *flâneur*

By turning to Benjamin's writings on Baudelaire (1973) now, we can get a sense of how this works as a critical strategy, even though these writings are of a more conventional style than those comprising either 'One Way Street' or the *Arcades Project*. This will also allow me to retrace the route to the present investigation of his ideas on intoxication and their importance for his method.

For Benjamin, the modern condition is one of cultural slumber – a big sleep in which modern industrial life and life in the city is characterised for the majority by alienated labour and commodity fetishism. In his work on Baudelaire he approaches the question of the relationship between modern subjectivity and the material forms of its existence by means of literary-critical techniques which are not at all aimed at recuperating Baudelaire's 'meaning' but rather at exposing the *modus operandi* of the production of consciousness in the mid nineteenth century. For this purpose Baudelaire serves as a useful 'example' and a literary context precisely because, as a lyric poet surviving into the modern era, he is sufficiently 'out of time with the times' to enjoy, by virtue of this disjuncture, a degree of immunity to the overwhelming force of modern identification, namely, with the massing city crowd on the one hand and on the other its counterpart, the newly burgeoning and mesmerising commodity culture. However, the single most important thing by far about Baudelaire for Benjamin is that he is 'a connoisseur of narcotics' (1973: 56).[6] Just why, I shall explain shortly.

Although the work on Baudelaire ostensibly takes the form of a kind of literary sociology of high capitalism in the nineteenth century, it simultaneously presents an exposition and a critique of the mimetic theory of representation as this applies both to literature and to everyday cognition and experience. It is a work which destabilises the very distinction between sociological and literary representation by examining the manner in which literature and experience are reciprocally and historically determinative of one another. Adorno is entirely correct when he points out that 'Benjamin did not respect the boundary between literary writers and philosophers' (1970: 16, cited in Buck-Morss: 443 n. 50). Not to do so, I suggest, is neither a philosophical oversight nor an analytical weakness on Benjamin's part. It signals rather a deliberate attempt to undermine, at the level of literary praxis, the artificiality of any such boundary. Such a move is central to Benjamin's 'anti-disciplinary' approach to the study of modernity. What is evidently at stake in view of the artificiality of such a genre distinction is consequently more than a critical assessment of a literary text or even 'literature' *per se*. At stake is the expression of the very nature of reality; the relationship between interiority and exteriority; the subject and object and history – a terrain traditionally claimed by the discipline of philosophy and communicated in rarefied, if not arcane, forms of philosophical discourse. In the Baudelaire essays (1973) Benjamin *shifts back* such philosophical issues, firstly into a literary context – 'Baudelaire' – but ultimately back into the streets of the nineteenth century. Figuring prominently in the Baudelaire book is Poe's famous story 'The Man in the Crowd',[7] which serves there as a (dialectical) counterpoint to the several accounts of the *flâneur* and the fate of the *flâneur* described by Benjamin in relation to various literary sources for this figure (for example, also in Dickens, Dumas and Hugo). Benjamin conjures a sense of the subjective experiences to be had in different cities, describing how these correlate to respective material aspects of the cultures of the street; in terms of such things as of street-lighting, traffic and changing nature of public spaces, and so forth.

But who or what is the *flâneur*? The term literally means 'stroller', 'idler' or 'dawdler', but it is also a figure which symbolises a certain ambivalent 'perspective' on everyday life in the city and represents a certain *way of seeing* attained by belonging to and being at a distance from that life at one and same time. The *flâneur* represents then a particular abstract, notional 'type' of social subject or individual which Benjamin's uses to develop his critique of nineteenth-century 'cultural narcolepsy'. His literary sociology does not aim to recoup from these literary sources an empirically examinable subjectivity which, save for the historical distance, might otherwise have been approached on an empirical basis. The *flâneur* is rather a figure which is able to give access to the newly developing condition of capitalist high modernity and the subjectivity which was in the process of emerging in relation to it. The *flâneur* is an inherently unstable figure who slips in and out of the guises of participant and witness to the process of historical transition itself. It could therefore be said to be the name given to a special form of historically contemporary subjective response. Literature (and other forms of culture) can of course, following Marx, be read as a reflection or depository of the historical details of the material substrate of social and economic change. But Benjamin's reading of Baudelaire shows the way in which any mode of literary representation is always related to the experience of *seeing*. Consequently, neither 'realism' nor, for that matter, any other epistemological framework of that 'vision' can be considered fixed, unchanging or true in any final sense. The very idea of 'reality' and its epistemological construction are thereby destabilised in his analyses. The 'literary sociology' of the Baudelaire study treats the figure of the *flâneur* as something which is at once a literary trope and an abstract figure of social existence in the nineteenth century. In other words it operates at the border between the literary and the sociological. The *flâneur* is thus a 'liminal' figure in several senses and for this reason is able to serve the role assigned to it in Benjamin's critique precisely because he finds it in Baudelaire to be in a ruinous state: it is being driven to extinction both in literature and as the prevailing model of 'vision'.

Questions of the epistemology of the literary text and the epistemology of vision are explored by Benjamin on the basis of the *demise* of the *flâneur*. This demise is characterised by what I referred to above as the deepening 'sleep' which can be discerned with precision in the very specific collapse of the *flâneur* onto the spectacle of the commodity, whose narcotising effects Benjamin is at odds to demonstrate.[8] Who better then to turn to for an insight into these processes than Baudelaire, who by virtue of his acquired *tolerance to narcotics* is able to resist, at least in some measure, the effects of the narcotic times in which he lives? Baudelaire resists these effects both in terms of the literary style to which he is habituated and on the basis of his extensive experience of actual narcotics. In Benjamin's estimation, Baudelaire is a narcotic thinker of the first rank.

> Jules Laforgue said about Baudelaire that he was the first to speak of Paris 'as someone who was condemned to live in the capital day after day'. He might have said that he was the first to speak of the opiate that was available to give relief to men so condemned. The crowd is... the latest narcotic for those abandoned. The *flâneur* is someone abandoned in the crowd. In this he shares the situation of the commodity. He is not

> aware of this special situation, but this does not diminish its effect on him and it permeates him blissfully like a narcotic that can compensate him for many humiliations. The intoxication to which the *flâneur* surrenders is the intoxication of the commodity around which surges the stream of customers. (1973: 54–5)

The *flâneur* is emblematic both of Benjamin's critique of the traditional literary theorising he rejects and of the narcotising effects of commodity capitalism: the two are considered to be symbiotic. 'Empathy is the nature of the intoxication to which the *flâneur* abandons himself in the crowd', says Benjamin, and he continues, quoting Baudelaire:

> The poet enjoys the incomparable privilege of being himself and someone else as he sees fit… if certain places seem closed to him, it is because in his view they are not worth inspecting. (1973: 55)

Baudelaire was able to experience being at one with the crowd without being overwhelmed and succumbing to the experience. It is this 'poetic ability' both to be subject to the narcotising effect of the commodity and yet to remain 'awake' whilst under its influence which is of key importance. By exploiting this poetic ability Baudelaire was able to play the role of *flâneur* and to be amongst the crowd without simply becoming a part of it. Benjaminian critique works by tapping into Baudelaire's highly qualified poetic 'reserve' of narcotic knowledge and then extending it to the commodity. He recognises the value of such a narcotic strategy for producing a kind of reverse articulation of the commodity *itself*, allowing it to become 'the speaker' (1973: 55). This takes Benjamin one step further towards one key aspect of narcotic illumination which had escaped Baudelaire himself: namely 'the charm displayed by addicts under the influence of drugs' and how 'commodities derive the same effect from the crowd that surges around and intoxicates them' (1973: 55).

Benjamin similarly develops his particular style of materialist dialectics by entering, as if from under the cloak of the strolling Baudelaire, into the narcosis of commodity capitalism in order to launch a critique from the perspective of the commodity itself. Whilst Baudelaire dallies along, Benjamin is gathering data on the characteristics of 'Baudelairian vision'. This is a highly original literary stratagem for revealing the interrelationship of the fate of the commodity and the fate of the modern subjectivity which arises in contiguity with it. He can do this under the guidance of Baudelaire precisely because Baudelaire is a 'connoisseur of narcotics'. His connoisseurship is not merely a reflection of his experience as a serious user, an experimenter with drugs and as member of a famous literary clique with a club dedicated to narcotic experimentation, the Club des Haschischins.[9] It is a reflection equally of his narcotic expertise as this is evidenced by his allegoric style. Baudelaire was able to write from the perspective of the *flâneur* on the basis of empathy: 'empathy is the nature of the intoxication to which the *flâneur* abandons himself in the crowd' (1973: 54–5). Baudelaire wrote out of such empathy, but without fully identifying with it.

The crowd for Baudelaire, then, is a narcotic phenomenon in which the distinction between the individual subject and the commodity is overcome in an experience of *pleasure*. Although this experience for Baudelaire is instructive with respect to the role of the imagination in the production of meaning, actual intoxication, including hallucination in particular, does not in itself give access to genuine allegorical meaning. It merely provides a model of the creative interaction between the perceiving subject and the object of perception – or, with reference to Baudelairean poetics, between the reader and the literary object or text. The Baudelairean *flâneur* does not succumb to the seduction of the commodity, nor does he mistake the drug-induced high for true insight. As Alexandra A. Wettlaufer notes, for Baudelaire 'the allegorical production of meaning lies in the *process* of translation, and in the *recognition* of the fundamental alienation between subject and object, perceiver and perceived' (1996: 395).[10] My point here, however, is to recognise the significance of the fact that although Baudelaire famously refuses the 'authenticity' of narcotised experience in relation to poetic and aesthetic creativity, it is only on the basis of intoxication that this thesis can be formulated in the first place. Baudelaire can, in effect, arrive at such a thesis only because he is armed with narcotic expertise gained through the use of actual narcotics. This insight concerning pleasures of narcosis and the nature of the crowd is not historically decisive, at least not in Baudelaire's time, as the narcotic pleasures of commodity capitalism are as yet restricted to the bourgeoisie. But it is none the less significantly instructive with respect to how the relation to the commodity figures in the production of social relations in general. The question Benjamin answers with striking originality concerns *the possibility of critique* itself and how this must be viewed in conjunction with the possibility of *resistance* to the (socially and culturally) narcotising effects of the commodity.

Through his reading of Baudelaire, Benjamin gains insight into how the pleasures of consumption have emerged as the driving force for the development of culture at large. He also finds a model for demonstrating how the pleasures of consumption since the nineteenth century are increasingly accompanied by the attachment of value to the culture of consumption itself. On the basis of his literary-historical researches, he isolates the moment in which the otherwise clearly limiting aspect of commodity culture turns itself into an all embracing, comatose pleasure which is valued above all others:

> It was self-evident, however, that the more this class wanted to have its enjoyment *in* this society, the more limited this enjoyment would be. The enjoyment promised to be less limited if this class found enjoyment *of* this society possible. If it wanted to achieve virtuosity in this kind of enjoyment, it could not spurn empathising with commodities. (1973: 59)

'Empathy' with the commodity thus goes hand in hand with an essentially insatiable desire to consume and to possess as a way to indulge in commodity intoxication (and later I shall look closely at how Benjamin uses the hashish 'trance' to examine this phenomenon critically.) This is an extraordinary insight of crucial importance for the critique of modern consumer culture – firstly, because 'orthodox' Marxist theory has failed to divert the energies of commodity intoxication in such a way as to turn it against itself or to neutralise it and, secondly, because there are no longer any existing socialist states in which experimental alternatives to consumerism might be explored. It should perhaps be recalled at this point how significant Benjamin's experience of Moscow and 'Soviet Russia' had been for him:

> At the turning point in historical events that is indicated, if not constituted, by the fact of 'Soviet Russia', the question at issue is not which reality is better, or which has greater potential. It is only: which reality is inwardly convergent with the truth? Which truth is inwardly preparing itself to converge with the real? Only he who clearly answers these questions is 'objective'. Not towards his contemporaries (which is unimportant) but towards events (which is decisive). Only he who, by decision, has made his dialectical peace with the world can grasp the concrete. (2000: 177)

Grasping the concrete, or the 'objective', requires not a knowledge of supposed 'facts' but an activity of *invention* stirred into action by concrete circumstances. And it appears to be precisely such an ability that Benjamin attributes to Baudelaire, who exercises it in another historical moment. As already noted, Baudelaire's ability to handle the effects of the commodity, the crowd and the pleasures associated with them was due to his historically dislocated literary style coupled with his knowledge of narcotics. Consequently, Baudelaire's 'enjoyment' of the society he observed was that of 'someone who had already half withdrawn from it' and for whom the crowd was a 'spectacle':

> The deepest fascination of this spectacle lay in the fact that as it intoxicated him it did not blind him to the horrible social reality. He remained conscious of it only in the way in which intoxicated people are 'still' aware of reality. (1973: 59)

I shall now extract this Benjaminian motif of *an intoxication within which an awareness of reality is preserved* – this image of consciousness in a state of drugged lucidity and use it as a pointer to his attempt in another context, to develop his account of intoxication and its implications for cultural analysis. This is to be found in the famous essay *Surrealism: The Last Snapshot of the European Intelligentsia* of 1929 (Benjamin, 2000: 223–39).

## Surrealism: dreaming the revolution

> To win the energies of intoxication for the revolution – this is the project about which surrealism circles in all its books and enterprises. This it may call *its most particular task*. (Benjamin, 2000: 236, *my emphasis*)

*Surrealism* is widely considered to play a pivotal role in Benjamin's move away from the thinking, approach and concerns which characterised his early conventional academic work on baroque German drama, *Trauerspiel* (1928), toward the determinedly materialist outlook of 'One Way Street', published in the same year, and the *Arcades Project*. The importance he attached to distinguishing his own ideas from those of surrealism is decisive for understanding the subsequent trajectory of his contribution to the critical theorisation of culture. The thinking of 'intoxication' in relation to the possibility revolutionary politics is identified as central to both the surrealists' and his own critical projects. Benjamin saw surrealist experimentation, which included the use of psychotropic drugs, as providing insights relevant to his own concerns with the soporific effects of commodity capitalism. But given that his critique of modernity is fundamentally a critique of the condition of 'intoxication' in the first place – namely, that it regards the effects of commodity overload as a form of 'narcosis' itself – a more complex account of drugs and their effects was vital if the 'energies of intoxication' were ever really to be 'harnessed for the revolution' – as Breton had famously suggested they must be. So it is not surprising that intoxication lies at the heart of Benjamin's troubled identification with surrealism. Whilst his use of Baudelaire in tracking the fate of the *flâneur* was to all intents and purposes a literary stratagem adopted to investigate the narcotic structure of modern 'vision', aimed at revealing its fixation on the commodity, the earlier essay *Surrealism* sets out to criticise the surrealist attempt to enlist 'actual' intoxication into the service of revolutionary politics. At the same time he also acknowledges surrealism as the indispensable source of his own ideas on the problems of overcoming the capitalist perceptual regime. He gives expression to his ambivalence toward the surrealist project in a letter to Gerschom Scholem of 1928 (a time during which he was systematically experimenting with hashish – see below) that an 'all-too ostensible proximity to the Surrealists could be fatal' for him (Buck-Morss 1989: 5). He considers that this proximity would continue to threaten his own thinking so long as the important differences with respect to intoxication were not adequately worked out. His account of surrealism – and consequently the true significance that the *Surrealism* essay plays in the trajectory of his thinking as it moves from idealism to materialism – is really one about the 'critical value' of intoxication and its usefulness for understanding and challenging contemporary norms of both the social life and the psycho-existential interiority of the modern subject under the condition of commodity capitalism.

    *Surrealism* has a complex structure. In it Benjamin applauds the intellectual achievement that surrealism represents whilst carefully critically distancing his own thinking from it. The essay begins with an image of the critic as a hydro-power plant harnessing the energy of the flows of intellectual currents. This image plays on the soon to be quoted line from Breton, which speaks of 'winning the energies of intoxication for the revolution'. Indeed this will turn out to be the very point at issue. What does this suggestion actually propose? How can this be done and what are the dangers that it presents? The danger facing all revolutionary thinking is that of counteracting the forces of bourgeois nullification and recuperation. Benjamin is able to observe the effects of these forces on surrealism itself at the same time as appreciating its capacity for resilience. However, in this essay Benjamin not only poses a question the future direction of surrealism and of how it can serve revolutionary critique: his concern is how critical thinking might appropriate surrealism so as to protect itself from the same kind of nullification. He suggests that this vulnerability to de-energising forces generally results (and not just in the case of surrealism) from incomplete or faulty under-standings of intoxication. Of course surrealism is far from being the most obviously culpable agent of narcotic misunderstanding; on the contrary, Benjamin indirectly acknowledges that it places itself in the front line of 'narcotic research' and provides the most advanced insights. Indeed, that is why it is of superlative importance and interest to Benjamin and why he subjects it to the closest scrutiny. He unequivocally acknowledges his own indebtedness to the intellectual well-spring of surrealist thought, and its unprecedented (save perhaps for Baudelaire) recognition of the central importance of intoxication *per se.*

The essay's opening figure of the power plant gives prominence to the question of critical positioning – of being and not being in the flow of things – and the critic's relation to the energy flows of culture. This is the heart of the matter for Benjamin, namely, the danger of being over-whelmed, of identifying too closely. Just as the gaze of the consumer can collapse onto its object, the thinking of the critic can similarly degrade into an uncritical 'seeing' which takes itself for true illumination. And here we arrive at the matter of Benjamin's disquiet with the surrealist view of intoxication. Despite the fact that surrealism undoubtedly repre-sents a decisive disruption of capitalist 'vision', and that it advocates narcotic means to destroy the imagination/world opposition central to its epistemology of this 'vision', surrealism none the less too easily becomes complicit in the dissipation of its own revolutionary potential by rechannelling its energies back through individual subjectivities. The early or 'heroic' stage of surrealism, says Benjamin, was characterised by individual expressions of the 'poetic life' being pushed to the limit, but the real political potential of the movement cannot simply flood into the supposedly 'low' plains of culture at large from the mountainous heights of its artistic and poetic endeavour without suffering a loss of force. The surrealist impulse was a philosophical probing of modernity and modern culture of a comparable nature to Benjamin's but pursued by artistic means. It was anti-*l'art pour l'art*, and was able to wreak great devasta-tion upon the canonical aestheticism of traditional art. Benjamin supple-ments this observation, however, with the suggestion that the ideologies of the *l'art pour l'art* movement were never simply what they seemed: 'it was almost always a flag under which sailed a hidden cargo' (2000: 231). This is typical of his subtle infusion of critique mixed with admiration for surrealism. Surrealism clearly was able to be such an effective agent of destruction because it had available to it the weapon of psychoanalysis. In particular it placed great emphasis on the key psychoanalytic ideas of the unconscious and of the dream, and Benjamin's critique of the surrealist account of intoxication can best be approached by considering how dreaming figures in relation to both revolutionary consciousness and what he calls 'profane illumination'.

For those drinking at the well-spring of the surrealist movement, he says, 'life only seemed worth living where the threshold between waking and sleeping was worn away in everyone as by the steps of multitudinous images flooding back and forth' (2000: 226). It is in relation to this that drugs were a vital technological aid to the surrealists in their experimental research, and many individuals in the movement are known to have not been averse to taking copious amounts of them in the name of art and revolution. Drugs were taken as a means to practical thought-experimentation and a tool for unfettering the imagination. But Benjamin's aim is neither simply to praise such 'heroic' use of narcotics by the surrealists nor merely to reiterate a claim about their significance for a critique of modern 'vision'. It is rather to set the surrealist use of narcotics – and the supposed insights of such experience – against the background of a more encompassing, and hopefully politically effective, philosophy of narcosis, in which 'actual' narcotics would be but one ingredient. The important thing for Benjamin is to work out how to build on the surrealist insight that whatever facilitates dreaming promotes a loosening of the normative, regulating idea of the sovereign individual subject.

> In the world's structure, dream loosens individuality like a bad tooth. This loosening of the self by intoxication is, at the same time, precisely the fruitful, living experience that allowed these people to step outside the domain of intoxication. (2000: 226)

Drugs were used by the surrealists on Benjamin's account – whether they saw it in this way or not – subversively, as an antidote to the narcotising effects of modernity. Most significantly for Benjamin, in doing so they were fighting one narcosis by means of another. This is what Benjamin as critic of surrealist drug use was able to recognise. Two points arise here: firstly this is easily overlooked, but, more importantly, overlooking it may lead to falsely supposing that surrealism is simply the art of anti-rationality (and therefore purely destructive and nihilistic) or, alternatively and equally falsely, that surrealism and its art are simply 'about' the contents of dreams, psychological life and the unconscious, or even alternative, esoteric or mystical realities. All of this, moreover, would be to suppose falsely that surrealism was still stuck in a mimetic mode. The issue posed by Benjamin in *Surrealism* is that of the most 'politically decisive' understandings of narcotics and their place in the armoury of cultural critique: this is something that can be approached productively, he says, only on the basis of their actual role in relation to the 'surrealist experience' itself.

> [Surrealist] writings are concerned literally with experiences, not with theories and still less with phantasms. And these experiences are by no means limited to dreams, hours of hashish eating, or opium smoking. It is a cardinal error to believe that, of 'surrealist experiences', we know only the religious ecstasies or the ecstasies of drugs… the true creative overcoming of religious illumination certainly does not lie in narcotics. It resides in the profane illumination, a materialistic, anthropological inspiration, to which, hashish, opium, or whatever else *can give an introductory lesson.* (2000: 227, *my emphasis*)

In other words, the surrealist narcotic experience is unquestionably insightful, but that does not imply that those most directly involved in it (and who take the most drugs) are necessarily the most able to recognise its bearing on surrealism's 'most particular task'. Benjamin's point is that more important than the authenticity of any individual 'surreal experience' is what can be learnt from within it about the nature of narcosis itself. The real task and challenge is actually to politicise the experience. This is not achieved simply on the basis of – and even less in the form of – the drugged experience itself.

This now takes us right to the point around which the difference between surrealist thinking and Benjamin's critical harnessing of it revolves and to the meaning of the 'introductory lesson' he says narcotics are held to provide. What needs to be learned, and which is of overriding political importance, is how to bring about a 'critical awakening', and this in turn requires, and is to be understood in relation to, the development of new forms of 'narcotic expertise'. The lesson to be learnt from the use of drugs, as Benjamin will attempt to show, is on how to think whilst asleep and awake at the same time, or, to extend the metaphor, how to become a lucid-dreamer.

Benjamin believed that the historical role of critical thinking in his time was to provide such a wake-up call to European modernity, to arouse it from the narcoleptic slumber into which it had drifted; to raise the alarm which, in the sentence which concludes *Surrealism,* he says must 'ring for sixty minutes in every hour' (2000: 239). Central to this is the idea that intoxication and sobriety, or sleep and wakefulness, are not be taken at face value: in order to awake one must understand first the nature of sleep and know the difference between mere somnambulant narcosis and the kind of 'critical awakening' in which dreaming becomes properly critical and, consequently, politically decisive for emancipation.

Enlightenment, or 'illumination', in either its religious (mystical) or its secular (rational) forms, is never free of the hypnotic effects of the commodity. The 'dialectics of intoxication' are indeed 'curious' precisely because *thinking itself proceeds on an 'eminently narcotic' basis.* Critique must acknowledge this general condition of modernity as narcosis and develop different forms of 'narcotic intervention' through experimentation. 'Is not perhaps all ecstasy in one world humiliating sobriety in that complementary to it?' (2000: 229), asks Benjamin rhetorically. But the belief in the possibility of sobriety, or the sobriety of Reason itself, is now evidently questionable, too, on the grounds of the political decisionism of the false antithesis between sobriety and intoxication. The 'hidden cargoes' of bourgeois cultural forms deliver the narcotic which keeps the modern subject in a state of political torpor.

In this way critical thinking is singularly indebted to surrealism's account of intoxication, but Benjamin's account of it takes on a critical edge surrealism itself lacks: for him the question is *how best to use* narcotics to counteract the stupefying effects of life under capitalism.

At the outset Benjamin locates surrealism between the poles of an anarchistic fronde and a revolutionary discipline: it aims to be a revolutionary discipline but none the less remains a kind of shock tactic; it detonates a powerful bomb, but not one powerful enough to bring down the edifice of bourgeoisie 'vision'. Surrealism succeeds in fracturing this, but it fails to overcome it and it continues in various states of ruination to be enraptured by the commodity. Benjamin's materialism is aimed at surpassing surrealism by insisting on the origin of ideas (including those of surrealism itself) in the actuality of the events as these are born of the matrix of material relations. And whilst Benjamin credits the surrealists for being the 'first to liquidate the sclerotic-moral-humanistic ideal of freedom' (Benjamin, 2000: 236), he does so in order to ask whether they have succeeded in binding revolt to revolution. This he soon concludes they have not done so effectively, despite moving to the left and toward communism. This is still an intellectual move, one which fails to become a revolutionary political praxis. The 'serious exploration' of surrealistic phenomena is, none the less, still a vital step on the way to refuting all 'inadequate' and 'undialectical' conceptions of intoxication.

> For [the surrealists] it is not enough that, as we know, an ecstatic component lives in every revolutionary act. This component is identical with the anarchic. But to place the accent exclusively on it would subordinate the methodical and disciplinary preparation for revolution entirely to a praxis oscillating between *fitness exercises* and *celebration in advance*. (2000: 236)

The problem that surrealism faces is the draining of its energies by bourgeois culture. He continues:

> [H]istrionic or fanatical stress on the mysterious side of the mysterious takes us no further; we penetrate the mystery only to the degree that we recognise it in the everyday world and by virtue of a dialectical optic that perceives the everyday as impenetrable and the impenetrable as everyday. (2000: 236)

These criticisms serve both to describe the limitations of surrealism and to work as a bulwark against its backward slip toward confusing the surrealist experience of narcosis with 'profane illumination', which Benjamin insists is not accessible by drugs alone. What is required is critical reflection on that experience of the materialist kind he is all along attempting to demonstrate. Surrealism is therefore in danger of making the leap from intellectual 'fitness exercises' to 'celebration' without ever becoming truly historical.

Despite the fact that Benjamin apparently understood this better than anyone, the charge has often been made that his own thinking oscillates between messianic mysticism on the one hand and a positivism of the object on the other. But what we see here is in fact an attempt to overcome precisely the 'esoteric', the 'phantasmagorical' and the 'occult' (his words), which he is able to explain are never seriously explored because, as with surrealism itself, they rapidly degenerate in the wider cultural context, into systems of irrational belief or bohemian dalliances. An oscillation between the analytical poles of subjectivism and objectivism (intellectualism/realism, idealism/empiricism, and so forth) is precisely the legacy of the tradition which he is attempting to disinherit. Recognising the necessity of working between those poles in order to further the materialist thrust of his own thinking, Benjamin attempts to speak from the perspective of the object without theologising or super-valorising the subjective act of negation (that is, reification) into the secular origin of the world. Thus between religious illumination and the rationalist secularisation of tradition, his critique of surrealism directs us to what he understands as the now-time (*Jetztzeit*) of 'profane illumination' – something of which surrealism allows a glimpse, but not something the surrealists' use of drugs simply gave them access to. What surrealist thinking lacks is a 'dialectical optics' of the experience of narcotics and what could be called 'critical narcotic practice'.

> [T]he most passionate investigation of the hashish trance will not teach us half as much about thinking (which is eminently narcotic), as the profane illumination of thinking about the hashish trance. The reader, the thinker, the loiterer and the *flâneur* are types of illuminati just as much as the opium eater, the dreamer the ecstatic. (2000: 237)

In other words 'drugs' (such as hashish, opium, mescaline, or whatever) are not the only narcotic vehicles available to the thinker who recognises the 'eminently narcotic' nature of thought itself. This does not deny that drugs have a singularly significant role to play in the critique of modernity; it just says that they do not 'alone' deliver 'profane illumination'. Furthermore, to suppose that they do is a mistake which leads directly back to forms of traditional, bourgeois entrancement, including traditional forms of critique.

So, to reiterate briefly: it's not the experience alone but the specific critical appropriation of the experience; it is about the relationship between thinking about the experience and the experience itself and about critical practice...

*WARNING*: at this point we are approaching, perhaps appropriately, a stoned logic, which, as we shall see in a moment, Benjamin had explored 'experientially'. The experience of hashish was arguably one of the most important influences on his thinking. In fact he had once planned an entire book about hashish and it is well-documented that his experiments with drugs were undertaken over a period of several years – with episodes both before and after all of his texts referred to here. The book was never written, but fortunately the famous essay *Haschisch in Marseilles* allows us a remarkable insight into Benjamin's efforts to pursue his narco-critical thinking to ever greater heights and to appropriate the experience it records.

## Benjamin on hashish and the love of things

Benjamin opens the essay *Haschisch in Marseilles* with a description of the onset of the hashish high with a 'preliminary remark' taken from a contemporary piece of psychopharmacological literature, *Klinische Wochenschrift*. He quotes it at some length as follows:

> *Preliminary remark:* One of the first signs that hashish is beginning to take effect 'is a dull feeling of foreboding; something strange, ineluctable is approaching... images and chains of images, long submerged memories appear, whole scenes and situations are experienced; at first they arouse interest, now and then enjoyment, and finally, when there is no turning away from them, weariness and torment'. (2000: 215)[11]

This first sentence, which notes the oscillation between 'foreboding' through 'arousal' to 'enjoyment' turning into 'weariness' and 'torment', echoes strongly the structure of the 'intoxication' which comes upon 'the subject of modernity' as depicted in the paragraph from the *Arcades Project* with which this chapter opened. Furthermore, Benjamin's abbreviation of the cited text allows him to use it to indicate several of his own interests and motivations in relation to his experiments with narcotics: it speaks of 'inspiration', 'illumination', the 'continual alternation of dreaming and waking states'. But perhaps one of the things that Benjamin was most approving of in this account of intoxication is that it recognises that '"the most admirable description of the hashish trance is by Baudelaire (*Les paradis artificiels*)"' (2000: 216). None of it in any case would have been too surprising to Benjamin as the article was in fact written by two physicians who were personal friends of his with whom he had experimented with hashish on several occasions.[12] On the evening in question, however, Benjamin is flying solo, apparently deliberately seeking out a situation where he is not likely to be disturbed by anyone who knows him – which may have been a problem as he had a long association with the town.

Perhaps the first thing to note (or is it the third?) is that his retelling of his evening's wanderings is not presented, as sobriety after the fact might be considered to warrant, in the form of a logical sequence of events; and the narrative unfolds according to a non-linear chronology. In fact the whole session is recorded on the basis of a kind of snakes and ladders sequential logic. It would be unremarkable to begin at the beginning – in his hotel room, awaiting the onset of the hashish 'trance' – except that the recollection begins with a moment of hesitancy as to the strength of the effect and whether he should leave his room at all. But 'at last' he leaves, 'the effects seeming non-existent or so weak that the precaution of staying at home was unnecessary'. If Benjamin had decided to stay in his room this recollection published as *Haschisch in Marseilles* would have been quite different and he would have been a different kind of thinker. It was what was happening in the streets of Marseilles rather than in his head that was of greater interest to Benjamin – whatever the circumstances. I shall attempt to shadow his movements – as best possible.

No sooner has he set off from his hotel room on the way to his first 'port of call', the bar around the corner, than we are treated to the first of a series of digressions, this one about his changing perception of space and time and about how humorous it seemed to him that at Basso's restaurant – where, in the chronological order of things, he has not yet been – he was informed that the hot kitchen was closed at the very moment he was feeling he had 'just sat down to feast on eternity'. On reading what comes next we are presented with a scene which, in all likelihood, had given rise to this thought about time and space. The narrative at this point concerns the difficulty he had encountered trying work out where he might sit in the restaurant. From the outside he had spied a suitable spot on the second-floor balcony, but by the time he was inside he had obviously forgotten about that entirely and in any case changes his mind on finding that the *first*-floor balcony seats are occupied. He then opts to sit at a newly cleared 'very large' table. But this situation makes him feel too awkwardly 'disproportionate' in relation to the table on account of his being alone. So, he gets up and sets off again 'across the entire floor' to the opposite end, towards a table that only 'became visible' as he reached it. At last, he is calmly seated in the restaurant – a kind of narrative precaution; a 'now we are sitting comfortably', before embarking (beginning again as it were) upon the trial of relating the story of what preceded his arrival in the restaurant, namely his 'first' port of call, which was in fact a bar just around the corner.

Only minutes, one can assume, after deciding the effects of the hashish were too weak to warrant the precaution of staying in his room, he now stands outside the bar already on the brink of 'retreating in confusion' because he suspects there is a brass band playing inside: 'I only just managed to explain to myself that it was nothing more than the blaring of car horns'. Once inside – although the inside/outside distinction is rapidly becoming redundant – the hashish only then *begins* 'to exert its canonical magic'. He becomes transfixed by the faces of those around him, entirely absorbed in the spectacle of their 'physiognomies' in a way which is clearly reminiscent of the vision of the *flâneur*: 'It was a very advanced post, this harbour tavern' – just around the corner. Later on, he will recall the time in the tavern again whilst telling us about the 'dark side' of the trance: at one point he had felt a physical discomfort, a pressure in his diaphragm which he had tried to relieve by 'humming' – this despite the fact that he was also trying hard, he tells us, not to draw attention to himself. Reminding himself as he prepares to leave not to overtip 'for fear of attracting attention by extravagance', he ends up making himself 'really conspicuous' by doing the opposite. It is at this point he 'actually' moves on to Basso's restaurant where his attention will become so entranced by the menu that he will order everything 'out of politeness to all the dishes that [he] did not wish to offend by refusal'.

Seriously stoned, seriously suffering the munchies, he eats up resolving to dine a second time elsewhere. The narrative now circles around itself once again: we return to a point before his feast and to the walk to the restaurant, which (assuming the humming had worked for his stomach cramps) was not without its pleasures, for instance the powerful feelings of 'empathy' toward objects, namely the small boats moored along the key, which are 'wonderful and beautiful' to him. They receive his empathy according to their names; the only distinct lack of empathy was for *Aero II*, owing to the name reminding him of 'aerial warfare' – which he passes by 'without cordiality'.

Let us take a break here to ask what is happening.

In the trance, his consciousness collapses, time after time, onto objects; onto people's faces, onto dishes on the menu, onto the moored boats. Trying not to draw attention to himself is a struggle; a struggle against an at times overwhelming attraction to 'things'. 'Objects' mill around him rather as does the crowd in the arcades around commodities: his intoxication is fuelled *by them* not by the hashish. Although the hashish has undoubtedly brought about the volatility of his relation to the object into *experience*, the experience does not accomplish a transition in this relation. What the intoxication does provide is an insight into this from an otherwise unobtainable perspective. There is here an experience of loss of self, but this is absolutely not something mystical; it does not suggest an elevated form of existence. It does not strip away a chimerical reality, it rather facilitates an experiential relation to the object which gives over the control of the relation, at least in part and sometimes almost completely (for example his experience of the large table which threatened to swamp him), to the object itself. This 'loss of self' does not result in the kind of alienation that the subject experiences in a flight into solitude (which he describes so powerfully in the *Arcades Project* fragment cited above). Indeed he speaks of how he 'was incapable of fearing future misfortune, or future solitude, for hashish would always remain'. The non-solitudinous engagement with the world around him is instantiated in his rather Baudelairean state of being 'a painter of the life' around him:

> Upstairs at Basso's, when I looked down, the old games began again. The square in front of the harbour was my palette, on which the imagination mixed the qualities of place, trying them out this, now that, without concern for a result, like a painter day-dreaming on his palette. (2000: 219)

His canvas is the square below, which has a life of its own in that it changes with every figure which enters, leaves or moves. The canvas is not lacking in form or in need of formal representation by Benjamin's 'painterly' thinking: it is already a scene containing the forms of the harbour loafer, the pimp, the prostitute, a Chinese in blue silk trousers, a girl in a white dress, whose visibility is intensified in proportion to their observer's diminishing 'desire'. Benjamin's consciousness becomes the canvas on which these 'objects' paint themselves, without interference or resistance from the ordinary conceptual, regulating mind. He says he feels he is 'obliged to think' by them, that is, moved to thought by the scene itself. The scene as a whole is able to impose itself as if entirely of its own accord rather than according to the actions of Benjamin's personal imagination. Indeed it is the 'I' which finds itself among things: 'I felt flattered by the thought of sitting here in a centre of dissipation, and by "here" I did not mean the town but the little, not very eventful spot where I found myself' (2000: 221).

Setting aside the question of the route Benjamin had taken to this balcony seat – which must always remain a confused matter (rather like his method of cultural analysis as a whole); despite every effort made to follow that thread, let us rejoin him at the 'centre of dissipation', for it is from there that he is able to grasp the critical benefits of a realm of lucidity between wakefulness and sleep: '[E]vents took place in such a way that the appearance of things touched me with a magic wand, and I sank into the dream of them' (2000: 221).

This zone of lucidity and vision of things and ability to relate to things solely on the basis of their 'nuances' (2000: 220) was something which informs Benjamin's study of culture throughout, and I have attempted to show how this involves developing a relationship to intoxication. The hashish trance was for him a laboratory for investigating the nature of 'dialectical imaging' and for developing this as a technique. It was a place in which the mind was inclined, perhaps to an extent determined by the dose of the intoxicant involved, to forget its education. At one point towards the end of the essay Benjamin recalls – though he is unable to remember exactly how it happened – that he 'permitted' himself to tap his foot to the beat of some jazz music: 'This is against my education, and it did not happen without inner disputation.' This may be a humorous quip, but it is also emblematic of resistance to and suspicion of popular cultural forms as legitimate objects of critical attention – something not only due to bourgeois snobbery, but also an aspect of Adorno's approach to and analysis of the 'culture industry'. In fact it reminds us of the very different nature of Adorno's highly reconnoitred philosophical targets and those typical of Benjamin's writings. On the other hand, Benjamin does attempt in a manner Adorno unequivocally approved of, to think 'at every moment both within things and outside of them' (Adorno, 1978: 74). The 'profane illumination' gained contra-education involves the novel perspective on knowledge Benjamin associates with Baudelaire: knowledge is 'piecemeal', a 'jumble of arbitrarily cut pieces from which a puzzle is assembled' (1999: [J80, 1] 368). In *Haschisch in Marseilles* Benjamin has not yet attained a fully dialectical perspective and his vision is still close to that of the Baudelairean *flâneur* than it was later to become; and, it shows very directly the value Benjamin attached to 'Baudelairean knowledge', which, as we have seen, was always a negotiation between one intoxication and another. Certainly Benjamin was well established on his way of attempting, as Adorno astutely notes, 'in ever new ways to make philosophically fruitful what has not been yet foreclosed by great intentions' (Adorno, 1978: 152).

I shall not attempt to foreclose the 'hashish trance' either of Benjamin or of any other user any more than he does. In keeping with the 'minor intention' of this chapter, arriving at the end of *Haschisch in Marseilles* we leave Benjamin on a much happier note than we began here: he is not rushing back to a 'disconcerting and unwelcoming room' in need of an antidote. His narcotic control over the evening rivals that of Baudelaire in more senses than one, and we last see him turning the next corner 'to have a final ice-cream' – of which he gives us the following lick:

> When I recall this state I should like to believe that hashish persuades nature to permit us… that squandering of our own existence that we know in love. (2000: 222)

There may appear to be little of significance for revolutionary politics in Benjamin's record of his stoned meanderings in Marseilles. But then such a criticism is commonly directed at the outpourings of the cultural theorists and philosophers of culture in general. What I have tried to show here is how an experimental drug-induced narcosis enabled Benjamin to explore the structure of his 'vision' – which, as we have seen, in other contexts, he already understood in terms of an intoxication brought on by commodity capitalism. What he appears to have gained from this is neither a mystical form of insight nor a wakening up from that other kind of narcosis. The experience provides him with a model for the *critical intervention* of theory in a world held together by the prevailing regimes of perception and representation. The hashish trance serves as a narco-dialectical optic through which this given totality – 'the great normal' – can be distorted for a duration at least, and thereby brought into view differently. At the same time, the task of dialectically re-imaging the narcotic condition of modernity and modern subjectivity is advanced.

For Benjamin the experience of intoxication was not one of the empowerment of the imagination to infinity – as the surrealists claimed on the basis of their own narco-logic, but rather one of a loosening of the imagination's power over the object. The imagination is humbled before a world which threatens to overwhelm it at any moment. Perhaps the most significant aspect of the experience for Benjamin, and something which he notes in *Haschisch in Marseilles*, is that it has an impact on the process of recollection (of the experience) itself:

> What one writes down the following day is more than an enumeration of impressions; in the night the trance cuts itself off from everyday reality with fine, prismatic edges; it forms a kind of figure and is more easily memorable. I should like to say it shrinks and takes the form of a flower. (2000: 220)

This 'flowery' logic informs the narrative structure of the essay we have just been looking at. Its twists, turns, folds and temporal leaps are not in any sense the result of a poor memory. Benjamin's experience of being high in Marseilles is recalled on the basis of meandering, lateral associations between visual, sonorous and other bodily sensations of things and things happening which we see as if the were making their own connections, so as to form a picture of the experience of the evening as a whole. The details of the evening are in fact remembered with an astonishing clarity and impeccable, if unconventional, coherence. Such peregrinations of thought are typical of Benjamin's approach to the critical reconstellation of cultural residues in his work in general. And what I have attempted show here is that this 'method' is a form of what I am calling narcoanalysis, in that it is both indebted to and concerned to examine the nature of 'intoxication'. This is not to suggest that Benjamin's method is derived from, or even inspired by, the experience of the hashish high above all else, but rather that drugs and intoxication were in several ways central both to Baudelairean *flânerie* and surrealism as well as to the original critical pathway of Benjamin's own distinctive materialist cultural critique.

## Notes

1 *Haschisch in Marseilles* was originally published in December 1932 in the *Frankfurter Zeitung*. Benjamin experimented with hashish, the hallucinogen mescaline and with the pharmaceutical opiate Eucodal between 1927 and 1934. These experiments were often supervised by various friends of his who were physicians and serious medical researchers with interests in psychopharmacology. Benjamin had intended to dedicate a book length study to hashish which he never produced. His experimental protocols and notes are gathered in Tillman Rexroth (ed.), *Walter Benjamin Über Haschisch* (Frankfurt am Main: Suhrkamp Verlag, 1972). For a useful discussion of the subject see Thompson (1997).

2 Cf. Nietzsche on Ranke in 'On the Use and Disadvantages of History for Life' (1983: 59–123).

3 Between 1939 and 1942 Benjamin wrote and presented around thirty broadcasts on German radio which were for children and early teens. See Mehlman (1993).

4 In a letter to Gerschom Scholem Benjamin writes: 'The literary forms of expression my thought has forged for itself over the last decades have been utterly conditioned by the preventive measures and antidotes with which I have had to counter the disintegration constantly threatening my thought… And though many – or a sizeable number of my works have been small-scale victories, they are offset by large-scale defeats (Scholem 1992).

5 In his articulation and concern with 'the present' Benjamin is closer to both Nietzsche and Foucault than he is to any other philosopher, including those associated with the Frankfurt School.

6 Baudelaire's 'connoisseurship' is testified to by his writings on hashish, wine opium gathered in *Les paradis artificiels* (1860). As far as hashish is concerned, Sadie Plant for example describes Baudelaire as 'the drug's most self-conscious and deliberate explorer' (1999: 35).

7 Edgar Allan Poe, *Complete Tales and Poems* (New York: Modern Library, 1938).

8 Various versions of 'commodity intoxication' as an updating of the Marxist notion of 'commodity fetishism' for the age of the commodified Sign, the image and 'information' exist. For example in the work of Guy Debord (1977): 'The spectacle is a permanent opium war which aims to make people identify goods with commodities and satisfaction with survival that increases according to its own laws' (chapter 2 sec. 44). Baudrillard speaks of the cultural condition of 'permanent auto-intoxication' (1988: 210) and others who have discussed the narcotising effects of modern media. See also chapter 8 below.

9 The Club des Haschischins was a literary salon which was dedicated to pleasures of hashish intoxication. It was established by Théophile Gautier around in 1845 and either frequented or visited by such figures as Nerval, Dumas, Balzac and Baudelaire, amongst other writers and artists, as well as by the physician and medical researcher Jacques-Joseph Moreau, who published a study on hashish in 1845. The classic account of what went on there, and one no doubt written to nurture mystique and a sense of exoticism surrounding the salon, is by Gautier himself and was published in *Revue de Deux Mondes*, 1846. Further details and discussions of the Club can be found in Mike Jay (2000), Boon (2002) and Plant (1999).

10 The Baudelairean model of *flânerie*, as Wettlaufer correctly points out, remains 'entirely psychological in nature' and, whilst his activities are outdoor and in the public domain, his essays 'often remain ensconced indoors and at home' (1996: 389). This is in aspect of the contrast between Baudelaire's thinking and Benjamin's materialism. The section below on *Haschisch in Marseilles* illustrates how Benjamin's way of working can be regarded as a 'thinking outdoors'.

11 This opening paragraph is from an article by his friends Ernst Joel and Fritz Frankel (1926). An English translation is available: 'The Hashish-*Rausch*: Contributions to an Experimental Psychopathology', trans. S. Thompson [Walter Benjamin Research Syndicate]: www.wbenjamin.org/contrib-1926.html.

12 Namely Joel and Frankel.

# 6    Hallucinating Sartre

> To ask oneself whether the world is real is to fail to understand what one is asking, since the world is not a sum of things which might always be called into question, but the inexhaustible reservoir from which things are drawn. (Merleau-Ponty, 1965: 344)

## Philosophy and/or intoxication

The intellectual endeavour of theoretical reflection seems obviously antithetical to intoxications of all kinds. Sobriety and being in control of one's own thought are naturally bound to one another, whereas intoxications, such as drunkenness, reverie, being high and hallucination, are clearly breaches or disturbances of normal consciousness, clear thought and common sense. Modern philosophy has tended to see itself as a sort of 'science' as opposed to an artistic, creative practice licensed to give free reign to the imagination and irrationality. And whereas modern artists and literary writers often have a celebrated history and reputation for indulgence or experimentation with drugs of one sort or another, and such habits are associated with the fuelling of their creative energies and productive imaginations, the same is not generally true of those engaged in the production of theory – least of all progenitors of systematic philosophy. This is not to say that individual philosophers and theorists are unknown to have partaken of intoxicants, but this is not associated with serving their critical practice or the formulation of their ideas. Such theory in fact assumes the burden of accounting for the imagination – its function, its structure and its operation in relation to such things as understanding, experience, perception, as well as artistic creativity and so forth – and to perform this task the sobriety and separation of the thinker from the phenomenon in this undertaking is generally taken for granted.

The phenomenon of intoxication, as has become clear in each of the chapters of this book so far, appears time and again though, in one form or another, as a feature within reflexive theorising rather than as something which can be said to be wholly distinct or excluded from it. We have seen that various forms of intoxication have found a role in the production of theory – either directly or indirectly – in the senses I have so far illustrated. Directly, for example, in the way that cocaine did for Freud, hashish did for Benjamin and mescaline did for Michaux and indirectly by having a figurative role, for instance in the form of the 'pharmakology' at work in Derrida's discussion of Plato and writing (and, as I shall later show, in relation to the communicative possibilities of language in my discussion of Foucault and Deleuze).

In this chapter I turn my attention to the phenomenon of intoxication and the question of what it might be considered to reveal about the relationship between the subject and its sense of reality of the world it inhabits in the context of the theory of consciousness and existential phenomenology. I am specifically interested here in the role the discussion of hallucination plays in the development and direction of such theory as represented by Sartre's early work on the imagination, especially his *The Psychology of Imagination* (published in 1940) and Merleau-Ponty's response to that in his *Phenomenology of Perception* (published in 1945). I shall look specifically at how their accounts of hallucination – which I consider to be a peculiarly dramatic form of intoxication – prove crucial to overcoming the rationalist/empiricist hiatus which the phenomenological approach aims at accomplishing.

Whilst existential phenomenology has in recent decades been subject to implicit and explicit critique within structuralism, post-structuralism and psychoanalysis – each of which in a distinctive way refuses the notion of an experience fully present to itself at the heart of meaning production – its enduring legacy ought perhaps to be measured in terms of what it contributes to understanding how the examination of experiential component of life is both indispensable and deeply problematic. From the phenomenologists' perspective it is indispensable simply because the affective experience of the subject is what is most immediate and undeniable: it is the 'given' starting point of reflection itself. And it is historically problematic within the history of thought because it refers to 'the gap' between subjective life and the objectivity of the world it inhabits. Following Husserl, on the basis of the evidence of the phenomenon alone, such phenomenological theory seeks a renewal of philosophy as an activity – as Merleau-Ponty sees it, it is an instance of philosophy's 'ever-renewed experiment in making its own beginning' (1965: xiv). The relationship between the subject and the world, no doubt, always stands in need of renewed elaboration as this is something which is fundamentally transitional. But is 'experience', in the final analysis, to be taken as the ultimate evidence for this?

It is axiomatic of the phenomenological approach as originally expounded by Husserl that the evidence for theory is ultimately to be found in the experience of the phenomenon alone, and I shall explain why an adequate account of hallucination proves to be crucial to Sartre's general theory of consciousness. In an experiment which bears testimony to Sartre's own philosophical commitment to the basic premises of Husserlian phenomenology (albeit often at odds with Husserl's own thinking) – in 1935 he took an experimental dose of the hallucinogenic drug mescaline. Whether the experiment proved successful for his purposes or whether it illustrated, on the contrary, the limitations of phenomenology itself, I shall discuss in due course and finally in the light of Merleau-Ponty's critique of his conclusions.

I will begin by setting the scene.

## The value of intoxication

In *The Prime of Life* Simone de Beauvoir recalls a conversation she once had with Sartre whilst out walking along the Seine in 1934: it revolved around the subject of the usefulness or otherwise of intoxication for examining 'life'. At the time Beauvoir was experiencing melancholic depressions and tells us that if she drank too much alcohol in the evening she was liable to burst into tears: 'hankering after the absolute… I would become aware of the vanity of life and the imminence of death. I would reproach Sartre for allowing himself to be duped by that hateful mystification known as "life".' She continues:

> Sartre denied that the truth could be found in a flood of tears and wine; according to him alcohol depressed me physically, and it was a fallacy for me to explain my condition in terms of metaphysics. I maintained, on the other hand, that intoxication broke down those controls and defences that normally protect us against unpalatable truths, and forced us to face reality. (Beauvoir, 1965: 207–8)

The situation is commonplace and in many respects the exchange banal. Of course, we cannot know for sure whether his response to Beauvoir represents simply straightforward, practical and personal advice – 'cut down on the drinking and you'll feel better' – or whether it represents also an expression of his developing philosophical perspective on how what are conventionally referred to as 'psychological states' do not stand in need of explanations as to their 'ulterior' meanings as they are, on closer phenomenological examination, already fully expressive of their own significance.

Certainly on the basis of the specific version of phenomenology Sartre was developing in his many studies of that decade, he would want to reject the sort of reflective, transcendental 'explanation' of lived experience aimed a revealing the truth supposedly behind it. He might, therefore, have retorted more harshly that Beauvoir was fooling herself if she thought her drink-fuelled mood could reveal anything about the human condition, as there was no hidden meaning or truth behind the experience of the world as it is revealed through the consciousness of we have of it. On the face of it, the exchange as she remembers it appears to present Sartre as rejecting the linking of 'metaphysics' – which can be read here as a synonym for philosophical thinking in general – and everyday experience, but this would not actually square with Sartre's diverse deployments of the phenomenological theory he was developing at the time. Indeed, this broadly embraced the idea that phenomenology promised to 'return' philosophy to the worldliness of everyday life, but it aimed to do this by taking the phenomena of everyday experience as the primary objects of all inquiry rather than postulating a hidden truth behind them. It would make more sense, therefore, to assume that what Sartre really meant was that one ought not to look to philosophy for the explanation of experiences and actions but rather to these things themselves. So, I want to suggest, it is not so much the case that he would refuse *per se* the idea that intoxication is a potentially philosophically instructive phenomenon and one worthy of examination, just that the 'philosophical truth' of intoxication must be looked for, quite literally within it. The critical judgement and interpretation of life as it is lived is always an intellectualisation of an initial engagement with the world – which the phenomenologist insists must be taken as the primary object of study.

It may seem odd to suggest that one of the great public intellectuals of the twentieth century would be opposed to 'intellectualisation'. However the word is used in the very specific sense here with reference to the theoretical distinction and opposition between rationalist, idealist and subjectivist ways of thinking on the one hand and empiricist, materialist and objectivist ways of thinking on the other. The phenomenological approach that Sartre identified with at the time, and developed in his own work, sought to reject both of these two traditional conceptual frameworks and their ways of thinking about the relationship between the human individual and the world, seeing them as abstractions which cut thinking off from life as it is lived and experienced. So, taking intoxication as an example, 'intellectualisation' means all those ways of looking for the meaning of it, for instance in literary terms of the play between Apollonian and Dionysian forces, or for an explanation of it in early family life, or for that matter giving an account of the phenomenon in anthropological or sociological terms. It is not that such intellectual concerns do not have their own coherence, value or role in shaping cultural perspectives and social agendas and so on, just that from a theoretical point of view, according to the phenomenologist, all intellectual theorisation must ultimately be grounded in the experience of life and the world as that relationship is lived. And the phenomenologist holds that to be as true and relevant to the enterprise of theory as much as it is to any other aspect of 'life': 'ideas must be *dramatically* asserted, if necessary through the most extreme manifestations of "compelling subjectivity"' (Mezaros, 1979: 32–3, *my emphasis*).

In line with this, in terms both of theory and method, Sartre's interest at the time was much more in the 'nuts and bolts' of conscious life. Though he referred to his general project in the 1930s as 'philosophical psychology', it was in fact deeply anti-psychological in the ordinary sense of the term. Traditional psychology, like all forms of intellectual explanation organised by sets of concepts (and *arché*-concepts – such as the 'psyche'), would remain purely subjective unless grounded in a phenomenological account of consciousness. Sartre set out to provide such an account as the basis for steering a middle course between forms of idealist intellectualism, on the one hand, and empiricist realism of the so-called objective sciences, on the other. And, in order to investigate the 'middle' between the subject and object it would be necessary to direct attention to experiences which on close inspection were able to reveal consciousness itself as an existential act of appropriation of the world, rather than as a form of subjective apprehension of a pre-existent set of objective facts and states of affairs pertaining to it.

Husserlian phenomenology had provided the impetus for Sartre's inquiries of this period, and, before I turn to Sartre's experimental examination of his own consciousness with the aid of mescaline, I shall briefly outline the key theoretical ideas he was working with at the time.

## The evidence of consciousness

Sartre became acquainted with the ideas of phenomenology in the early 1930s and this set the course of his thinking for that decade.[1] In the most general terms, Sartre's attraction to Husserl's thinking was based on the prospect it apparently held of a 'liberation' from the 'intellectualism' of traditional philosophy, or 'metaphysics', by proposing a refounding of philosophy on a return to 'the things themselves'; to the phenomena of experience. Sartre credits Husserl with having discovered something of great significance for philosophy in general, namely that all theoretical reflection was secondary in relation to original 'lived experience'. This discovery ought not to be regarded merely as an abstract detail of a putative theory of consciousness though; it was, rather, an aspect of the philosophical enterprise itself as a conscious 'activity', and this was, so it seemed, an irreducible fact. Sartre identified closely with the reloca-tion of the origin philosophy itself in the phenomena of experience alone, and was determined to follow through on the implications of this for his own philosophical practice. This approach was in a way, Beauvoir tells us, what Sartre had been looking for even before he heard what Husserlian phenomenology could offer. She says, he had wanted

> to describe objects just as he saw and touched them and to extract philosophy from the process ... phenomenology exactly fitted with his special preoccupations: by-passing the antithesis of idealism and realism, affirming simultaneously both the supremacy of reason and the reality of the visible world as it appears to our senses. (Beauvoir, 1965: 135–6)

The two key ideas of Husserl Sartre initially took to heart (but which he would also criticise) were the methodological principle of the 'phenomenological reduction' (or, to give it its Greek name, the *epoché*) and 'intentionality'. The principle of *epoché* is that reflection must reject by 'bracketing out' everything which is known of the object of inquiry from theoretical (intellectual) reflection (Cf. Husserl, 1962: Sec. 31–4). This move itself is supported only by the evidence of the pre-reflective, or, as Sartre sometimes calls it, 'non-thetic', experience, which is claimed to be not merely logically but ontologically prior to the second order, intellectual reflection which may or may not arise in relation to it. By this he is referring to that awareness of things, actions and the world in general which exists but does not necessarily become an object of reflective consciousness. In *Transcendence of the Ego* Sartre supplies descriptive examples of how when consciousness is absorbed in activity, for instance such as performing a mental or physical task, there is a pre-reflective awareness of the circumstances and details of the activity which can readily be described and accounted for if at any point the 'I' (the conscious subject) is called upon to do so.(Sartre 1957: 46–7). This notion of pre-reflective awareness is absolutely crucial to the theory of consciousness he develops, as it is this which guarantees the transparency of consciousness to itself and does not allow of any delusion on the part of consciousness with respect to its self-knowledge. (This will prove central to the analysis of the account of hallucination given below.) Secondly, Husserl's notion of 'intentionality': this refers to the way in which 'the given' object of a consciousness (such as the thing, the world, relations and so on) in perception, imagination or cognition, is what it is for consciousness in its being-posited by that consciousness. This idea is also expressed in Husserl's famous dictum that consciousness is always 'consciousness of...' something.

Providing an account of the objects of consciousness 'themselves' on the basis of a reflection on the conscious experience of them alone, Sartre surmised, would achieve a liberation, once and for all, from the so-called 'problem' of what was internal and what was external to consciousness, rendering all epistemologies of representation obsolete and paving the way for a more 'worldy', philosophical engagement with the realities of human affairs. This thought is given dramatic expression in Sartre's well-known minor essay of 1939 bearing the title 'Intentionality: A Fundamental Idea in Husserl's Phenomenology', in which he emphasises the implications of this discovery for the general experience of being in the world: it implies the corollary that 'consciousness and the world are given at one stroke; essentially external to consciousness, the world is nevertheless essentially relative to consciousness' (Sartre 1970: 4). The promise and excitement of a new philosophical vitality arising out of the deployment of such a phenomenological method is expressed in the following:

> Husserl has restored to things their horror and their charm. He has restored to us the world of artists and prophets: frightening, hostile, dangerous, with its havens of mercy and love. He has cleared the way for a new treatise on the passions which would be inspired by this simple truth, so utterly ignored by the refined among us: if we love a woman, it is because she is lovable. (Sartre, 1970: 5)

The promise of Husserlianism, so construed at least, was the 'restoration' of 'objectivity' to the world of objects as they are experienced – something

Cartesianism would not allow. The imagination had been for Descartes, on the contrary, an obstacle to the act of self-reflection performed by the cogito and the image itself 'no more than a quasi-material residue of sensory experience' (Kearney, 1988: 161–2). From a phenomenological perspective there is simply no need for the image to represent objects in the world to reflective consciousness, for the world substantively originates in conjunction with the acts of consciousness: hence it is neither subjective nor objective in the traditional senses of these terms.

This 'restoration' of exteriority to the object in its entirety has its counterpart according to Sartre in the total evacuation of all content from consciousness; consciousness 'itself' thus comes to be regarded as pure emptiness, or 'nothing': it is rather a purely negational 'act' (*néantisation*). Each negational act of consciousness is a positing of that which it itself is not. Indeed, in *Transcendence of the Ego* Sartre attempts to follow through on the radical implications of the Husserlian notion of 'intentionality' and thereby to deliver the phenomenological *coup de grâce* against the subjectivist metaphysics which supposes the immanence of a consciousness (an 'I think') folded in upon itself and containing the objects of its own reflections. Against such immanentism, Sartre champions the Husserlian dictum that consciousness is always consciousness of something other than itself. In fact he takes this so far in that work as to conclude that even 'self-consciousness', or the ego, must be nothing more than a transcendent object of consciousness: 'I find myself out there a thing amongst things a man amongst men' (1980: 5). In other words, all of 'reality' is unequivocally located on the side of the object. The descriptors 'real' and 'imaginary' when applied to objects, rather than indicating an epistemological or ontological hierarchy, refer now instead to the acts of the consciousness which posit them 'originally'; which, literally, originate them. Most importantly, this 'fact' of consciousness as a relation to the object is not in the first instance an item of knowledge belonging to a consciousness at all, but rather the very movement of consciousness itself. For Sartre reality 'happens' at the level of such non-thetic consciousness engagement with the world. Reflective, 'thetic' consciousness, of which philosophical reflection is one species, occurs 'after the fact' of the existence of consciousness; or, in other words, of a contextualised action in the world. Sartre's best-known and later expression of this idea is given in his *Existentialism and Humanism* in the phrase 'existence comes before essence' (1973: 26).

Sartre's aim in all of this is to 'restore' the priority of such a situated consciousness – now to be identified with the phenomenon itself – as the object of inquiry. Hence the phenomena of 'imagination' are taken to be the primary source for any theory of imagination. All the varieties of 'mental images', experienced in waking life, in dreams or intoxicated states, are the only sources out of which a theory of consciousness must be constructed.

The consequences of accepting the 'intentionality' thesis are clearly far reaching and go far beyond establishing the loveableness, or otherwise, of particular women: 'the passions' and emotions, moral and aesthetic judgements as well as science and mathematics would all need to take into account the intentional nature of their objects. No longer should the propriety, efficacy and privilege of certain forms of knowledge, methodology and inquiry be considered to be legitimated on the basis of a notion of an objectivity attributable to the object as something existing independently of the intentional acts of consciousness, for intentional objects are no less 'real' for being posited by consciousness. What does or does not 'in fact' exist (that is, what is real as opposed to imaginary) only becomes an issue for a reflective consciousness; the pre-reflective consciousness precedes any intellectual distinction between the subject and object, or between what is real and what is unreal. It would be wrong on this basis to continue to refer to this moment of consciousness as 'subjective' and as standing opposed to the 'objective' reality which it grasps. Such terms, as Heidegger in his phenomenological studies of the being of Dasein had in fact already made clear, need to be avoided. Derrida would later argue, following Heidegger's lead, that the effects of such binary terminology need to be tackled in relation to the context of the operations of language. But rather than concern himself with the problems of language *per se*, Sartre's final appeal, very much in the spirit of the Husserlian phenomenology of intentionality which inspired his approach in the first place, is to the phenomenon itself and to the systematic investigation of it. He was committed to the view that all of the pertinent evidence for an account of 'human reality' is ultimately to be found in the court of experience itself. In this court, the law of experience is not presided over by a judging transcendental 'I think' as for Kant; the evidence of experience alone is not, according to Sartre, subject to judgement at all.

This is at least the spirit of Sartrean phenomenology and his inquiry into the imagination.

## Hallucination as a 'stumbling block' for the theory of consciousness

Given Sartre's various appropriations of Husserlian ideas in his studies of the1930s and his applications of them to 'psychological' phenomena such as the emotions, the ego and the imagination, the exchange Beauvoir recalls with him about 'drinking habits' and 'life' is perhaps pregnant with significance.[2] And perhaps Sartre did indeed take to heart something of what Beauvoir said after all – not concerning the subjective 'hankering after the absolute' she suspected drinking brought to the surface, but rather the much more technical proposition that it contains – that it is 'the breakdowns' in the 'controls and defences' of sobriety that could reveal something of the nature of the relationship between consciousness and the world. In any case it was only a couple of months later that Sartre decided that as a way of pursuing his own philosophical investigations into the workings of the imagination, he should try an experimental and rather extreme form of 'intoxication' in the form of a shot of the hallucinogenic drug mescaline. The aim of the experiment seemed straightforward: to experience first hand a form of consciousness that he considered vitally important to account for in the context of his work on the imagination. The general research question posed in what was eventually to be published as *The Psychology of Imagination* was the following: 'What are the characteristics that can be attributed to consciousness from the fact that it is a consciousness capable of imagining?' which he expands as follows:

> This question can be taken in the sense of a critical analysis under the form: of what nature must consciousness be in general if the construction of an image should always be possible? And no doubt it is in this form that our minds, accustomed to raising philosophical questions in the Kantian perspective, will best understand it. But, as a matter of fact, the problem in its deepest meaning can only be grasped from a phenomenological point of view. (Sartre, 1972: 207)

Sartre's methodological commitment to investigating consciousness on the basis of its intentional structures is clearly expressed here. Since Husserl, the way was now open, as he says in the conclusion to his first book on the imagination, 'to start afresh attempting above all to attain an intuitive vision of the intentional structure of the image' (1962: 75), and he dedicated the later *Psychology* to this task.

It involved the systematic, phenomenological study of instances of the mental image, as these are intuited in experiences of them, and he argues throughout on the basis of the description of these that there is in fact no such *thing* as a 'mental image', moreover that consciousness has no content at all. What reflection finds are only acts of consciousness which are different forms of relation – perceptual, oneiric, hallucinatory – to transcendental 'objects of consciousness': 'there is not a world of images and a world of objects. The two worlds real and imaginary are composed of the same objects: only the grouping and the interpretation of these objects varies' (Sartre, 1972: 20). This is not the place to go into the very detailed phenomenological descriptions of each of these which are offered in support this conclusion. I want rather to cut straight to the problem Sartre's thesis encounters in the case of hallucinating consciousness. The following points are of most importance to note here:

(1) Sartre insists that each mode of consciousness is necessarily a pre-reflective awareness of its own nature: its status as imaginary or perceptual can always be checked by reflective consciousness.

(2) All modes of consciousness are mutually exclusive: 'perception and imaginative consciousness are two alternating attitudes' such that 'hallucination coincides with a sudden annihilation of perceived reality' (1972: 172–3). His arguments for this conclusion and the basic distinction between perception and imagination are quite simple: when I perceive an object then the object is subject to a multiplicity of perspectives and my perception is always open to correction by the object. When I imagine something, be this a perceptible object (such as a chair) or a purely imaginary object (such as a centaur), then the object is given as complete. The phenomenon of hallucination poses several problems in relation to this analysis. Firstly, it does not obviously fit with this bipartite division of the modalities of consciousness. Secondly and methodologically, hallucination is not an everyday form of consciousness which is available to any other than the 'mad' or the 'sick' – in fact it is not surprisingly identified by Sartre as a 'pathological' form of consciousness. Not only does hallucination need to be explained in a way which is consistent with the basic idea at the centre of Sartre's theory of consciousness, namely that 'consciousness and the world are given at one stroke', but hallucinating consciousness must contain a pre-reflective awareness of the status of its hallucinations. For this, hallucinatory consciousness must be found to have an immediate (and unmediated) self-knowledge of itself as being consciousness of its object. In other words, in being a 'self-consciousness', self-consciousness is a 'knowing', too, of the nature or 'truth' of its object – in the case the hallucinator, of the hallucinatory image as an imaginary object.

(3) If this were not found to be the case then it is not only the hallucinator's grasp on reality which is insecure but in principle that of every consciousness. Only if it is true in every case that on the pre-reflective (or, non-thetic) level consciousness can never be wholly self-deluded, can consciousness ever know that it knows anything with certainty. Sartre's pre-reflective *cogito* serves as guarantor of the possibility of both the *knowing* of the image *qua* object and the *knowledge* of the image *qua* image. It can indeed serve this function according to Sartre as on pre-reflective level these amount to being the same thing. Hence there can never be a consciousness which is wholly deluded.

So it is against this background that hallucination is recognised as presenting a philosophical 'problem' of some urgency: Sartre asks explicitly '[D]o we not take the risk of finding our stumbling block in the problem of hallucination?' (1972: 171). On the face of it there is hardly anything more urgent for a philosophical project than to secure the distinction between the real and the unreal, between dream and wakefulness, sense and nonsense. As Hammond *et al.* have noted: 'if one cannot account for the difference between hallucinations and experiences of the real, then there is always the possibility that all our perceptions are illusory: that there is no transcendent reality' (1991: 201). Hallucination is thus a form of consciousness which could be said to mark a specific limit of philosophical inquiry in general. Without this hypothesised absolute transparency of consciousness we would really be no better off with Sartrean phenomenology than we are with the Cartesian *cogito* (which required the invocation of God as its guarantor).

## Sartre and Lewin

Though Sartre's interest in all of this was not at all in the neurochemistry of consciousness processes, if he read anything about the effects of mescaline in advance of his experiment, he more than likely was familiar with the work of Louis Lewin. Lewin was a pharmacologist, toxicologist and medical historian who had written the seminal classificatory text in 1928 on psychotropic drugs and their effects. In his *Phantastica, Narcotic and Stimulating Drugs* Lewin classifies drugs according to both anthropological descriptions of their cultural uses and their psychological effects. In view of the well-documented evidence for their use throughout the ages and across many cultures, Lewin proposes that such substances in the brain, which occur either naturally or arrive there through introjection, are evidently the material basis for what modern psychological discourse identifies as 'visions and hallucinations' as well as other psychological phenomena such as mood. The evidence of drug-induced hallucinations, which are 'abnormal' or 'pathological' and caused by 'foreign influences', led him to hypothesise that 'visionary states' and mental disorders – whatever the cultural determination of their meaning and significance – must have their basis in 'substances produced in the organism': 'The action of these substances brings about in the individual subjectively felt realities, which should not be subject to reproach of fraud or untruthfulness' (Lewin, 1964: 91).

In his own way, then, Lewin suggests that hallucinations are something empirically 'real' – they are not only a 'subjective' reality for the hallucinated person, they evidently exist 'objectively' too, in that there is some neurochemical counterpart to this experience, namely a chemical alteration brought about in the brain which gives rise to them.

> If, in order to investigate how these internally caused perceptions appear and to which cause we must attribute them – false projection of ideas, unreal happenings, or non-existent objects – we must limit the problem to what we can actually observe, we are immediately faced with a tangible cause to which psychologists and alienists ignorant of the facts have paid little attention... [namely] the action of chemical substances capable of evoking transitory states without any physical inconvenience for a certain time in persons of perfectly normal mentality who are partly or fully conscious of the action of the drug. (Lewin, 1964: 91–2)

Whilst Lewin's interest is ultimately in the neurochemical basis of the phenomena of what he refers to as perception, imagination and cognitive processes in general, it is the possibility of engendering deliberate, temporary alterations of the underlying psychopharmacological processes that leads him to conclude that there is a role for psychotropic drugs (or 'phantastica' and 'hallucinatoria', as he calls drugs which give rise to 'sense illusion') in researching the 'disturbances' to mental life. Sartre may well have taken his cue, as far as the use of mind-altering drugs for researching consciousness was concerned, from these remarks of Lewin. I say this because taking a drug such as mescaline offers a simple, practical method of effectuating a change of consciousness, the central subject–object dyad of Sartre's phenomenological inquiry. Lewin himself seems accutely attuned to the fact that, in his own field of inquiry, experiential phenomena should be regarded as a 'doubling', or a point of contiguity of the subject and object. When psychotropic drugs reach the brain, the subjective experience of thought, emotion and meaning and the objective state of the biochemical human organism are viewed by him, effectively, as correlates of one another. What is particularly interesting about Lewin's discourse on drugs in this context is that when he speaks of 'limiting the problem to what can be observed', he has both the evidence of the halluci-nated person (what the hallucinated person 'sees', 'feels' and says) in mind as much as he has the evidence of neurochemical mechanisms. 'Phantas-tica' and 'halluninatoria' are for him equally approachable as he puts it, as both chemical and thaumaturgic agents. He says for instance:

> The importance of the Phantastica and Hallucinatoria extends to the sphere of physiological and semi-physiological and pathological processes... If any light is ever to be shed on the almost absolute dark-ness which envelops these cerebral processes, then such light will only originate from chemistry. (1964: 93–4)

and yet, on the other hand, that

> [this] point of view does not pretend to be the only one applicable to known processes of life. Others assume with equal justification, that a religious impulse, a truly divine emotion which makes the soul vibrate in its most profound depths, may be transmitted as a wave of excitation, and may influence centres which call forth internal impressions, false perceptions, hallucinations, etc. (1964: 93–4)

It is precisely the *division* of enquiry into an empiricism of mate-rial processes on the one hand and a subjectivism of psychological expe-rience on the other that Sartre's phenomenological approach, too, in its own, albeit quite different way, is opposed to. Where Lewin's discourse of the double-sidedness of the phenomenon is quite unlike Sartre's, is that it has already decided in advance, so to speak, the nature of what it sets out to discover – namely, how neurochemistry is related to psychological processes. Sartre's intention, at least, is to assume nothing at all, but rather to take the experience of hallucination as primary. Lewin's scientific inquiry and his proposal for the investigative use of hallucinogenic drugs are concerned with how the affected brain gives rise to certain subjective states – thus the *dualism* of intellectual processes and the realism of the world of material processes remains his underlying 'metaphysical assump-tion' (which is not something Lewin is in the business of subjecting to critique). Sartre's account of consciousness, on the other hand, is at pains not to reimport such metaphysical distinctions back into the inquiry in this way. None the less, Sartre's decision to experiment with mescaline at least shares the strategy of disrupting the processes of consciousness as a means of bringing into view, in the sense of into affective phenomenological proximity, that which normally remains hidden, namely the 'act' of consciousness itself . What he pays attention to is how, in the pre-reflective 'act' of consciousness, such distinctions as those between the subject and the object or the real and unreal have not yet arisen or acquired any significance. It is the transitions or transformations between modes of consciousness that Sartre was especially interested in and which he recognised could be rendered accessible only *in the processes of their formation and dissolution.*

What Sartre needed to show was that objects only ever exist as correlates of specific acts of consciousness by which they are posited. His bigger question (explored fully in *Being and Nothingness*) concerns what consciousness must be such that it exists only as one of a spectrum of modes of relatedness to its objects. In this respect the *Psychology* was a preparatory work for the Sartrean project of existentialist philosophy, which is ultimately rooted, as Sartre's prefatory note to the text states, in the phenomenological description of 'the great function of consciousness' which is 'to create a world of unrealities, or "imagination", and its noetic correlative, the imaginary' (1972: vii). It is useful to recall at this point too what is said there about the use of the term 'consciousness' as he deploys it in the *Psychology*: 'The term "consciousness" will be used… not only to designate the unity and the totality of its psychical structures, but to indicate each of the structures in its concrete particular nature' (1972: vii). The significance of this is that it is an indication of how each case, or instance, of consciousness must exemplify the general thesis concerning the transparency of consciousness to itself. There can be no exceptions.

As Sartre's fundamental idea of phenomenology is based on the self-examination of consciousness, the following questions he poses have both a methodological and a theoretical dimension to them – in fact these two dimensions of his 'theory and practice' are, precisely, inseparable:

> How do we abandon our consciousness of spontaneity, how do we feel ourselves passive before images we ourselves form; is it true that we confer reality, that is, actual presence upon these objects which occur to a sane consciousness as absent? (Sartre, 1972: 172)

It seems entirely reasonable to suppose that imaginative consciousness would lend itself to a more detailed 'observation' by the phenomenologist, if it were possible to bring its activity to the fore 'at will' by dissolving the (conscious) distinction between the wilfulness and passivity of consciousness. It seems reasonable, too, to suppose that mescaline could facilitate such a dissolution as, depending on the dose, it is a powerful hallucinogen. It also has the specific advantage, as Lewin records, that whilst under its influence 'the subject is fully informed as to his state. He exhibits a desire for introspection, asks himself whether all the strange things he experiences are real' (Lewin, 1964:103). Under the influence of mescaline, this description suggests, consciousness preserves a philosophically reflective inclination. This would no doubt have been reassuring to Sartre as he embarked upon his experiment in so far as it promises both a measure of 'objectivity' and a preservation of his own rationality during the hallucinatory experience it produces. There was evidence elsewhere in the psychological literature of the time that mescaline was suitable for such an experiment. Through his conversations about hallucinations with his friend the physician Daniel Lagache (who had just completed a book *Les hallucinations verbales et la parole* (1934)), Sartre may well have been familiar too with the work of Berenger, whom Lewin cites as an example of an 'unprejudiced' experimenter who had provided details of his 'wonderful experiences' whilst under the influence of mescaline (Lewin: 1964: 104n.1). The advantage, then, of an investigation of hallucination aided by a shot of mescaline, Sartre would have been aware, is that it seems likely to allow the hallucinator direct access to the phenomenon of hallucination whilst allowing also, and crucially, a degree of immediate reflection. Any drug which produced temporary but predominantly delusional experiences of utter hallucinatory and confusion would allow, at best, only a *delayed* reflection on the memory of the experience.

## Sartre's mescaline trip

So, it was amidst these and the aforementioned philosophical preoccupations with the intentional structures of consciousness and the relation of consciousness to its objects that in February of 1935 Sartre decided to take up an offer from Lagache, of a dose of mescaline to be administered by injection.

Hallucination could be seen as a kind of test case and a means of examining precisely the 'breakdowns' of various modes of consciousness and the points of transition between them. Hallucination is ambiguously located on the border between perception and imagination, apparently existing as some hybrid, half-way-house consciousness. As clearly stated elsewhere in the *Psychology*, it needed to be approached in the same way as other phenomena of consciousness were, through the identification and description of its characteristics.

Given Sartre's clearly expressed commitment to philosophise from the perspective of the phenomenon alone, it is easy to see why an experiment of his own in the form of a foray into a temporary hallucinatory state was in order. At the beginning of the *Psychology* he announces that, at the outset of his inquiry at least, 'the method is simple: we shall produce images, reflect on them, describe them; that is attempt to classify their distinctive characteristics' (1972: 2). So, despite the advice he dispensed to Beauvoir about the suspect character of alcohol intoxication as a possible source of philosophical insight into 'life', he appears to have decided that potentially there was something to be learned from a drug-induced derangement of the philosopher's mind after all, at least in relation to a phenomenological investigation of lived experience and in so far as this was aimed at discovering 'the characteristics that can be attributed to consciousness from the fact that that it is a consciousness capable of imagining' (1972: 202).

With all of this in mind, we have to imagine Sartre arriving at St Anne's hospital where his friend Lagache worked and had arranged for the use of dimly lit room for the day's experiment. The experience was from the outset thus located in relation to the pathological, and Beauvoir may well be right when she suggests that Sartre's experience as a whole may have been influenced by this setting and by Lagache's warning to him that it would be a 'mildly disagreeable experience' and that he could expect to 'behave oddly' for several hours after the effects of the drug had subsided. As she recalls the episode later

> He had not exactly had hallucinations, but objects he looked at changed their appearance in the most horrifying manner: umbrellas had become vultures, shoes turned into skeletons and faces acquired monstrous characteristics, while behind him, just past the corner of his eye, swarmed crabs and polyps and grimacing things. (1965: 209)

When she had phoned him at the hospital he had told her 'in a thick, blurred voice' that her call had 'rescued him from a battle with several devil-fish that he most certainly would have lost'. Despite the fact that the effects of the mescaline must have passed after several hours (Beauvoir tells us that he was himself again the next day) a week or so later a stroll on the beach collecting starfish appears to have triggered some sort of flashback – the disturbance to his normal state had lingered, as Lagache had predicted, for several days. At one point this included the conviction that he was being followed by a lobster, a sure sign, he thought he recognised, of his succumbing to a 'chronic form of hallucinatory psychosis'. This was not on fact the case and the experiment did indeed provide Sartre with at least some phenomenological 'material' which he later was able to compare with various reports and discussions of hallucination to be found in clinical literature on psychotic illnesses.

Certainly, going on what Beauvoir describes of his 'visions' (I hesitate to call these hallucinations at this point for reasons that will become clear later), he must have felt there was indeed an evident correspondence between transformations of consciousness and the transmogrifications of its objects – some examples of which I have just noted. His experience, judging by this following snippet of first-hand description which he includes in the *Psychology*, appeared to confirm the thesis of the spontaneity of consciousness:

> I myself was able to observe a short hallucination when I administered to myself an injection of mascalin [*sic*]. It had exactly this lateral trait: someone was singing in the room near by and as I tried to listen – stopping completely to look in front of me – three small parallel clouds appeared before me. The phenomenon naturally disappeared as soon as I tried to get hold of it. It was not in keeping with the full and clear visual consciousness. It could exist only by stealth and as a matter of fact it occurred as such; there was, in the way in which these three small clouds appeared in my memory directly after they had disappeared, something at once inconsistent and mysterious, which, it seemed to me, only translated the existence of these freed spontaneities on the margins of consciousness. (Sartre, 1972: 182)

This is Sartre's only published commentary on his mescaline experience. It places the hallucination very precisely between perception and dream. As he describes it in the *Psychology*, perception is characterised by a pre-reflective consciousness accompanied (immediately) by a reflective consciousness, whereas dreaming is a pre-reflective consciousness in relation to which no reflective consciousness is formed (the pre-reflective consciousness is, so to speak captive to itself). So a hallucination is found by him to be like a dream image, but it is one which (almost) immediately passes into conscious memory. The dreamer does not normally form such immediate recollection of his oneiric images as dreaming consciousness is wholly captivated by them and so sleeps on. What Sartre observes in his hallucinatory state is that the hallucinated object – the three clouds, for instance 'disappear' into his (conscious) memory (of them). This transition he holds to illustrate the thesis that pre-reflective consciousness of the image and the image are the same thing (whether in the hallucination or in the memory) but also that such hallucinated clouds (as distinct from remembered hallucinated clouds) cannot withstand the attention of a reflected consciousness. They are said to exist 'by stealth' on 'the margins of consciousness' and, in that hallucinatory moment itself, as something entirely unreflected: this he says 'we may call the *pure event* of the hallucination' (Sartre, 1972: 184).

This 'observation' – that '*the hallucination happens as a phenomenon, the experience of which can be made only in memory*' (1972: 184, *my emphasis*) – which is gained from 'the experience' of hallucinating but referred to as being beyond experience, is intriguing. What it notices is that the 'hallucinatory event' always happens in the absence of the subject.

Just what is the significance though, of the discovery of the complete absence of the subject from the centre of 'its own' experience – which is by virtue of that enigma not truly deserving of the name 'experience' at all? This impersonal 'pure event' is a sort of black hole at the centre of the very experience he is (none the less) attempting to describe, though necessarily at a distance from it and through reflection and memory. What Sartre does not appear to notice is that as soon as he says that experience implies the existence of a thematic consciousness, he has in fact encountered the extreme limit of the phenomenological method which has got him to this point. He concedes, in effect, that there cannot be a 'phenomenology' of this pure event of the kind he all along proposes. On the one hand, mescaline does indeed deliver a limit-experience in the sense that he anticipated – of the border between the two principal species of consciousness (perception and imagination). What he discovers at this limit is that the hallucinator posits the hallucinated object as unreal: there is a pre-reflective awareness of the object's unreality. It is only when there is an accompanying thematic reflection upon this that the hallucinator comes to think of it as having been unforeseen and not subject to voluntary production, and hence can 'genuinely' claim to have experienced the hallucinated object as something external to himself or herself. With this same thematic reflection, the hallucinator is also aware that the hallucination was something conjured up by his or her own consciousness, and that pre-reflective consciousness did not 'know' the difference between the real and the unreal. *On reflection*, in other words, the hallucinator cannot maintain the view that the hallucination is something real, precisely because he or she realises that the immediate intuition of the hallucinated object was of *something unreal*.

Whilst this experience of hallucinating consciousness appears to confirm Sartre's account of the role of the pre-reflective consciousness as a consciousness which does not make a judgement as to the reality or unreality of the object, and that the hallucinator is never really duped by the hallucinations, he does not seem to realise that his own experiment has given rise to an experience of the limit of the phenomenological approach itself. At the heart of the 'experience' of hallucination Sartre identifies what he calls *the pure event* of hallucination as something which is, to all intents and purposes, *for ever absent*. At this point one has to remember that the distinction between the pre-reflective and thematic moments of consciousness is an abstraction. Sartre holds the pre-reflective to be the guarantor of the transparency of each consciousness to itself, but when, in the context of his experimental investigation of hallucination, he 'looks for it', it disappears – just as those three hallucinated clouds do. I say 'as' the three clouds do, but in fact the three clouds 'are' the manifestation of the pre-reflective conscious *in act*.

One is left wondering here what it is that Sartre has learnt from his experimental trip into a hallucinatory mode of consciousness. Everything he says could in fact have been said on the basis of the psychological literature on hallucination, some of which he weaves into his commentary in order to back up the claim that that 'patients' know their hallucinations are not real and that the behaviour and remarks of psychotics typically illustrate that hallucination only ever occurs as perception crumbles (Sartre, 1972: 172–4). I do not wish to question the efficacy of Sartre's paralleling of his phenomenological theses with clinical accounts of hallucination at all, but rather to reflect on how his phenomenological approach runs up against the buffers as far as the idea of drawing on the experience of the phenomenon alone is concerned.

Firstly because, as I have attempted to show, what he calls the 'pure event' of hallucination, by his own description, is in fact opaque rather than transparent to itself. Secondly because the distinctness and mutual exclusivity of the two key modes of consciousness, perception and imagination – which he holds in effect to be the condition of possibility for any 'true knowledge' of reality – seem to be questionable. Their mutual exclusivity and distinctness is said not to be 'found' (that is, found to be absent) at the pre-reflective level, but the pre-reflective level is at the same time found not to be truly examinable as such. The pre-reflective phenomenon and its characteristics are ultimately only a hypothesis of a thematic consciousness (an intellectualisation). So, somewhat paradoxically, the pre-reflective remains 'questionable' not for lack of 'phenomenological evidence' but rather because the evidence itself is ultimately a 'thesis' or judgement of reflective consciousness.

What I am suggesting here is that it is as if Sartre has already decided in advance what the significance of the experience of hallucination is for the theory of consciousness – and the evidence of his experience of hallucination *as he reports it* is held to bear this out. He encounters the 'limit' of his phenomenological inquiry in the opacity of the 'pure event' of hallucination. Moreover, when his thought encounters this limit, he turns away from it, back towards the terms of reference of his inquiry and ends up writing about his own experience pretty much as a clinical psychologist writes about the experience of the psychotic patient. It is notable that the only part of the experience he chooses to cite in his chapter on hallucination in the *Psychology* is an account of a hallucination (the three clouds) which appears – at least initially – to endorse his thesis about the distinctness and mutual exclusivity of the perceptual and imaginative modes of consciousness. We do not hear anything directly about those elements Beauvoir recalls for us – for instance that he did not appear to have had any hallucinations (!), his odd behaviour, or his paranoid flight from crustaceans and other fishy things. Selective memory one wonders? Perhaps, but that is not the issue I am raising here. Much more important given the place afforded to phenomenological reflection in Sartre's philosophy of this time is the question of whether it is possible at all to 'know' with certainty whether an experience is hallucinatory or not from 'inside' the experience when, as Sartre himself discovers, *the subject is always absent from the event of hallucination*? Is not the whole phenomenological strategy of turning to 'experience' itself as a programme for steering a middle ground between intellectualism and empiricism, therefore, rather like the experience of the three clouds itself – ultimately located at on 'the margins of consciousness'?

The conclusion I suggest he could have drawn – and in fact the 'lesson' that hallucinatory experience, and for that matter other forms of intoxication, teaches, as I have attempted to show throughout this work, is that the enterprise of theory is not itself immune to the effects of drugs. In a certain sense it can be counted amongst them. Is not the 'sobriety' of the reflection which accounts for the imaginal realm – in this case instantiated by an hallucinating consciousness – always a case of a withdrawal from it?[3]

## Merleau–Ponty: ambiguity and hallucination

In *Phenomenology of Perception* Merleau-Ponty provides a brilliant diagnosis of why the phenomenology of consciousness, such as that pursued by Sartre, will never escape collapsing back into the 'intellectualism' it seeks to escape. This is nowhere clearer or more succinctly expressed than in the section he devotes to a discussion of hallucination and the account Sartre had given of it in the *Psychology*.

Like Sartre he begins by acknowledging that neither empiricism nor intellectualism can provide an adequate account of the phenomenon. It has to be acknowledged that there is no sensory content to hallucination, but, by virtue of that fact, to suppose that the hallucinator makes judgements or holds beliefs about the hallucinated object is also plainly false:

> A hallucination is not a judgement or a rash belief, for the same reasons which prevent it from being sensory content; the judgement or the belief could consist only in positing the hallucination as true, and this is precisely what patients do not do.

Like Sartre, too, he invokes the clinical evidence of what patients say, but with Sartre's thesis in mind, he adds:

> In intellectualism, an effort is made to get rid of hallucination properly speaking, to construct it, and to deduce what it might be from a certain idea of consciousness. (Merleau-Ponty, 1965: 335)

What is wrong with this thinking according to Merleau-Ponty is that it is essentially Cartesian and subject to the well-known limitations of cartesianism, namely that 'everything which consciousness knows with certainty' it looks for and finds within itself. This intellectualism shares an unexpected kinship with the empiricism it is traditionally set against, in the emphasis it places on objective thought – what Sartre refers to as thematic consciousness. It is true that Sartre claims the existence of the pre-reflective *cogito* to be the fundamental characteristic of every form and instance of consciousness, but, as I argued above, it is clear from within his own analysis that the 'phenomenological evidence' for this is presentable only in the hypotheses of objective thought.

When Merleau-Ponty says 'we must not be satisfied with the opinions of sane consciousness on the subject of hallucinatory consciousness'

(337) he is not simply expressing a view on the clinical efficacy of a sympathetic ear for what the patient has to say of his or her hallucinatory experiences, he is making the point that every idea of reality and normality is the outcome of a communicative process of exchange with others, through which each arrives at his or her own sense of reality. This is in fact how I know that someone else is having a hallucination (and that I am not) in the first place. The hallucinator is identifiable as someone who 'sees' what is not visible to the others – what is truly visible is what is shared in intersubjective vision of 'the real', or the perceptible realm. Merleau-Ponty interrogates the structure and assumptions of the kind of experimental project undertaken by Sartre directly:

> If a philosopher produces hallucinations in himself by means of an insulin injection, either he yields to the hallucinatory impulse, in which case the hallucination is a living experience for him and not an object of knowledge or else he retains something of his reflective power and it will always be possible to challenge his testimony. (Merleau-Ponty, 1964: 337).

Sartre is at odds to account for the difference between hallucinating consciousness and the reflective consciousness which comes to account for the hallucination. But in concluding that the hallucinator posits the hallucinated as 'unreal' (and is aware pre-reflectively of its unreality as such), Sartre does not adequately account for the fact that the hallucinator may be deceived by the hallucination – as indeed is the case (and Sartre acknowledges this) – whilst 'living' that consciousness.[4] But Merleau-Ponty refuses such a solution on the grounds that it cannot explain why the hallucinator can be in a state of deception and either not be aware of it or, if aware of it, can remain in such a state (336). The charge of reducing experience to 'so many objects', thereby causing us 'to lose sight of the phenomenon of hallucination' (336), is applicable, and most likely being directed here at Sartre. Ironically, despite having sought out the phenomenon of hallucination itself in his mescaline experiment, Sartre, it is suggested here, ends up 'intellectualising' the experience to the point of losing sight of it altogether.

The major difference in approach between Merleau-Ponty and Sartre on hallucination is that the former emphasises how hallucination is one amongst the many possible ways of being in the world, whereas the latter remains deeply attached to the primordiality of psychic intentionality. It is this privileging of consciousness that Merleau-Ponty regards as the source of Sartre's error. Merleau-Ponty emphasises instead the body-world synthesis: 'we learn to know consciousness as we learn to know anything else' (1965: 336). It is through our embodiment – the form of our inhabitation of the world – that this happens. Merleau-Ponty's hallucinator does not inhabit the world of perception as fully as does the normal person, but his or her world of hallucinations is none the less 'superimposed' on the world of perception. The hallucination is not of the world of perception, to be sure, but the disjuncture between the hallucination and the world of perception is never exclusively of the hallucinator's design either. Hallucinators do not live in their own world: they repress the public world of perception by means of the hallucination they produce. But they none the less remain in that world in so far as they exploit their being in the world in order to carve a private sectors for themselves (343) and their own body are themselves visible, public objects (even if they may entertain the fantasy of their own invisibility). The 'world' is the environment of their lived experience, perceptual or hallucinatory, and it is this, rather than some quirk of the structures of consciousness which makes both perception and hallucination possible. The hallucinator summons up a pseudo-environment which is necessarily made up of elements of the real world.

Merleau-Ponty provides us with another (elsewhere unpublished) snippet of Sartre's account of his experience to add to the others:

> I perceive a world covered with swellings... It is as if my perception suddenly changed key to become perception in intumescence, as one plays a piece of music in C or B flat... Just then, my whole perception was transformed and, for an instant, I perceived a rubber bulb. Does that mean I saw nothing else? No, but I had the feeling of being transferred to a setting such that I could perceive in no other way. The belief took possession of me that the world is thus... Later another change took place... Everything seemed at once clammy and scaly, like some of the large serpents I have seen uncoiling themselves at the Berlin Zoo. Then I was seized with the fear of being on a small island surrounded by serpents. (Merleau-Ponty 1965: 340)

His comment is as follows:

> Hallucination does not present me with protuberances, or scales, or words like ponderous realities gradually revealing their meaning. It does no more than reproduce for me the way in which these realities strike me in my being and feeling of language. (Merleau-Ponty, 1965: 340)

What this implies is that there is in fact no such thing as a self-contained private experience and Sartre's mescaline experience is a case in point: what his hallucinatory experience teaches about hallucination is not something he, by virtue of being the one experiencing the phenomenon, has privileged access to the truth thereof. Even his own words are a matter of the possibilities of the public language in which his sentences are formulated. The content of his experience is never identical with his consciousness of it: it is always contextualised and always a function of his relation to what is beyond his consciousness. In the case of Sartre's mescaline experience, this includes his philosophical preoccupations of the time and the reading he had made of Lagache's and other works discussing hallucinations – but these are all 'dialogical'. It also includes the pathological background to the experiment, in terms of the clinical literature but also in terms of the 'set and setting' of the experiment; of injections and the dimly lit room in St Anne's hospital. Beyond that still should be counted those elements of 'the experience' which are inscribed in Beauvoir's comments and observations and indeed in the discussion of it given in Merleau-Ponty's own text. These and other elements of 'Sartre's experience' indicate the sense in which a subject is not in a privileged position in relation to its own experiences. The hallucinator may be the one who 'lives' the hallucination, but in so far as he, Sartre, considers (or places) himself in this position, he takes part in an event which is constituted by a 'situation' constituted out of a set of relations of which 'the hallucinator' is only one part.

'Hallucination' does therefore indeed remain a 'stumbling block' for his theory of consciousness as transparent to itself, but it does so because it brings to light the limitations of the phenomenology of consciousness as such. So, it is instructive in this sense at least: what it reveals, as Merleau-Ponty puts it, is that 'I know myself only in my ambiguity' (1965: 345).

In the context of the loosening of control over the grip consciousness has on reality which drugs can produce, this brings to light how there is always an ongoing negotiation *in language* about the distinction between the real and the imaginary. This negotiation always has social, cultural, institutional, personal, and no doubt other, parameters to it.

## Hallucination as a literary sort of high

In a short story entitled 'The Room', written around the time of his multifaceted project of 'philosophical psychology', Sartre himself illustrates this last point particularly clearly. 'The Room' is about a couple, Eve and Pierre. Pierre is suffering from some kind of psychotic disorder, probably schizophrenia, and he is regularly visited by statues which fly around the room buzzing and making fishy eyes at him. Eve loves Pierre and in loving him tries to identify with his madness, including having discussions with him about 'the visitors' to their room: "I'm afraid of the statues," she thought. It was a blind, violent affirmation, an incantation. She wanted to believe in their presence with all her strength' (Sartre, 1960: 106). At the same time as she attempts to enter into his insanity, she also wonders why it is that he always knows well in advance when it is that the statues will come, and she remembers something Pierre's doctor had once said to her concerning her doubts as to whether Pierre believed in the existence of them: 'But my dear Madame, all mentally unbalanced persons are liars; you are wasting your time if you're trying to distinguish between what they really feel and what they pretend to feel.' The story expresses the complexity of the 'phenomenon' of hallucination, which is not isolable from the set of relations, between Eve, Pierre the doctor and so on, all of whom have a different kind of investment in their 'reality'. The psychiatrist, for instance, makes his living out of the madnesses of others, Eve and Pierre are in a power struggle and Pierre's hallucinations are something he is 'doing' to get his way, whilst Eve needs to love Pierre in order to be happy and so on. So the phenomenon of hallucination is not the exclusive property of any 'science'; not of psychiatry and not of phenomenological psychology either, no more than a particular hallucination is the exclusive property of the hallucinator.

Another instance of literary representation of hallucinatory experience in Sartre is to be found in his novel *Nausea*. The hero Roquentin is driven in the course of the novel toward what might be described as a kind of revelatory psychotic episode, brought on in this case by the toxic effects of bourgeois life in Bouville. Sartre's account of Roquentin's experience in the park, from which the following is excerpted, is perhaps the finest literary condensation of the fundamental phenomenological impulse that was to become central to the development of his existential thought.

I was in the municipal park just now. The root of the chestnut tree plunged into the ground just underneath my bench. I no longer remembered that it was a root. Words had disappeared, and with them the meaning of things, the methods of using them, the feeble landmarks which men have traced on their surface... And then, all of a sudden, there it was clear as day: existence had suddenly unveiled itself. It had lost its harmful appearance as an abstract category: it was the stuff of things, that root was steeped in existence. Or, rather the root, the park gates, the bench, the sparse grass on the lawn, all had vanished; the diversity of things, their individuality, was only an appearance, a veneer. This veneer had melted, leaving soft, monstrous masses, in disorder – naked, with a frightening, obscene nakedness... *Superfluous*: that was the only connexion I could establish between those trees, those gates, those pebbles... And I – weak, languid, obscene, digesting, tossing about dismal thoughts – *I too was superfluous*... The word Absurdity is now born beneath my pen. (Sartre, 1965: 182–5)

This literary account of a hallucinating consciousness is presented as providing a moment of existential insight to its writer, namely into the irreducible absurdity of Being. But it is only because words had 'returned' – and eloquently so – by the time Roquentin sat down to make this remarkable entry in his diary that this can be claimed to be the case.

Indeed, all literature is in this way 'after the fact', and even the most committed phenomenologist aiming at the impersonal articulation of impersonal experiences cannot avoid the logic of the necessary withdrawal from the 'non-thetic' immediacy of things, which Roquentin's written recollections, by their very nature, are evidence to. That writing supplements experience in this way, however, ought not to be so much regarded as an intractable obstacle or *reductio ad absurdum* for phenomenology *per se*, as it should be considered to indicate how the consciousness or world unity experienced in the event of existence is already, as Merleau-Ponty says, 'the social with which we are in contact by the mere fact of existing, and which we carry about inseparably with us before any objectification' (1964: 362). In the case of Roquentin this primary sociality is in the form of writing his diary.

## Notes

1 In *The Prime of Life* Beauvoir tells us that this was first through discussion with Aron, but his first serious reading of Husserlian ideas was through his discovery of Levinas's book of 1930, *The Theory of Intuition in Husserl's Phenomenology*.

2 These studies in 'philosophical psychology' appeared in the form of series of major essays and books written between 1934 and 1940. These were *The Transcendence of the Ego* (written in 1934, published in 1937); *Sketch for a Theory of Emotions* – written in 1936, published in 1939; the book-length critical study of contemporary theories of imagination, *Imagination: A Psychological Critique* (*L'imagination*) – written in 1935, published 1936; followed shortly afterwards by the Sartre's own original account of the imagination *Psychology of the Imagination* (*L'imaginaire: psychologie phénoménologique de l'imagination*) – begun in 1935, published in 1940. It ought also to be noted that by 1934 Sartre had also been working for four years on his novel *Nausea* (published in 1938) and that collection of short stories published in 1939 in the volume *Intimacy*, as these literary works also give expression to his 'philosophical psychology'. I juxtapose this list of Sartre's publications of this period in order illustrate the extensive range of Sartre's work on 'philosophical psychology' in the decade prior to the production of his opus Being and Nothingness (1943) for which he is best known. As this later work rests on the theory of consciousness worked through in all of its details, the significance of the problem of hallucination is greater than might be expected, and hence this background and Beauvoir's recollection of the conversation with Sartre about intoxication set the scene for this chapter.

3 Marcus Boon makes a related observation when he says: 'It does not seem to have occurred to [Sartre] that the phenomenological space of inquiry, far from being objective, is an imaginal realm, much like any other mental realm, and subject to the same kinds of behaviour as the "irrational" world of imagination he wished to study' (2002: 236). However, Boon, in my view, implies there is no logical alternative to the intellectualism Sartre at least sets out to overcome. In the next section I shall discuss how Merleau-Ponty's critique of Sartre on this issue arguably succeeds in resolving the problem Sartre is attempting to address.

4 This idea of 'self-deception' (*mauvaise-foi*) comes to figure prominently in the existential phenomenology of his later opus *Being and Nothingness*.

# 7    Foucault and Deleuze on acid

## Drugs and the orbit of madness

In an interview in 1984 on the work of Raymond Roussel, which had been the subject of Foucault's early book *Death and the Labyrinth* (1963), the discussion touches on the subject of Roussel's use of drugs. Foucault says that 'the study of the culture of drugs or drugs as culture in the West' was something that interests him greatly and that he would have liked to have undertaken a study of the drug culture which was 'so closely tied to the artistic life of the West' (1987: 182–3). Unfortunately he never did. The idea behind this chapter initially arose out of my wondering just what sort of an account of the culture of drugs Foucault might have produced given the nature of the few, minimal, passing, almost entirely marginal remarks and exchanges he made on the subject. I realised immediately that whatever he might have written on drugs would have depended on just when in the course of his overall intellectual trajectory he had undertaken such a project. One writes in order to become something other than what one is, he once said, and taking drugs – as a theme or just as they come – resonates with this. Foucault's books never failed to surprise as much as they delighted, and it is not my intention here to speculate on what he might actually have had to say. What I shall do in this chapter is pick up on and open up further a dialogue on the subject of drugs, madness and philosophy that can be traced in several texts by Foucault and Deleuze which are at the same time of a more general interest with regard to their understandings of each other's thinking.

This discussion of Foucault's and Deleuze's (and toward the end of the chapter, Deleuze's and Guattari's) thinking on drugs addresses the question of the relationship between drugs, literary art, 'artistic life' and the processes of theorising itself in the context of their own intellectual movements away from the humanistic modernity which Foucault refers to as 'the age of man'. The aim is consider how drugs and drug effects may be considered to figure in their respective attempts to overcome anthropocentric modernity, which traditionally claims the artist and the work of art, moreover the individual creative intelligence and its product, as the source of culture. I shall not attempt to draw a general map of the relation between Foucault's and Deleuze's work. As elsewhere in this book, the single thread marking the contour it follows is the drugs theme alone: it continues the drugs culture 'series' of the previous chapters (borrowing in advance from Deleuze's terminological tool-box) with the theme 'drugs and madness'. It is this conjunction which directs us to a point of connection and interaction between Foucauldian and Deleuzian theorisations of 'the limits of Reason' with their analyses of sense and nonsense and their thinking of the relation between interiority and exteriority. The connection between Foucauldian and Deleuzian thinking is identified here on a narcoanalytic basis, and, setting out from the most marginal of drug-mediated exchanges between them, I aim to show that the drug effects which circulate in culture at large (or cultural exteriority) are related to specific materialisations of individual existence (or cultural interiority), providing another specific instance of how drug effects are inscribed within the production of theory.

One of the most influential ideas of Foucault's early work is the notion of historically discontinuous 'systems of thought' – the epistemic-cultural totalities he refers to as *epistemes*. Within each *episteme* prevailing ideas of truth and falsity, the normal and the pathological, sense and nonsense, Reason and Unreason and so on, order the cultural whole and are materialised in cultural practices and institutions. His 1961 study of 'the history of madness in the age of reason', *Madness and Civilisation*,[1] with its declared aim of allowing madness to speak for itself,[2] revolves around two key themes: these are 'the impossible 'and 'desire'; the impossibility of translating Unreason into Reason *without remainder* and the desire for 'the other', or what exceeds, or is outside of rational thought.[3] These are the enduring parameters of the Foucauldian *oeuvre*, and it is his thought concerning the relation to alterity (rather than the socio-politics of mental health management) that informs my approach to his texts here and which will enable me to exploit the connection with Deleuzian schizo-analysis. By means of this bridging, which is done here with the aid of 'drugs', we can get a sense of how their own critical practice is already a part of the 'culture of drugs'.

The Foucauldian and Deleuzian projects meet in the orbit of madness. I propose the figure of the 'orbit' to express the tenuous relation between rational theorising and the 'other of reason', whose separation is maintained in their theorising solely on the basis of a certain notion of 'speed', or 'speed of thought'. It is 'speed' which prevents their theorising collapsing into the 'madness' which it addresses.[4] To those with no taste for such of speedy thinking, their thought might well appear in places to be characterised by flights of fancy, and, as we shall soon see, rationality is in any case regarded as but a line of thought drawn between the two co-ordinates of madness discernible in language and in the body.

Deleuze's encounter with Lewis Carroll, for example, in *Logic of Sense* (1990), results in something that looks at first sight like 'philosophy on acid': the text is a madhouse of cultural forms and figures, discursive contagions, impossible encounters and Alice-like distortions of space-time, and often seems fundamentally out of control. But this popular idiomatic expression, 'like X on acid', if it *means* anything at all, means something only in relation to its opposite, 'X not on acid' – as if the 'not on acid' is something constant, identifiable and normatively coherent or 'straight'. But such constancy could only belong to, and make *sense* itself in, a system of thought which by rights could be regarded as 'normal' in some enduring and foundational manner. But this is a notion which Foucault and Deleuze both expose to unrelenting contestation in the first place. So the very characterisation of 'X (on acid)', as with any other 'function' of analogical or metaphorical characterisation of normality, (which assumes 'X (not on acid)' returns a constant) cannot be recursively calculated: the function never 'bottoms out', as the idiomatic language of computational mathematics says, on some fixed, transcendent realm. Or, in philosophical terminology: the acid-effect which the idiomatic expression makes a joke of cannot be theoretically attained by thought by means of a hermeneutics – which is the 'literary' form of mathematical recursion. As Deleuze says (at another point close to talking about drugs and to which we shall return) 'experimentation replaces interpretation' (1988: 284). For this reason it cannot seriously be anyone's aim to attempt either to derive a *theory* of drugs and drug effects or to calculate a *value* for 'the meaning of drugs' from a reading of the works of either Foucault or Deleuze. We can only approach the subject of drugs in their work on the basis of the traceable effects of 'drugs' within it.

If Foucault had taken on the project of a work on the culture of drugs, would it have been similar to the earlier 'archaeological' studies? Would he have approached drugs in the context of analysing the carceral society and its institutions of control and perhaps focused on the use of drugs to subdue the incarcerated, to execute murderers and generally to render the body 'docile' and manageable? Alternatively, had he under-taken a study of drugs and culture at later stage in his trajectory would it have considered how drugs figure in relation to 'technologies of the self', and looked at the role of drugs as a part of the cultural milieu in which drug-centred cultural practices are the backdrop for what he called self-styling?

Instead of idling around this sort of conundrum, I shall focus on how the drugs theme figures in the often discussed *shift* between Foucault's earlier work and later work. That shift is from the earlier quasi-historical studies of discontinuous and irruptive cultural constellations, *epistemes* and 'regimes of truth', which theorise impersonal 'structures' of exteriority, to the later studies of interiority, or individual forms of 'subjectivation' (*d'asujetissment*), 'self-styling practices' and 'aesthetic existence', which emerge in the books on sexuality, and other later writings on 'technologies of the self'. My reasoning here is that, given Foucault's expressed view about how the work (*oeuvre*) is always a part of a process of self-transformation through an encounter with alterity in one form or another, then a work on drugs (from a Foucauldian perspective at least) would have been interesting to the extent to which it dealt with and contributed to such a transition and transformation – of both theory and life.

I frame what follows, then, with a question about how the themes of drugs and the culture of drugs span the difference between Foucault's identification of the 'artist' as a liminal figure in his earlier work and his later focus on 'aesthetic' practices of the individual self, in which each self becomes the artist of its own existence. For reasons that will emerge, Deleuze's reading of Foucault, and Foucault's reading of Deleuze, starting from a rather strange and marginal exchange between them on the subject of drugs, will be my way in to considering how drugs and theorising might be seen to connect with one another. 'Drugs' are the signpost pointing to a specific juncture of their thinking on the interrelatedness, or co-becoming of 'the subject' and 'culture'. The series linking the subject to the culture of drugs below will follow the sequence: Foucault on Deleuze, Foucault on LSD and Deleuze, Deleuze on Foucault on LSD, Foucault (actually) on LSD, Deleuze and Guattari on Foucault on drugs.

### LSD in the *Theatrum Philosophicum* – 'What will people think of us?'

I begin in the *Theatrum Philosophicum*, a text by Foucault which presents a celebratory, rather than a conventionally critical, review of two books by Deleuze, *Nietzsche and Philosophy* and *The Logic of Sense*.[5] 'What will people think of us?' is the text of a footnote Deleuze appends to Foucault's text at a point at which Foucault offers a brief assessment of the relation

of drugs, their effects and their significance, to the enterprise of philosophical thinking, all in the context of his reading of Deleuze (Foucault,
1977: 191n. 20). Here the effects of drugs (LSD and opium are specifically
mentioned) are suggestively invoked as a model for representing, and as a
potential means for upsetting, the machinery and conventions of Reason,
the prevalence of which, says Foucault, maintains thought in state of
'catatonic rigidity' (Foucault, 1977: 191). In effect, Foucault credits both
LSD and Deleuze's work at that time, by means of a seemingly casual
comparison, with the power to disrupt this 'catatonic rigidity' of thought
by virtue of the 'difference' they both give rise to.

It is hard to imagine that either Foucault or Deleuze might be
genuinely concerned with what people might think of them, in the sense
of incurring bourgeois disapproval, for bringing illicit drugs into a discussion of the philosophical pursuit of truth and for considering the philosophical significance of the effects and experience of such drugs. It is true
that taking drugs seriously and simply discussing them can be confused
with personal interest in taking them in another sense, and that talk of
'experimentation' in this context can sound like a programmatic proposal
– both of which may draw opprobrium. But in any case, as Deleuze was
later to write in his book on Foucault's thought, Foucault often asks his
readers to admire certain infamous individuals 'by virtue of their misfortune, rage or uncertain madness' (Deleuze, 1988: 95). 'Infamy' was something which Deleuze was later to say Foucault often actively claimed,
though in his view 'strangely, implausibly', for himself. Foucault's bid for
(or incidental accrual of) infamy in a biographical sense is not at all my
theme here, but let us take a moment to consider why Deleuze says that in
Foucault's case courting infamy would be strange and implausible. Going
with this sideways slide now, as one line of thought crosses another, may
lead to a more interesting approach to Deleuze's peculiar footnote.

The reasons why Deleuze thinks it strange and implausible for
Foucault to 'identify' too closely with those figures who operate in the
proximity of madness, are in fact the same reasons why Deleuze might
well have wanted to add his footnote to Foucault's text: would people
think that Foucault's remarks implied that 'drug-crazed thought' provides
a model for the orbit of madness in which the Deleuzean and Foucauldian
projects encounter one another and for the exorbitant philosophising
they engage in? Furthermore, if this is in some measure the risk entailed
by thinking in the proximity of Unreason (whatever its sources), would
this orbit even be philosophically tenable? Or would it result, rather, in

a spiralling crash into 'Unreason itself'? Foucault's bringing the themes of drug taking and philosophising into general proximity in the context of a review of Deleuze's thought may be taken to imply that both it and drugged thinking do indeed have something in common (the text is after all ostensibly a 'response' of some kind to his work), or at least a significant connection. These questions are important for the dialogue between Foucauldian and Deleuzian thought: they concern the connection between philosophising and those 'drug effects' akin to madness, specifically in the context of Deleuze's work and indeed with respect to the relation between his and Foucault's projects in general.

In an interview three years prior to the publication of Foucault's review of Deleuze's texts, as his biographer Miller citing him notes, Foucault had 'defended the value of certain drugs as a means to breach certain cultural limits, allowing a person to enter into "a state of *nonreason* in which the experience of madness is outside the distinction between the normal and the pathological"' (Miller, 1994: 248). In his comparison of Deleuze's thought with the LSD effect in *Theatrum*, Foucault reiterates the idea of a link between drugs and the kind of critical 'experimentation' contra Reason, characteristic of Deleuze's writings. Taking a lead from Foucault in *Theatrum* now: to understand what such a connection (of being *outside the distinction* between the normal and the pathological) amounts to, one must first reject the misunderstanding of any supposed drugged insight as the revelation of 'truth': 'only to fortune-tellers' do drugs 'reveal a world "more truthful than the real"' (Foucault, 1977: 191). This caution echoes the Baudelairean rejection of the idea of intoxication as a means of transcendence and access to 'truth'. But in the cases of both Foucault and Deleuze, we are not with this statement of reserve and rational suspicion to be done with drugs: where to idealist thinking drugs appear as the enemy of truth and the friend of artifice, to materialists like Foucault and Deleuze drugs and drug-effects are at least potential means for countering 'regimes of truth' and the self-assertion of Reason. Let us look at the finer detail of what is perhaps one of Foucault's most explicit and interesting characterisations of the philosophical enterprise in general. It requires some unpacking.

It begins with a juxtaposition of 'intelligence' (philosophical observation), 'stupidity' (*bêtise*) and 'thought'. How are these three related to one another and how does their interrelation bear on the self-understanding of the philosophy which emerges? The big issue is how 'stupidity' can be confronted. 'Intelligence does not respond to stupidity, since it is stupidity already vanquished. The scholar is intelligent. But it is thought which confronts stupidity and the philosopher who observes it' (Foucault, 1977: 190). Although philosophical 'observation' takes itself to be what faces up to stupidity, and considers 'thought' to be merely a medium of expression of both stupidity *and* intelligence, in facing it it becomes mesmerised by a negative image of itself. Intelligence sees in stupidity its own 'death mask': 'At the limit, [such philosophical] thought would be the intense contemplation from close up – to the point of losing oneself in it – of stupidity' (Foucault, 1977: 190). This gives rise, says Foucault, to a 'catatonic theatre' of 'immobility'. When thought is restricted to such a contemplation of its antithesis, Unreason, then philosophy takes its role and its function to be the production of critical, transcendental *judgements* concerning truth and falsity. Foucault then proposes an alternative model for philosophical thought, one which presents the prospect of openness to 'the shock of difference':

> the philosopher must be sufficiently perverse to play the game of truth and falsity badly: this perversity, which operates in paradoxes, allows him to escape the grasp of categories. But aside from this he must be sufficiently 'ill-humoured' to persist in his confrontation with stupidity, to remain motionless to the point of stupefaction in order to approach it and mime it, to let it grow within himself (this is probably what is referred to as 'being absorbed in one's thoughts'), and to await, in the always unpredictable conclusion to this preparation, the shock of difference. (Foucault, 1977: 190)

This is not, emphatically, an alternative philosophical path to 'truth': the conclusion to the preparation is a 'shock' to which the philosopher (still the Man of Reason) responds in a reactive way. No sooner is 'the shock of difference' felt than it is accommodated by the resolve of philosophical thought to overcome difference, or to judge. So, if the passage cited above describes a formula for kick-starting the differentiation engine of thought, then, according to Foucault, such an approach succeeds only in turning this engine over, it still cannot get it into gear: 'Once paradoxes have upset the table of representation, catatonia [still] operates within the theatre of thought' (Foucault, 1977: 190).

It is at this point, without any warning or explanation, that Foucault introduces some other gear, namely, LSD.

> We can easily see how LSD inverts the relationships of ill humour, stupidity, and thought: it no sooner eliminates the supremacy of categories

> than it tears away the ground of its indifference and disintegrates the
> dumbshow of stupidity; and it presents this univocal and acategorical
> mass not only as variegated, mobile, asymmetrical, decentred, spiraloid,
> and reverberating, but causes it to rise, at each instant, as a swarming of
> phantasm events. (Foucault, 1977: 190)

'LSD' is introduced in this context as if it were a synonym for 'Deleuze's
text'; and it stands there at least as an agent of perversity and mimicry
of the kind played out in *Logic of Sense*. Mimicry, mask-play, silence and
improvisation are all 'theatrical' devices deployed to perversely disrupt
the play of Reason unfolding according to its own logic and its traditional
script. Leading players in the cast of the Deleuzian 'theatrum' of *Logic of
Sense*, alongside its perverse and ill-humoured philosopher-director, for
instance, are figures such as Lewis Carroll, Antonin Artaud (a star actor
by any measure), alcoholics, schizophrenics, jabberwockies, little girls and
so on. They play in differing combinations in scenes involving shitting,
eating, falling, grinning, and are made to engage in outrageous linguistic
copulations with ancient and modern philosophers, psychoanalysts,
poets and artists. Opium, too, is credited by Foucault with establishing
a ground 'that no longer stupidly absorbs all differences but allows them
to arise and sparkle as so many minute, distanced, smiling, and eternal
events' (1977: 191). *Logic of Sense* stages such a 'theatrum' of events,
whose scripting is compared to the 'phantasm-events' Foucault links to
the effects of LSD on thought:

> As it slides upon this surface at once regular and intensely vibratory,
> as it is freed from its catatonic chrysalis, thought invariably contem-
> plates this indefinite equivalence transformed into an acute event and a
> sumptuous apparelled repetition. (Foucault, 1977: 190–1)

Superficiality and delirium are staged in *Logic of Sense* in such a way that
'the stupid' will invariably tend (on the basis of a false opposition of the
clinical and critical dimensions of madness) to mistake them for signs
of actual superficiality and delirium. Staging such delirious movements
across the surface of a literary-philosophical cultural landscape populated by the mad, by philosophers and by fictional characters crashing
into one another, is made, in Foucault's commentary, to resonate with
the idea of a drugged-up, dissembling, out-of-control state. But this resonance does not have the status of a truth claim. It does not claim that
Deleuze's style is based on the *experience* of taking LSD, or that taking
LSD in itself produces comparable drug-induced insights into the nature

of thought, only that the kind of sliding, associative movements of thought it compares with the effect of LSD illustrate very well the kind of technique Deleuze employs throughout *Logic of Sense*. The lines of connection which chaotically bundle *Logic of Sense* together do not map out or frame any disciplinary territory; they pursue, rather, connective links and 'series' – all of which remain open. Here we have an account of what Deleuze describes as 'surface effects', which characterise what I will call the *horizontal* dimension of the Deleuzian 'literary' enterprise. I shall address in detail the perpendicular axes of the horizontal surface and vertical depth in *Logic of Sense* in a moment, but just before that let us revisit that Deleuzian footnote to Foucault on drugs, which is becoming a refrain here, too!

All of this suggests that the footnote could be read as Deleuze's wondering about what will be made of this sort of wide-ranging associative practice, which on one level, by dropping the drugs LSD and opium into the discussion, Foucault's remarks are simply 'joining in with': they show, rather than theorise, how the Deleuzian project is *open to extension*. In other words, in linking-in some remarks on drug effects, Foucault demonstrates how to respond to Deleuze; and that this is what the Deleuzian text allows, is open to or even calls for. To use a musical metaphor, Foucault is 'jamming' with Deleuze, and Deleuze's one-line footnote 'jams' a little toot in return: 'What will people think of us?'

## Deleuze and Alice/D(odgson)

It would be wrong to suppose that drugs play a greater role than any other element in the ensemble of 'molecular' elements which comprise Deleuze's *Logic of Sense*. They are not in any case isolable as such; they are rather discernible in the connections they forge. Various drugs appear and in multiple guises in Deleuze's writings, by way of the use he makes of the likes of Burroughs (junk) Artaud (peyote), Michaux (mescaline), Fitzgerald (alcohol), as well as in his later direct comments on drugs (discussed below). Deleuze is undoubtedly very interested, and overtly so, in at least the cultural 'side-effects' of various drugs, especially their figuring in relation to literary-artistic productions of the 'high culture' of the West. Given the focus in *Logic of Sense* on the writings of Lewis Carroll, their 'side-effects' are clearly not approached principally in terms of biographical expressions of individual experience – say, of the authors of the texts referred to – they figure rather in a 'series'; a series linking 'literature' or 'literary culture' to culture in general. Drugs and their effects are relevant to the Deleuzian philosophising which conjoins with them, and which Foucault admiringly claims holds the power to explode the 'catatonic theatre', or stage (in both senses) of the philosophy of Reason – producing as radical an alteration of the modern way of thought as, say, does LSD on the 'normal' cognitive processes of the individual user. Drug effects reorganise and disrupt the production of 'sense'; they both represent and actually figure in the challenge to Reason that Foucault identifies closely with. They cross over the literal/metaphorical and actual/virtual divides and confuse the issue of whether actual drug effects and figurative or cultural side-effects can ever be disentangled. There is a meditation here on the 'difference' drugs make.

Drugs and drug effects unquestionably figure in the Deleuzian scenario, and Foucault's 'comparison' of Deleuzian thought with the effects of drugs, we must assume, primarily serves as his explanation of the effect of Deleuze's writing on the thinking that attempts to come to terms with it or to 'do' something with it. The reference is also, clearly, not merely a rhetorical device – it is not simply a metaphor, and the LSD in question does not play a purely analogical role. Drugs 'proper' unleash a chain reaction along the series, and their 'reality' is, as in the case of everything else, in Deleuze's schema, *a function of their operation within the series* as such. Drugs are incorporated within the 'series of culture' (an idea not a million miles away from what Raymond Williams identified as the 'cultural formation'). This is a matter of the series itself; of the series' materiality, and independent of the detail of whether Deleuze or Foucault personally incorporate such substances into their own physical bodies. The point is that the 'culture of drugs' is discernible in the traces it leaves everywhere. The distinction between the inside and outside of literature, for Deleuze, refers only to locations within the series constituting culture as a whole. In this sense there is no escaping drugs and drug effects for they have entered into the chains of connectivity, the very material of the language and the concepts by which we communicate and think.

## Deleuze's mathematisation of the series and the function 'LSD'

Foucault's reference to LSD, then, is neither unwarranted nor as casual as it may first appear: it is not simply an aside to readers who might be 'in the know', nor is it an appeal to 'experience' at all. In fact, 'curiouser and curiouser', as Alice says, it links in with something Deleuze proposes concerning the nature of 'events' in *Logic of Sense*, specifically in the section 'Ninth Series of the Problematic'. This link in the thirty-four series (plus appendices) comprising the work as a whole opens with the question 'What is an ideal event?', which is then answered with reference to Lewis Carroll's 'recreational mathematics', which in turn is linked at a single point in the text, anchored perhaps, to LSD: '*("LSD, a function of great value...")*' (Deleuze, 1990: 56). The pararentheses, italics and dots are all Deleuze's: the function of LSD is actually emphasised by means of every typographical possibility at his disposal. But, before we get to the 'function' (of) 'LSD' and to the questions of what a 'function' – mathematical or pragmatic – is or can be used for, and what the limits of its use are, we must recall the function of this Ninth element in the series of *Logic of Sense*.

The problematic addressed in the 'Ninth Series' chapter of *Logic of Sense* deals with the functioning and the connectivity of the series as such, and with the 'singularity' of the event. It begins thus:

> What is an ideal event? It is a singularity – or rather a set of singularities or of singular points characterising a mathematical curve, a physical state of affairs or a psychological and moral person. Singularities are turning points and points of inflection; bottlenecks, knots, foyers, and centres; points of fusion, condensation and boiling; points of tears, and joy, sickness and health, hope and anxiety, sensitive points. Such singularities, however, should not be confused either with the personality of the one expressing him- or herself in discourse, or with the individuality of a state of affairs designated by the proposition, or even with the generality or universality of a concept signified by a figure or a curve. (Deleuze, 1990: 52)

Each point both belongs to the series and is the source of another, adjacent series. In so far as the Ninth Series theorises the infinite connectivity of the series as such, its (own) singularity is defined by this highly, if not purely, 'theoretical' function – but without compromising its status as being 'just' a part of the series. The theory and practice of *Logic of Sense* are not, therefore, two different things. More importantly, they serve to show that the connectivity which it addresses denies the traditional epistemological distinction between 'literature' and 'the world' (of persons, sufferings, joys, places, situations and so on). Each and every series is equally to be regarded as *a specific 'materialisation' of the world*.

Once again then to that footnote, once more unto the breach of ill-humour: Deleuze's comment, coming as it does in the context of

Foucault's celebratory characterisation of his philosophy as operating between the horns of perversity and ill-humour, may be also be read as articulated laughter – and a species of philosophical 'good humour' – at the apparent suggestion that his thought flows from a drugged-up state of mind. It also expresses a certain solidarity and acknowledgment of the appropriateness of Foucault's dropping LSD into the text at the point at which he does this. Foucault is following suite, as it were, with Deleuze's reference to LSD in Ninth Series, which identifies it explicitly as a 'function of great value'.

If we suppose, somewhat eccentrically, though with the 'support' of both Deleuze and Foucault as outlined so far, that the *Logic of Sense* can be said to anchored around the half sentence '*("LSD, a function of great value...")*', then it is indeed anchored, paradoxically and provocatively, to one of the most potent symbols, and indeed most potent substances, known, for bringing about a 'cutting free' of thought from normal sense; from reality, sanity, selfhood and everything traditionally regarded as being dependent on a (normal) logic of sense governing our concepts and the unity and continuity of the subject who thinks them. And, it is by way of the 'LSD logic' which the *Logic of Sense* itself espouses and exploits that the following link in the 'series' of this chapter will now be made: I cut to Zabriske Point.

## Zabriske Point

The film *Zabriske Point* (Antonioni, 1969) provides one of the most enduring images of the will to destroy the modern: the explosion of an ultra-modern desert dwelling, symbolic at once of the mastery over nature which goes hand in hand with alienated, domestic consumerism. To the music of Pink Floyd, the magnificent symbol of consumerist-domesticity, the ideal home, is exploded and re-exploded into millions of projectiles colliding in slow motion. For this reason alone, there could not have been a more appropriate place than this for one of modernity's most radical and enduring critics to have undergone his 'most severe exercise in depersonalisation' (Miller 1994: 245, citing Deleuze) – by pharmacological means.

Foucault's first and reportedly only LSD experience, in Death Valley (in May 1975), as his biographer Miller records, came many years after the quirky introjection of LSD into the discussion of Deleuze's thought in *Theatrum* (Miller, 1994: 247). There was in those remarks, therefore, strictly speaking, no 'comparison' being made with an 'LSD-experience', nor, I suggest, any appeal to 'experience' as such. This is significant because in so far as 'LSD' figures in Foucault's engagement with Deleuze's thinking at the time, the 'function of LSD' was an event of pure figurality: that is to say, his remarks make sense, like all statements which make sense (as Foucault's early works show) within a discursive system – the relevant subset of which could be called 'the hallucinogenic-drug-effect-idiom circa 1970'. Communication and exchange between Foucault and Deleuze and their readers via the LSD function is possible owing to the degree of the investment of each in the currency of such a drug-effect idiom (the ways of talking about drug effects, for which the participating speaker does not need to be 'experienced' drug user at all) and, of course, also because 'LSD' is a 'function' of the *Logic of Sense* itself. Deleuze's discourse and the idiom of the LSD effect share in a certain logic, and consequently each can be used to communicate something of the other. Foucault's reference to LSD merely picks up on something of general significance with respect to that function of sense that Deleuze himself had already identified with LSD. Dropping LSD into the commentary is a 'reverberatory' sort of thing – a word Foucault uses to describe it and a word which resonates with the 'LSD-logic' of Deleuze's philosophy. It amplifies the associative possibilities Deleuze's text proposes. It also represents the possibility of an 'inversion' or 'slippage' within the order of discourse which determines the logic of the relation between the philosopher and thought in general.

Foucault's work had shown in considerable detail how the self was a function of the discursive 'order'. To think of the thinker in terms of his or her individual incarnation, as an author with a proper name, is the mark of a deeply 'humanist' tendency, and one which Foucault always resisted. By (re)introducing LSD into the discussion, and suggesting how Deleuze's thought is organised by an LSD-logic, he highlights its resources for resisting this tendency to return to author-ity and the practices of 'interpretation' and hermeneutical thinking aimed at the recovery of meaning.

## From the self as a function of discourse to self-stylisation

Foucault's work up to around 1975 and the time of his LSD trip had, in different contexts and in relation to his wide-ranging critique of the human sciences, shown how the idea of 'man' functioned as the organising principle of humanist knowledge. Man, as the 'subject' of humanist knowledge at the centre of modern disciplinary forms of inquiry, he famously found to be a 'recent invention' (Foucault, 1970:386–7). The seemingly natural sense of self at the heart of the humanist cultural enterprise deriving from the Enlightenment was a contingent 'effect' of the specific cultural totality in which it appeared. Making sense of the world and modern self-understanding were, within a given system of thought, correlative to one another. *The Order of Things* impressively demonstrated this in its detailed analyses of other historico-cultural constellations – 'The Renaissance', 'The Classical Age' as well as 'The Age of Man'. It showed how meaning and selfhood are in each case related and configured by the cultural whole. The decentring of the subject as a feature of postmodern cultural critique is heavily indebted to this aspect of Foucauldian thinking, which shifts the epistemological privilege away from self-consciousness toward the discursive materiality of 'statements' and *epistemes. Logic of Sense*, read against this background, exemplifies the possibility of a form of creative subversion of the prevailing discourse and its controlling systems of 'sense'. And, as I have noted, it investigates the manner in which this 'subversion' is played out horizontally on the 'surface' of language (for example, in Lewis Carroll), but it also proposes a dimension of verticality, or 'depth' (explored, for example, by contrasting Carrollian and Artaudian poetics in the 'Thirteenth Series of the Schizophrenic and the Little Girl'). It is to this dimension of depth that I shall now turn, linking the discussion so far to the theme of Foucault's encounter with LSD proper.

The symbolic function of LSD for Foucault in *Theatrum*, or the value the LSD function 'returns' (as mathematicians say), is that it has the power to zap the centre of control governing the grammatical and syntactical 'surface' of language. This neutralisation of the logical centre of sense and, conterminally, the self-centring notion of 'Man' in the production of sense, I now wish to argue, plays a key part in redirecting Foucault's thought toward 'the self' as he came to speak of it later. This 'self' in the later Foucault is not at all the self configured on or at the surface of discourse, it is rather, as he develops his notion of it in the *History of Sexuality* series, 'the self in relation to itself', or as he comes to call it, the *oneself*. When Foucault experienced his acid trip at Zabriske Point, the 'logical', horizontal vector with respect to LSD became one of 'depth' and verticality, in that it could be described as an exercise on that supremely localised element of the 'series', the materialised cultural practice of 'the self in relation to itself' or *oneself.* The power of LSD to 'depersonalise' the subject and to induce a state in which the coherence and stability of individual identity are shaken is well known. To expose oneself to its effects in this direct, chemical manner through bodily incorporation is to expose oneself to an experience of the unbridled contingency of the processes by which coherence and identity come to appear fixed and natural *in the body itself.* It is an extreme, experimental undertaking and a wilful intervention in the processes by which one maintains oneself as oneself. No matter how reckless it may *be judged* to be, it is an experiment of some significance when viewed against the backdrop of Foucault's claims that the humanist subject is a socio-historical and cultural contingency and an epiphenomenon of the prevailing system of thought.

Whilst Foucault, up to this point, may have established the basis for *understanding* the possibility of a subject otherwise than it is, such thinking cannot 'think' the processes of *becoming otherwise.* Actually taking LSD is an experimental leap into an abyss of 'self-destruction' and an actualisation of becoming-otherwise.

In what follows I intend to regard the 'LSD' trip at Zabriske Point, *figuratively* at least, as a turning point in Foucault's thought in the direction of becoming *otherwise* – something I shall approach here with the help of Deleuze. I stress 'figuratively' because I am not claiming that Zabriske Point was an intellectually decisive 'experience' for Foucault 'personally', above all others, such that it serves as a pivot around which the relation between the earlier and later Foucault might perhaps now be understood, biographically. I am merely suggesting that his later thinking subsequently came to consider directly the 'vertical', or depth axis of the body–discourse relation. In fact I am suggesting that such a redirection of his thought was possible only on the basis of the materialist theory of discourse both he and Deleuze had already critically expounded and explored: only because of such decentrings of the humanist subject and rejection of the regimes of truth and sense which give rise to forms of modern self-understanding could the dimension of 'depth' be redefined otherwise than in terms of the various manifestations of 'depth-psychology'. This was possible only after the 'poststructuralist' critique of the 'deep self' conceived on the basis of essentialist metaphysics. I am not therefore interested here in speculating about Foucault's subjective response to actually trying LSD.[6]

Taking the drug LSD allows direct experimentation on the nerve centres of the self and on its singular connection with Reason. Everything that Foucault had said about 'madness' served to explain its meaning and

manifestation within the *episteme* of Reason. The 'madman' was identified as a figure of 'excess', as exorbitant and transgressive, a figure to
whom Reason responds by institutionalising, controlling, excluding and
designating as its 'other'. He was not concerned with the experiential
or psychological condition of madness, as if these notions were independent of the discourses in which they operated. In fact, the very notion
of an 'interiority' of either madness or Reason is ontologically undercut
in Foucault's earlier work, and interiority, in the ordinary sense of the
word, is regarded as an effect of the constellation of modern discourses
constituting the 'age of man'. For this reason Foucault's later concerns
with individual existence and 'technologies of selfhood', which have been
perceived as a 'return to the subject' in his work, may superficially appear
to go against the basic thrust of his view of the materiality of discourse.
For example, it has been argued that to the degree to which Foucault's
thinking had rejected *any* notion of intentional, volitional autonomy for
the individual subject, he had effectively closed off the prospect of an
emancipatory account of the human condition. I wish to argue, however,
that the rotation between horizontal and vertical axes of 'discourse' and
'practical self-experimentation' in Foucault's earlier and later work can
be understood on a narcoanalytical basis – in this case taking LSD as the
*logical* point of 'inversion', rather than as a personal, biographical detail.
The 'LSD effect' links, rather, the horizontal and vertical dimensions of
'language' and 'the body' respectively.

    This 'inversion', which in his comments on Deleuze in *Theatrum
Foucault* attributed to the LSD-effect ('LSD inverts the relationships of ill-
humour, stupidity and thought'), involves not a 'return' to the humanist
subject but a redirection of thought along another axis, one which led
him to consider the processes by which the self exists as a *oneself*. Rather
than thinking of this as an act of autonomous subjective self-reflexivity
and an immanent movement of interiority, in the second and third
volumes of *The History of Sexuality* (Foucault, 1985, 1986) in the contexts
of Greek and Roman antiquity, Foucault attempts to show how the *oneself*
fashioned itself out of its 'cultural exteriority'; out of the cultural totality
and the ethos of its time. In support of this materialist view of a self which
is formed by a fold of exteriority, he provides examples of how such 'self-
styling' can be independent of the 'deep self' that modernity considers to
be the manifestation of a universal human essence. He finds evidence for
this view in the literature of antiquity which records forms of selfhood
realised purely through *external* relations to *external* standards; pure

*praxes*, or 'conducts', related to such things as diet, training, the home, marriage, and especially in sexual practices. The *oneself* in such conducts becomes what it is prior to its becoming an object of reflection in the human sciences. Individual existence is thus described as a 'stylisation of conduct', performed by individuals wishing 'to give their existence the most graceful and accomplished form possible' (Foucault, 1986: 250–1) – hence Foucault's description of such individualities as forms of existence in an *aesthetic* mode.[7]

This axis of 'depth' (as defined thus with reference to Deleuze's terminology in *Logic of Sense*) does not refer, then, to a notion of the 'deep self', rather to a highly localised domain of cultural practices, namely those of *the body*. The body is not the container of the person or the mind but the medium of cultural activity and a site of various cultural practices. Intention and volition are not, therefore, conceptually distinct capacities of the intellect as opposed to the practices the subject engages in; they do not come 'first' or lead to action.

Ironically, much critical reading of these Foucauldian texts has sought to 'translate' them back into the discourses of 'the social' and into the language of the sociologised Foucault which has dominated Foucauldian studies; readings which in one way or another are preoccupied with the sociological anatomy of the 'docile body'. But the approach I have taken here, on the basis of Deleuze's reading of Foucault especially, seeks, by way of the drug theme, to stick with the active 'self-styling' dimension of *becoming-oneself*. This distinction, and these two dimensions, I contend, cannot be translated into one another. This is something that Deleuze makes clear in his treatment and comparison of that theatrical, self-styled, ethno-pharmacologist and prodigious drug experimenter Antonin Artaud and the nonsense poet Lewis Carroll.

## Artaud and the artistry of depth

To get a better sense of what is at stake in the difference between surface and depth effects – a perspective attained by means of LSD – let us return briefly to *Logic of Sense* and to how this distinction is made in Deleuze's exploration, in the Thirteenth Series, of two kinds of nonsense. The two antithetical species of nonsense are presented in the work of Carroll and Artaud: nonsense for little girls and schizophrenic nonsense. This juxtaposition permits Deleuze to make a remarkable comparative investigation of the nonsense which depends on the surface effects of language, which a 'clever' poet such as Carroll is able to exploit, and the nonsense which is emitted from the depths of a 'schizophrenic body' such as Artaud's. Artaud's 'translation' of Carroll's poem *Jabberwocky* [8] serves to highlight how the body, language and meaning are connected and how surface and depth are related to one another.

Briefly: Carroll's mastery of lexical, syntactic and grammatic systems, his use of portmanteau words and a full range of linguistic figures and so on, is nowhere better illustrated than in his poem *Jabberwocky*. Deleuze, reiterating Artaud's own diagnosis, says that the poem is the work of a 'little pervert, who holds onto the establishment of a surface language, and who has not felt the real problem of a language in depth – namely, the schizophrenic problem of suffering, of death and of life' (Deleuze, 1990: 84). Artaud describes Carroll's relation to language as intellectual and snobbish, and *Jabberwocky* as 'the work of a profiteer who, satiated after a fine meal, seeks to indulge himself in the pain of others' (Deleuze, 1990: 84). He sees in Carroll's relation to language a reflection of his social position and sense of being at home in the bourgeois culture of his time. In stark contrast, the 'genius' Artaud suffers his every utterance in his body: 'for him there is not, there is no longer, any surface' and his 'body is no longer anything but depth' (Deleuze, 1990: 86–7). Meaning is a function of the movements of his 'flesh', his muscles, bodily retentions and ejaculations, quivering expulsions of breath, giving rise to gurglings, screamings, gruntings, all painfully shaped into sound-words, breath-words, which are despatched to the surface where the rest of humanity will hear them often only as gibbering 'nonsense' – not at all the best kind of wordsmithery for entertaining children. Artaud's discourse is clinically schizotypal: it contains articulation disorders, timing and rhythm disorders, vocal disorders and symbolisation disorders. Artaud was a schizophrenic who was often unable to operate at the surface at all and, quite literally, he suffered the consequences.

The example of Artaud's relationship to language stands to illustrate how both language and life are experienced when they are articulated and lived almost entirely along the axis of depth. And the LSD-effect can similarly be viewed with the emphasis on the vertical dimension of the body and related to the work of the later Foucault. Foucault's account of individual 'aesthetic existence' of the 'self-styling subject' who fashions itself through the 'performance of conducts' involves the management of the surface/depth axis of individual life. Somewhere between the two extremes, of joining the 'catatonic dumbshow of stupidity' and wearing the straitjacket of conformity on the one hand, or 'going mad' and being straitjacketed by social service authorities on the other, each individual undertakes the creative work of becoming *oneself.* Foucault's later interest in subjective individuality is far from a 'return' to the subject of Enlightenment humanism he had so thoroughly sought to displace; it describes rather an involution of the surface of the discursive cultural whole through the 'practices' of selfhood. It is through such 'practice' that the dimension of depth is formed. And, to 'know' something of this depth, one must undertake, at least to a degree, an encounter with the other of Reason and expose oneself to certain experiences of 'madness'. If Deleuze's work might at times be called a kind of 'philosophy on acid' then it is very explicitly so. It is a conscious effort to philosophise in a way which neither plummets to Artaudian psychotic depths nor skims fatuously across the Carrollian surface of culture.

In Foucault's earlier studies, the artist was often privileged as a figure of such liminality: operating at the limits of a given *episteme* the artist's creative act, the artwork, exposes something of the processes of epistemic totalisation characteristic of the age, especially along the fault-lines of transition. Foucault's later focus on the cultural practices of self-hood verticalises and localises that liminality in the individual body. This body is the materialisation of each individual becoming, or self-styling of (each) *oneself,* out of the cultural whole. LSD-logic, we have seen, can function to disrupt the patterns of meaning which flow across the surface of language and the cultural landscape of meaning, but when LSD is taken directly into the body, causing alterations at the level of its substantive materialisation, then it has the power to collapse the surface of meaning completely; it may plunge the user into another dimension. This does not mean that it necessarily produces a full-on psychotic or schizoid disorder, or that the user will experience Artaudian suffering. But, to the degree to which it launches its user into the orbit of madness (to an altitude where one is likely to come across a panoply of philosophers, artists, cultural theorists, actors, hippies, party-goers and others), it causes an oscillation in the subject between the axes of surface and depth. The self experiences itself as a gradient between these, and whether it gives rise to an egoless skimming across the surface of communications or to a plummeting into the depths of solitudinous paranoia is perhaps a contingent matter, and a measure of the risk involved in experimentation. What it reveals is something of the dimensional components of the self and its becomings in the self–world constellation.

In Foucault's account of 'self-styling' this dimension of depth is something an individual accomplishes; one fashions oneself, not out of the depths of suffering (as in Artaud's case) but by giving oneself depth by means of a 'folding' of the surface: forming oneself by exploiting the difference between surface and depth, or, as Deleuze puts it, in his reading of Foucault, forming an inside by making folds in the 'outside', by 'bending' the outside. This kind of 'self-creation' figures at the level of the individualised or localised field of cultural practice known as 'the body', but it does not imply that such an individual transcends the prevailing, historical, 'impersonal' formations of culture in general. The *oneself* morphs itself out of the available cultural material. Deleuze represents the distinction between Foucault's earlier analyses of socio-cultural totalities and his later emphasis on the self-styling *oneself* in terms of a shift of location along the surface/depth gradient. Thought traverses a sort of cultural and historical surface, but the artwork of the artist and the self-artistry of every individual also 'bends' this surface of rational 'normality' into new forms, producing new meanings and a specific dimension of depth. In this respect, as Deleuze's account of Artaud contra Carroll shows, the 'critical', or horizontal, surface and the 'clinical', or vertical, depth, are formally and theoretically distinguishable and can be critically contrasted (this is indeed the work of the philosopher-commentator), but in the case of any actual *oneself*, they are in practice inseparable.

## The LSD function and the surface–depth gradient

Deleuze's diagrammatic and topological metaphors lead us to re-pose the question of the 'effects' of drugs along the vertical axis – of LSD, for instance, taken 'substantively', or directly into the body. Its potency is such that it may cause a fracture, a distinctive 'crack' in the meaningful surface, thereby shattering the self whose unity is experienced only on the basis of its being locked, horizontally, and 'safely', into meaningful structures of the syntactic and grammatical connectivity by which its world is materialised.[9] In *Logic of Sense* Deleuze provides a framework for graphing the two axes of nonsense and madness. LSD is a 'useful function' which can take these two parameters and compute the gradient of selfhood. The LSD gradient touches the 'degree zero' point of language and the body and of experimentation with respect to the self: its two co-ordinates meet (or at least can be extrapolated in reverse to the zero point of radical depersonalisation or nonsense). LSD serves both experimentally and logically (as it does in Foucault's commentary on Deleuze in *Theatrum*) to reveal how becoming a subject in relation to a discursively ordered cultural totality is always a matter of 'co-ordination' between the two. A singular point on the graph is always a function of the two co-ordinates. An individual may have a zero value on one of the two axes: for example a fictional character such as Alice is entirely without depth, Artaud (who is pure body) at the other extreme is without surface. Foucault's notion of 'self-styling' refers to the general process by which individuals 'locate' themselves and engage in practices of becoming. The living individual can thus be considered as the self-originating 'artist' of his or her own existence – whether deemed conformist or transgressive by others – without denying the historical and cultural reality in which the specific act of self-creation is accomplished. This 'oneself' styles itself in a comparable way to which the artist becomes who or what he or she is through the creation of an artwork. These axes of surface and depth are evident in Foucault's work, where the creativity of artistic production and aesthetic self-creation touch upon each other. Let's just recall what Foucault says about this notion of aesthetic existence: it refers to

> those intentional and voluntary actions by which men not only set themselves rules of conduct but also seek to transform themselves, to change themselves in their singular being, and to make life into an *oeuvre* that carries certain aesthetic values and meets certain stylistic criteria. (Foucault, 1986: 10–11)

This fusing of aesthetic and practical conducts in becoming oneself has its counterpart in the role assigned to art elsewhere in several of Foucault's writings, where he repeatedly returns to the figure of the artist or poet and the work of art (including 'literary art'), in references, for example, to Van Gogh, Goya, Bataille, De Sade, Blanchot, *Las Meninas*, *Don Quixote*, Roussel, Magritte and, of course, Artaud. The artist or poet and the artwork have a daimonic relation to the ongoing processes of rational totalisation (which gives rise to the historical 'exclusions' of the insane, the sick and the criminal and so on, with which Foucault was directly concerned). The work of art, according to Foucault, is produced within the orbit of 'madness' and in the approach to alterity, and it must repeatedly differentiate itself from it. The field of forces within which the work of art operates becomes apparent at those points at which it is nearest to a collapse into madness; the point at which its extremity constitutes both its resistance to the place assigned to it by Reason and at which the risk of its tether to Reason finally breaking are greatest.

> A work of art opens a void, a moment of silence, a question without
> answer, provokes a breach without reconciliation where the world is
> forced to question itself... The madness in which the work of art is
> engulfed is the space of our enterprise, it is the endless path to fulfilment,
> it is our mixed vocation of apostle and exegete. (Foucault, 1965: 288)

Art is accredited with accomplishing a reflexive moment which exceeds
'the age' to which it ostensibly belongs. It generates a discursive movement which is somehow surplus to history and a new space is thereby
constituted. Such an artwork works at the borders of systems of thought
without being drawn back into them. In *Order of Things*, in his account
of the discontinuous series of *epistemes*, it is to Cervantes's figure of
*Don Quixote* that Foucault turns to illustrate the transition between
the Renaissance and the Classical Age, and it is Velázquez's *Las Meninas*
which bears the trace of the moment of transition between the Classical
Age and the Age of Man. These works of art function in this way, trans-
gressively; without being wholly caught up in either the preceding or the
coming system. The work of art works outside of historical time, the time
of continuity; it works on the borders and in 'in-between time' marking
like a dye the limits of the systems of thought Foucault delineated.

It is not surprising that the workings of the work of art on the
borders between systems of thought later continues to serve as the principal trope by which he attempts to think, non-transcendentally and non-
metaphorically, beyond the modern system of representation in order to
articulate the idea of the immanence of becoming oneself. To become
who one is, is to become something of an artist and a little mad: it is, to
borrow another expression from Deleuze's commentary on Foucault, to
fashion oneself creatively by 'folding' the 'outside of thought' (Deleuze,
1988: 94–123). 'Folding' is the exercise, or practice, of thought.

The LSD effect marks the zero point of the apostle–exegete
dichotomy: knowledge and desire are fused in the depths of the body of
the apostle (a clinical condition) but 'to speak' he or she must bend the
surface down to form this depth by articulating the exegetical (or critical)
co-ordinate. This is a project which is 'engulfed in madness' according to
Foucault. This is a dramatic claim and indeed and, on one level at least, a
'bid for infamy' on Foucault's part, but it also links back into the issue of
why Deleuze would think it 'strange and implausible' for Foucault to allow
his thought to become too engulfed in 'madness itself'. Foucault's thinking
is, of course, neither a rearticulation of aestheticist criticism, nor does it
aim to bring about an actual collapse into the depths of discombobulated

Unreason. Changing dimensions involves passing through the null point of this theoretico-practical dimensionality itself. Artaudian 'infra-sense' and Carrollian surveyance of surfaces are perpendicular to one another, and 'only the commentator', as Deleuze says, can address these crossed axiologies (Deleuze, 1990: 93). 'Commentary' – theory in effect – involves plotting a gradient between the two axes. Foucault's exploration of the depth axis of LSD, at Zabriske Point, complements, but is not identical to, Deleuze's experiments with LSD logic. That this event or experiment roughly coincides with the redirection of his thought toward the practical exercises he later associates with *becoming oneself* begs the whole question of how 'drugs' which 'alter thought' might also be considered to a practical technology of such becoming.

### Deleuze, drugs and the 'folding of thought'

In the chapter of his book *Foucault*, entitled 'Foldings or the Inside of Thought (Subjectivation)', Deleuze presents a remarkable account of how the many different aspects of Foucauldian thought relate to one another on the basis of the paradoxical topology of interiority and exteriority. 'Foucault's thought' is presented not as a cartography of the surface of culture but as an originary *distortion* of that surface:

> It is as if the relations of the outside folded back to create a doubling, allow a relation to oneself to emerge and constitute an inside which is hollowed out and develops its own unique dimension: 'enkrateia', the relation to oneself that is self-mastery. (Deleuze, 1988: 100)

'Aesthetic existence' in Foucault is that involuted form of artistic creation, the surface folded in such a way as to produce the 'interiority' of the self. And I now wish to consider, on the basis of this Deleuzian theoretico-topology of 'folding', the idea of drugs as a technology of self-formation.

The drug LSD is a chemical means of plunging oneself into the depths of pure intensity, on an almost vertical gradient, almost parallel to that of the schizophrenic – therein lies its experimental (clinical) value and the correlated (critical) significance of Artaud to Foucault and Deleuze alike. It represents a possible means of experimentation in Alice-like free-fall and the opportunity to crash test fictionality into the wall of material thought. To have any chance of making any sense of the outcome of such an experiment, the test data must be processed in the critico-clinical frame of reference, which I have derived here from Foucault and

Deleuze, precisely for this purpose. The LSD experience is not, as noted at the outset, one of the revelation of a truth: such 'revelations of truth' are but provisional 'truth effects' which circulate on the surface of language. In other words, such 'truths' – whether identified as rational or mystical – are examples of the infinite number of pure fictions. This does not amount to an *a priori* denial of the power of the drug to impact on the processes of critical thought and what critical thought comes to 'understand' differently as a consequence of experimenting with a drug such as LSD. But to use the drug's effect as a technological aid to becoming-oneself is to acknowledge its power to distort the horizontal surface of sense to the point of making it crack or tear. In order to make 'critical' use of it then (rather than confusing its effects with miraculous revelations) one has to understand something of how its 'clinical' vector is accomplished by means of a 'folding' of that surface; in other words to think of it as a tool for re-forming thought *and thereby oneself.* The shift in approach of the later Foucault toward the subject's *mastery over* rather than *subjection to* desire can thus be seen in terms of a shift of focus from the 'docile' to the 'intensive' body.

On the basis of the discussion here so far, it appears there are indeed good reasons to suppose that LSD, and no doubt other drugs, can function as such technological agents of individual creative becoming. They have this power by virtue of the linkages they make and unmake between the intensive body (the 'body without organs', a term Deleuze adopts from Artaud) and the surface of discourse. And, it is therefore reasonable to suggest that drugs could serve the undertaking of making the subject-life of 'oneself' a work of art. Doing so, however, is a dangerous undertaking for it requires a certain mastery of the 'gradient' along which a fall into schizophrenic madness remains one extreme possibility and a fall into mysticism another. On the 'vertical' and often vertiginous axis of self-becoming, the evaluation of the 'usefulness' of a drug such as LSD would have to be measured purely in terms of the immanent processes of self-production or self-creation, in defiance of any external criteria of *judgement.* In fact an entirely new 'drugs expertise' is called for, one which is a form of 'life skill' with regard to 'experimentation and unforeseen becomings'.[10]

In the last section of this chapter, I shall turn to Deleuze's and Guattari's later discussion of drugs in order to discuss why Deleuze became thoroughly sceptical about the possibilities of drugs successfully being used in this way.

## Deleuze and Guattari on the limits, uses and abuses of psychotropic drugs

Deleuze returns directly to the subject of drugs, the use of drugs and 'drug users' in *A Thousand Plateaux*, in the section entitled 'Becoming-Intense, Becoming-Animal, Becoming Imperceptible', where he addresses explicitly the issue of drugs as 'agents of becoming' (Deleuze and Guattari, 1992: 232–309).

Deleuze and Guattari here argue against the discourses of drugs which tend to see in them the means of establishing and sustaining a 'plane of immanence', by fixing their meaning, overriding or erasing their differences and thereby producing a 'drug assemblage'. It would be a mistake, they argue, to suppose that drugs are constitutive of a 'plane' – a plane, roughly translated into a more Foucauldian idiom, is a discursively defined space, a 'world of drugs'; a coherent, self-defining 'materialisation' supportive of certain forms of drug heroics (such as those discernible for example in Castaneda, Artaud, Michaux or the Beat poets). Despite the implicit recognition of differences concerning the specificity of drugs and their effects (the 'molecular' plurality of drugs being reflected in the diversity of the drug culture texts such as the above authors are represent-ative of), there is a tendency, say Deleuze and Guattari, for everything to 'reconnect'. Such reconnection of elements into a discursive 'drug assem-blage' amounts to the *fusion* of perception and desire: perception seems filled up by desire as they coincide. No wonder then, they note, that 'there is a discourse on drugs current today that does no more than dredge up generalities on pleasure and misfortune, on difficulties in communica-tion', and 'the more incapable people are of grasping a specific causality in extension (that is, the specific materialisation of their lives), the more they pretend to understand the phenomenon in question' (Deleuze and Guattari, 1992: 283). They continue further:

> It is our belief that the issue of drugs can be understood only at the level where desire directly invests perception, and perception becomes molecular at the same time as the imperceptible is perceived. Drugs then appear as the agent of this becoming. (Deleuze and Guattari, 1992: 283).

This expresses the view that it is *only* in the closed discursive world of a certain 'drug culture', and only in the eyes of the user, that drugs appear as agents of becoming. Deleuze and Guattari think of the drugs plane as an insular plane, one which limits, rather than extends, the possibilities of becoming. They claim that the 'deterritorialisations' produced by drugs are 'compensated for by the most abject reterritorialisations', such as drug addictions and compulsions to repeat (as is the case with opiates, amphetamines, cocaine), but also with reference to Artaud and Michaux (who shared a taste for hallucinogens) they recall the 'negative effects' of loss of control, erroneous perceptions and 'bad feelings':

> Drug addicts continually fall back into what they wanted to escape: a segmentarity all the more rigid for being marginal, a territorialisation all the more artificial for being based on chemical substances, hallucinatory forms and phantasy subjectifications. Drug addicts may be considered as precursors or experimenters who tirelessly blaze new paths of life, but their cautiousness lacks the foundation of caution. So they either join the legion of false heroes who follow their conformist path of a little death and a long fatigue. Or, what is worse, all they will have done is make an attempt only nonusers or former users can resume and benefit from, secondarily rectifying the always aborted plane of drugs, discovering through drugs what drugs lack for a construction of the plane of consistency. (Deleuze and Guattari, 1992: 285)

Their thesis on drugs and drug users, despite its overwhelming rejection of drugs as a fuel for 'becoming', criticises but does not entirely deride the risk taking of others who attempt to use them in this way. They only deride the failure on the part of the user to recognise the dead end, or limits of the plane of drug effects, their use of drugs leads to. They recognise the cultural benefits of the experiments of others and sincerely pose the question of whether it is 'cowardice or exploitation to wait until others have taken the risks'. They answer their own question in the negative but also, rather unconvincingly, suggest that abstinence is 'joining in the middle, while changing the means'. It is only abstainers and non-users, they say, who are able to capitalise on what they can 'observe' of such experiments. By such a strategy the drugs theorist avoids the mistake drug takers often make – which is to keep starting over again 'from ground zero'. In other words, drug takers tend not notice that 'the drugs don't work'. That is, they don't ever 'reach the point where "to get high or not to get high" is no longer the question' (Deleuze and Guattari, 1992: 286). Drug takers will tend to be unable to affirm a 'line of flight' and make a positive choice in favour of (the materialisation of) life, and unable to see how drugs are linked to a line of 'death and abolition'.

On one level we must surely agree with Deleuze and Guattari: only on the basis of 'abstinence' can there be philosophy and critical thought – even if that thinking is 'anti-philosophical' in the sense in which this can be said of Deleuze's, Deleuze's and Guattari's, and Foucault's own thought. It is after all incumbent upon the 'commentator' to maintain the ability to 'change dimensions' (Deleuze, 1990: 93) without becoming stranded on a plane where he or she is duped into thinking that drug-induced 'becomings' are affirmations of existence: 'What good does it do', they ask, 'to perceive as a quick-flying bird if speed and movement continue to escape somewhere else' (Deleuze and Guattari, 1992: 284). This can be taken as meaning 'why would anyone want to waste their time trying this experiment more than once?' More importantly, why if others have undertaken such experiments does anyone really need to repeat them for him- or herself? Of course, this is a good enough argument in terms of a logic of 'experimentation' associated with their work. But does this stance not also indicate – and on the basis of everything that was earlier learned from Deleuze's juxtaposition of Carroll and Artaud and his own account of the surface/depth distinction – that the comments on drugs in *A Thousand Plateaux* represent a shift up the surface/depth gradient in the direction of the surface? The figure of the 'philosopher' – with whom this discussion began – is, after all, more of a 'little girl' than he or she is a schizophrenic. And are not these philosopher-commentators showing signs of being a little afraid of sinking too far from the surface, the only place where they can make a living? Do they not sometimes show signs of being 'perverts'? And was not that exactly the point at which Foucault provoked Deleuze in *Theatrum* with his reference to LSD?

In any case, that playful gibe, which was about philosophy and its tendency toward perversion and ill-humour, is a bit of dialogue between two thinkers as they both fly, at speeds required to maintaining their 'escape velocities', into the 'orbit of madness'. So this observation of my own is not in any way intended to derogate the brilliantly perceptive analyses of surface/depth in *Logic of Sense* or Deleuze's account of how philosophical thought can be located on a gradient between the two dimensions of nonsense and madness. Artaud, of whom Deleuze says he would not give one page for all of Carroll, becomes accessible to us only to the extent to which the depths of his body were transformed into a unique literary phenomenon: as Deleuze says – 'Artaud is alone in having been an absolute depth in literature' (Deleuze, 1990: 93). Perhaps the pages on drugs and the analysis of the 'drugs assemblage' in *A Thousand Plateaux* can be regarded as Deleuze's 'let me make it clear...' – a continuation of his footnote to Foucault, completed with the help of Guattari. But even so, they complexify rather than simplify the relation of theorising to drugs by linking drugs to a discussion of psychoanalysis. In drawing this chapter to a close now I shall reconstruct their critico-clinical commentary.

In 'The Thirteenth Series' of *Logic of Sense*, Deleuze had spoken of 'bad psychoanalysis' as the 'psychoanalysis of sense'. As it is on 'the surface' that 'the entire logic of sense is located', the psychoanalysis which concerns itself with sense, 'botches' the clinical psychiatric aspect and the literary critical aspect simultaneously. For this reason it is in effect of no use at all for treating Artaud in either clinical or critical terms (Deleuze, 1990: 92–3). The discussion of drugs in *A Thousand Plateaux* develops this view by linking drugs to the production of the plane of immanence of the unconscious, that plane which Deleuze and Guattari say psychoanalysis 'has consistently botched' (1992: 284). What gets 'botched' in both cases is botched by virtue of the *separation* of one plane from the other: the clinical from the critical, the conscious from the unconscious. The same is true, I have suggested in the course of previous chapters, of separating being on drugs and being abstinent. In other words, the botching results in the maintenance of a dualism. The plane of the unconscious becomes a plane of transcendence and that in relation to which psychoanalysis justifies its existence; the 'critical', or linguistic, surface of sense is opposed to the 'clinical', or bodily dimension of depth, and the drugged-up drug user perceives a plane of consistency, 'on drugs', which he or she opposes to the abstinent state of being straight. On drugs, say Deleuze and Guattari, 'you will be full of yourself, you will lose control, you will be on a plane of consistency, in a body without organs, but *at a place where you will always botch them*, empty them, undo what you do' (1992: 285, *my emphasis*). So, psychoanalysis, literary critique and drug use are all 'botched' at the point at which they cut themselves off, territorialise and enclose themselves, on 'planes of consistency'.

Despite this tone, let us be clear, this is not an anti-psychoanalytic, anti-critical, anti-drug invective. Deleuze and Guattari are in fact reaffirming the interconnectivity of all these would-be separate planes of consistency, which *in their work* are found, shown and even forced to cut across and interpenetrate each other. Take drugs as an example: firstly, I reiterate, according to Deleuze and Guattari 'drugs give the unconscious the immanence and plane that psychoanalysis consistently botched' – but they add that this botching can be traced to the point at which psychoanalysis defined itself in opposition to psychopharmacology: 'perhaps the famous cocaine episode marked a turning point that forced Freud to renounce a direct approach to the unconscious' (1992: 284). Secondly, literary critique territorialises the 'surface' of language, 'botching' this enterprise by cutting itself off from the 'clinical': it ends up abandoning Artaud to the psychiatrists. And yet, 'LSD', as we saw above, is said by Deleuze to be 'a function of great value' precisely when it comes to disrupting the 'logic of sense' and enabling the attunement of one's thinking to the dimension of depth. Lastly, to the drugs plane itself: on drugs, literally *on drugs*, high, tripping, stoned, pissed, chilling out and so on, perception coincides with desire and you will become inclined to stay there! Their point is that only as an ex-user or a periodically abstinent user will you get past the point of identifying with the phoney immanence of the drug's effect; the supposed immanence which the user apparently gains by swapping the rhetoric of transcendence for the rhetoric of the drug plane itself. Such a drug user may become a sort of 'body without organs', but in a stillborn, encephalitic form, on a plane largely populated by such characters as mystics, dreamers, dope-heads and lager louts and so on.

None of this denies the 'value' of *passing through* this plane, even repeatedly.

Their clinico-critical advice is, perhaps, keep an eye on the angle of incidence of your approach; don't end up on the horizontal and don't take the Artaudian vertical dive!

## Foucault, Deleuze and the power of drugs

In the context of the conjunction of Foucauldian–Deleuzian–Guattarian thought 'on drugs' it is possible to construct a sort of 'thesis' which refers drugs to a discussion of the inside or outside of thought; to the notional idea of interiority and its relation to its other, the outside. In his interlocution of Foucault in the book Deleuze dedicates to Foucault's thought, he shows how the shift in Foucault's attention from exteriority to interiority can be understood in terms of the reflexive folding of the 'outside of thought', which, he argues, Foucault's own thought accomplishes, leading to new understanding of the inside. He says that this was a 'permanent theme' in Foucault and was already analysed in depth in his book *Raymond Roussel*:

> For what Raymond Roussel had discovered was the phrase of the outside, its repetition in a second phrase, the minuscule difference between he two (the snag [*l'arroc*]) and the twisting and doubling from one to the other. (Deleuze, 1988: 98)

Although neither Foucault nor Deleuze have written much directly on the drugs theme, this chapter has shown that drugs none the less figure in relation to their contributions to understanding the becoming of the self-styling subject; and in fact that drugs were, in their cross-commentary, never very far away. With reference to Deleuze we have been able to extrapolate the Foucauldian idea of an inside, or interiority, whose 'identity' is produced solely on the basis of a localised intensification of (external) power (relations): 'in all his work Foucault seems haunted by this theme of an inside which is merely a fold of the outside, as if the ship were a folding of the sea' (Deleuze, 1988: 97). It is impossible to imagine a more perceptive reading of Foucault than that which Deleuze has provided in this book. However, Deleuze's own thinking on the production 'immanence' in work undertaken with Guattari, when it turns to the question of drugs as agents of becoming, makes it clear that there are no technologies of selfhood and becoming which are transcendent, 'wholly outside' or distinct from the 'molecules' of becoming constituting the life of an interiority. 'Drugs' are not simply a chemico-technology of becoming, and to suppose that they are (and to take them that way) would be to lock oneself into a plane on which the kind of self-*mastery* Foucault speaks of would actually tend to be abnegated, closing off rather than opening up thought. Drugs represent the risk of reinstating a plane of repetition and a metaphysical idea of 'truth': 'drug users believed that drugs would grant them a plane, when in fact a plane must distil its own drugs, remaining master of speeds and proximities' (Deleuze and Guattari, 1992: 286).

## Notes

1 M. Foucault, *Folie et déraison: Histoire de la folie à l'âge classique*, Paris: Plon, 1961, abridged and trans. R. Howard as *Madness and Civilisation: A History of Insanity in the Age of Reason*, New York: Random House, 1965.

2 Foucault's use of the phrase 'madness itself' in this work was to become the centre of a famous and protracted disagreement between Foucault and Derrida. Derrida's text 'Cogito and the History of Madness' (1978: 31–63), originally delivered as a lecture in 1963, presented a scathing critique of Foucault's project. Foucault eventually responded to this (1979). For a discussion of this dispute and Derrida's later engagement with Foucault's 'great book', in his lecture '"To Do Justice to Freud": The History of Madness in the Age of Psychoanalysis' (1998a: 70–118) see Boothroyd (2005).

3 See Foucault's meditation on the work of Maurice Blanchot and Blanchot's

reflections on Foucault's thought, both in Foucault and Blanchot, 1987. See also Deleuze (1988).

4 Amongst the many references to 'speed' in *A Thousand Plateaux*, Deleuze and Guattari say that 'all drugs concern speeds and modifications of speeds' (1992: 282).

5 All references to *Theatrum Philosophicum* are to the English translation in Foucault (1977: 165–96). All references to *Logic of Sense* are also to the English translation, Deleuze (1990).

6 See Miller (1994: 245–84, 437–8n.1) for further anecdotal details and possible sources of information on Foucault's subjective responses to the experience.

7 For a fuller discussion of this see Boothroyd (1996).

8 Artaud's wrote to his publisher in 1945 to tell him that Lewis Carroll's *Jabberwocky* poem was in fact a plagiarism of something he himself had written and lost, entitled *Letura d'Eprahi Falli Tetar Fendi Photia o Fore Indi*. His letter included the following sample of how a translation of the poem would look: 'ratara ratar ratara atara tatara rana otara otara katara otara ratara kana ortura ortura konara kokona kokona koma kurbura kurbura kurbura kurbata kurbata keyna pesti anti pestantum putara pest anti pestantum putr' (1974, vol. IX: 188).

9 Deleuze discusses the 'crack' in this sense in relation to the alcoholism of F. Scott Fitgerald (1992: 198–200). A different drug, a different text, but a comparable style of calculation of the 'gradient' I am talking about here.

10 See Daniel W. Smith's and Michael A. Greco's translators' Introduction to Deleuze (1998: liii): 'Life does not function in Deleuze's philosophy only as a transcendent principle of judgement but as an immanent process of production or creation; it is neither an origin nor a goal, neither an *arché* nor a *telos*, but a pure process that always operates in the middle, *au milieu*, and proceeds by means of experimentations and unforeseen becomings.'

# 8    Cinematic heroin and narcotic modernity[1]

> Who will ever relate the whole history of narcotica? – It is almost the history of 'culture', our so-called high culture. (Nietzsche, *The Gay Science*, para. 68)

When attempting to think the modernity of 'culture', in a particular form, as a whole, or as the relation between form and whole, be this in terms of historical unfolding, the history of ontology, or on the basis of any other critical thinking, then one can begin from anywhere and on the basis of anything. So, as Nietzsche appears to suggest, why not narcotics? Indeed one must always 'begin' the study of culture from some specific location, proposition, experience or event. The whole – *le Tout* in Deleuze – is necessarily approached on the basis of an opening perception of the singular; or, as Derrida has shown in numerous places and in relation to a range of themes, any deconstruction must always proceed by way of 'the example'. Reading Nietzsche's remark backwards, as it were, and with this in mind, it suggests, almost casually, that one could, just as well as from any other starting point perhaps, relate the whole history of the culture of modernity from the point of view of its relationship to narcotics; by thinking modernity as 'narcotic modernity', as Avital Ronell (1992) expresses this thought.

## From the heroin scene to the heroin screen

As a cultural context, or scene, in relation to which modernity's striving for progress, peace, health, efficiency, universality, well-being and so on, on the one hand, and its anxieties about everything it perceives as a threat to this *ethos*, on the other, the 'drugs scene' and narcotics in general have historically, and all too simplistically, been depicted as instantiating both an actual and a symbolic form of its antithesis – its alien other. In the case of opiates in particular, it is because what can alleviate pain can also be experienced as a positive pleasure that they appear to act directly in relation to fundamental human drives too. Consequently, opiates, especially the modern synthetic form heroin, are never only 'drugs' but also ciphers for the full scope of human possibility; for the risks, dangers and ecstasies of the human condition. Indeed, the very material 'empathy' of the human organism with opiates at the level of neurochemistry has always guaranteed them 'a place in advance' in the human cultures in which they have become known. In modern times, the phenomenon of 'narcotics' is extraordinarily diverse in terms of what it signals to us concerning the distinction, or perhaps non-distinction, between the material body and spirit or will. In many senses narcotics figure in our relationship to nature (in the sense of the neurochemical empathy just mentioned, but equally in literary or philosophical forms, such as the philosopher-poet Coleridge's opiated reflections on the sublime). Today, narcotics, especially heroin, are widely reviled as 'bad drugs' and, when used without medical author-isation, considered dangerous agents of social and moral destruction, addiction and delinquency. But the actual and symbolic ambivalences of heroin – for instance it is both the last pain relief of the dying and source of the sublime pleasure which is like 'kissing God'[2] – mark it as a cultural *pharmakon*: it is an undecidable poison or cure which exerts an extra-ordinary hold on the modern imagination, seemingly as strong as the hold it has over those addicted to it. It is unquestionably deeply rooted in our culture in both broadly socio-anthropological and artistic senses. No doubt then, the development of the self-understanding of modernity *and* its reflexive self-critique might be undertaken on the basis of its relation-ship to narcotics.

Whilst this book's project is clearly not aimed at an extensive history of 'narcotic modernity', it is, none the less, worth indicating briefly the kind of cultural contextualisation which belongs to heroin and its 'natural precursor' opium. In the second half of the nineteenth century opium was incorporated into a wide range of medicines and tonics and available on demand in its raw state in pharmacies. In 1897 Heinrich Dresser, working for Bayer, synthesised the drug first discovered by C. R. Wright in 1874 and christened it 'heroin' after the company workers he tested it on reported how it made them feel 'heroic'. Yet at the same time, the traditional, orientalist association between opium smoking and the moral lassitude and technical inferiority of the East prevailed. In the early twentieth century, the perceived threat of illicit or misused narcotics to modern societies was to the efficiency of labour and the work ethic. From the latter half of the twentieth century the threat posed by narcotics tends to be perceived as operating on two fronts simultaneously. Firstly, narcotics are an 'enemy within': they both fuel the dangerous hedonisms and recklessnesses of youth and sustain a visible underclass which, unable or unwilling to move through 'welfare to work', is forced to secure its supplies through crime. Secondly, narcotics represent the external enemy, or, rather, they become the weapon of the external enemy: narco-barons and international terrorists together open up a front against 'official' global capitalism in the form of an alternative black, global narco-economy capable of financing an unending economic and ideological 'war' against the modern West.

This kind of cultural history of opiates, which, amongst other things, illustrates the part they have played in the delineation of the modern borders between the licit, the proper and rational on the one hand and the illicit, the immoral and the irrational on the other, could be fleshed out in much greater detail and used to show the generally contested and conflictual character of a modern culture which, amongst other possible accounts of it, is 'opiated' through and through. With the modern technologisation of medicine, 'drugs' *as medicines* have never been more central to the pursuit of health, well-being and the evasion of pain. Along with this development, the distinction between medicinal and the non-medicinal uses of drugs may be seen as more value-laden than it has ever been. Lately, as molecular biology develops an ever more sophisticated technical mastery over the human organism itself in relation to the extraneous bio-chemical environment with which it interacts, its global business voice speaks the promise of 'better living through chemistry', and concomitantly the drive to bio-chemical manipulation and intervention has taken on a messianic character.

All of this serves to indicate how the phenomenon of 'drugs' in general functions as a screen upon which all the ambivalences of modern life – individual, social and geo-political aspirations and anxieties – can be projected and find expression. The generic forms of cinematic heroin range from the international crime heist such as *French Connection* (Friedkin, 1971) through to sci-fi such as *Liquid Sky* (Tsukerman, 1984); they include 'Bonny and Clyde' films such as *Another Day in Paradise* (Clark, 1998) and *Drugstore Cowboy* (Van Sant, 1989), the vampire film *The Addiction* (Ferrara, 1995); social commentary, *Christiane F.* (Edel, 1981), black comedies such as *Pulp Fiction* (Tarrantino, 1994) and *Gridlock'd* (Hall, 1997), 'literary' films such as *Naked Lunch* (Cronenberg, 1996) and *Performance* (Cammel/Roeg, 1968), and even historical drama, for instance *Pandaemonium* (Temple, 2001), a film about the narco-literary life of Coleridge.[3] In more traditional moral language, cinematic heroin articulates narratives of life, death, love, loss, hope, depravity, abjection, greed, desire, humour and violence, alongside the obvious frequent preoccupations with addiction, repetition and compulsion. Under the rubric of the 'heroin film', I propose including any film in which heroin has some significant role – whether a starring role, a cameo or bit part.

Methodologically, the root of the idea that modern culture's articulation *by* heroin (at least as much as by anything else) might be investigated on the basis of the heroin film is the supposition that modernity can also be identified, conterminally, as the age of cinema; as the age in which the whole of reality is made to pass through its lens. Whilst this expression is ostensibly metaphorical, Deleuze, drawing on Bergson, thinks of the emergence of cinema as nothing less than a techno-ontological transformation of perception itself – unsurprisingly provoking therefore, a philosophical rethinking of the subject/object distinction (Deleuze, 1997). The neo-Bergsonian strain in the thought of Deleuze and others does lead to the rejection of Kantian and neo-Kantian idealism. This spreading view – applied to the present case – entails ontological continuity between (what might once have been referred to as) the real world of heroin and the cinema of heroin. One way to understand this is to consider how heroin can be apprehended only through its material image effects, and how thought's conceptual arrival at what is called 'heroin' is only ever on the basis of its differing 'images'. In other words, heroin is 'differentiated' from everything else on the basis of all the image-effects it engenders. Its boundaries (within what is conventionally regarded to comprise its 'phenomenal range') such as those delimiting it as 'chemical substance', as 'narcotic', as 'film genre', as 'scourge of humanity' and so on, are empirical and offer connectable moments of available utility:[4] they neither express nor legitimate any ideal or hierarchical order of things. The sensations of being high in the user, the addict's frantic psychological anxieties about procurement,[5] the moral sentiments of third parties, the criminal activities surrounding supply and the threat of police seizure, through to the Newsnight symbolisations of the narco-economy, and all other, ever more extensive, heroin-associated phenomena, are all conjoined links in the 'material chain of heroin effects'; and 'cinema' can give us a sense of *thought's movement* along these material pathways. In short, the 'heroin film' is *a mode of access* to heroin.

With the advent of the cinematic technology, a new means for the distribution of narco-mythology had arrived: cinema extended the cultural scope of heroin. The entry of heroin into the world of the moving image began with Dickson's and Edison's Kinescope production *The Opium Joint* (1894), which, with its opium dream sequence, registers for the first time surrender to the specific cinematic temptation to illustrate states of narcotic consciousness. The development of this deceptively simple opportunity for the artistic imagination to enhance the significance of certain aspects of social reality by moving from describing to fashioning them as a framing device, is brilliantly illustrated by Sergio Leone's *Once Upon a Time in America* (1984), which opens with Noodles (Robert de Niro) drifting into an opium dream, through which the film's narrative will be laid out, unfolding its account of the American Dream through the lifetime relationship of Noodles and Max. Both the technical possibilities of film and a certain form of narcosis are thus evidently linked in the history of cinema in terms of the *denaturalisation of perception* made possible between them. Rather than this being a mere simile, it draws attention to an actual phenomenological connection between memory, cinematic perception and narcosis. Leone's film materialises the 'cultural memory' of the rootedness of American politics in vice and gangsterism through a technology which allows the past, present and future to happen 'all at once'.

It would no doubt be easier to argue for a connection between drugs, film and altered perception by reference to drugs films whose principal aesthetic effects are consciously aimed at the representation of pharmacologically altered sensory perception. 'Hallucinogen films', such as Roger Corman's and Jack Nicholson's LSD movie *The Trip* (1967); Kenneth Anger's *Inauguration of the Pleasure Dome* (1954); or 'underground' shorts such Jordan Belson's *Allures* (1961) and *Re-entry* (1964) and Standish Lawler's *Raindance* (1972), are all of this nature. In their use of psychedelic imagery, all of these are aimed at systematic *recreations* of sympathetic entrancement in the spectator. It is, however, simultaneously less obvious and more compelling that cinema in general involves a form of 'narcotic' entrancement; that it introduces, in a primary alteration, a new stage of 'creative evolution' of perception in general. To emphasise this affective aspect of the cinematic image, as Deleuze has done, is not to deny that every film is woven into the fabric of culture at large; that it is always 'of its time', for instance in the ordinary historical sense of its 'time and place' of production. Neither is it to deny its relation to the material system of its distribution and the contexts of its being shown and viewed. On the contrary, it is the inescapability of the 'materiality' of cinema that must be acknowledged. Whether treated in terms of the technical possibilities from celluloid to digitisation, or infrastructural developments from multiplex to pay per view, or questions of morality, aesthetics, taste and performance which may come into focus in various ways when it is taken as an art form, cinema is part of this very same material connectivity of culture 'as a whole' that elsewhere extensively incorporates 'narcotics' – the entire global phenomenon and industry of narcotics – as a part of *the same* cultural whole. It is, therefore, the organisation of culture 'as a whole', which includes both cinema *and* narcotics, which gives rise to the specificity of the cinematic representations of the latter and to the extensive, material context of their cultural mythologisation. The material connections engage and exceed 'cinema' understood simply in terms of films, directors, genres, stars and studios, picture houses and so on

Every film has a set of material circumstances which broadly contextualise it. The first decades of the twentieth century saw the rise of 'drugs menace' and 'drug hysteria' movies, which largely took the form of phoney cross-overs between 'drugs education' and sensationalist entertainment. These were produced outside of the dominant studio system of production and distribution and generally presented by film showmen at travelling 'roadshows'. Titles such as *Human Wreckage* (Wray, 1925) and *The Pace that Kills* (Parker, 1928) were typical of these highly popular anti-drug melodramas, which the authorities none the less feared and partly suppressed on the ground that, despite their overt intentions of demonising drug abuse, they might actually widen the public's nefarious interest in the activity of consuming narcotics, simply by exposing audiences to images of consumption. Danny Boyle's more recent *Trainspotting* (1995) created a mild form of such a 'moral panic': despite its depictions of the horrific consequences of addiction, it attracted popular media criticism for its ambivalent depictions of narcotic pleasures. Otto Preminger's *The Man with the Golden Arm* (1955) was perhaps the first attempt to deal with the drugs and addiction theme with a degree of psycho-sociological seriousness, whilst pushing at the 'material' boundaries of what was then legally permitted in terms of scenes showing characters taking drugs, and thus released without an MPAA certificate. Each decade since has produced its crop of heroin films, sited often enough with respect to more established film genres (crime, black comedy, social realism and so on), but nevertheless dealing more or less directly with heroin and its effects as a principal theme. These films have been produced, released and received within a culture in which illicit drug use, especially of heroin, is highly scandalised within the mass media as one of the great scourges of humanity. Rather than analyse such filmic material in terms of the cultural theory of 'media effects', or by either prioritising the forces of production and ideology as against those of audiences' pro-active consumption or by 'decoding' imagery and unconscious traces, as is prevalent in much cultural studies, is it possible to examine the filament that connects cinema directly to the drug? Can the 'heroin film' be critically approached as an *expression* of heroin 'itself'?

Heroin films express specific relations between elements within a heroinised cultural formation of which they are also part. This formation is typically treated as extraneous, but can be thought of as constituted by a process of 'internal differentiation' between material images of heroin. There is no *a priori* limit to the diversity of the material connections that 'heroin' might make, no limit to what may become linked into the 'heroin chain'. These materialised images of heroin may equally take the form of the propagandistic art of shock seen in various 'scandalous depictions' of heroin use, or they could exist for a very few in the private meeting that never took place to secure the financing of a film project with narco-dollars. What is at issue is the questionable distinction between 'film' and 'world'. In the age of cinematic perception, the nexus between world and representation, I want to argue, ought rather to be thought in terms of *lines of connection* within the *continuum* of culture. This cuts across traditional thinking of the boundary between what is internal or external to 'the film'.

## Deleuze and the cinema of heroin

Deleuze's application of Bergson's materialist account of perception to cinema invites us to think through the *continuum* between cinema and reality. Deleuze summarises the distinction of cinema as an art form as follows:

> The cinema can, with impunity, bring us close to things or take us away from them and revolve around them; it suppresses both the anchoring of the subject and the horizon of the world. Hence it substitutes an implicit knowledge and a second internationality for the conditions of natural perception. It is not the same as the other arts, which aim rather at something unreal through the world, but makes the world itself something unreal or a tale (*récit*). (Deleuze, 1997: 52)

He tells us how Bergson's first assessment of the 'mobile-section' or the 'movement image' (the image of movement itself) exposes an illusion of perception, one that can serve as a 'diagnosis of a crisis in psychology': it reveals how 'movement, as physical reality in the external world, and the image, as psychic reality in consciousness, could no longer be opposed' (Deleuze, 1997: Preface to French edition). For Bergson, movement is in perception and perception is in the perceived (movement); there is a contiguity of thought and thing such that they are not truly distinct from one another. Despite Bergson's own earliest assessment of the cinematic image as the continuation and repetition of an old illusion of movement, Deleuze argues that it is the cinema which ultimately gives rise to the perception of the movement-image as such: 'cinema does not give us an image to which movement is added, it *immediately* gives us the movement-image' (Deleuze, 1997: 2, *my emphasis*). And therein lies its techno-evolutionary novelty. In other words, the cinema, or cinematic image, gives us reality itself; it is not a *representational* medium; images, even as we ordinarily think of them, do not represent externalities. They are, rather, a record, or memory, of the serial process of internal differentiation (between images) *within* perception. Consequently, he proposes that the whole (*le Tout*) – the universe if you will – be considered as 'metacinema' (Deleuze, 1997: 59). This is an initial and enduring position of Deleuze's philosophy of cinema: there is no ground for an absolute distinction between 'things' and 'effects' – for these are undifferentiated within perception.

Since 'narcotic perception' cannot legislatively be restricted to association with any particular 'thing', it is not surprising that cinema has been seen as a purveyor of narcotic effects. F. R. Leavis (1930), as far removed from Bergsonism as he was from narcotics proper, famously complained of the dangerous narcotising effects of cinema on the general public. Marshall McLuhan (2001) directly engaging with the question of the cognitive impact of the 'visual', defined media technologies as 'extensions of the senses', and associated them with a certain 'narcosis'.[6] But there is a certain narrowness of understanding here. For materialism, thinking proceeds by moving along lines of connection between one phenomenon and another – in the Bergsonian idiom, between differing images *within* perception. The point here is that heroin provides a specific set of conceptual pathways for thinking relationships across culture in general, and without any necessarily fixed directionality. Heroin's primary existence is in the form of a network of multivalent connections within culture at large, not *essentially* as a prime mover and creator of cultural darkness. When a casual film review is aligned with F. R. Leavis in likening the cinema to heroin,[7] the power of the analogy should not be allowed to obscure the ontological assumptions underlying the comparison; and it is against these assumptions that Deleuzian–Bergsonian materialism applied to cinema would seek to ground the connection of cinema to heroin and vice versa in the field of sensation itself.

'Analogical thinking' itself is the experience of similarity grounded in sensation. In Deleuze's account of cinema, the movement-image gives us direct access to something as sensation: it is the most real (thing). Heroin the 'narcotic substance' is not external to the set (*ensemble*) of all its so-called 'images'. Film is neither simply an aesthetic treatment nor a sociological investigation of a subject matter: it is no less than a mode of access to the phenomenon. Deleuze's idea of cinema as a 'sensorium' which produces a perceptual transformation is key to this metaphysic: cinema engages us directly, through its intensities of light, sound, colour, movement, rhythm and so on; it is not primarily a *representational* medium requiring narrative interpretation. This is not to deny that there is a narrative dimension and structure to (most) films (one which does indeed call for, precisely, 'interpretation') but it is to privilege the relation to film as it is rooted in embodied sensation and experienced in the body.[8] 'It is through the body (and no longer through the intermediary of the body)', says Deleuze, 'that the cinema forms its alliance with the spirit' (2000: 189).

Rather than the materiality of 'sensation' in Deleuze being the basis for a theory of film spectatorship *per se*, it is identified, ultimately, with the movement-image itself: 'The movement-image is matter [*matière*] itself, as Bergson showed' (2000, 33). As his thinking of 'body' generally deconstructs, rather than assuming and simply inverting, the traditional binary distinction between sensation and cognition, or body and mind, it is the 'cinema', prior to the distinction between the viewer and the viewed, which is considered to generate signaletic material (*matière signalétique*). In line with this, I suggest, the distinction between 'heroin' and 'images of heroin' is always in the process of being made (unmade and remade) – we *know* heroin only on the basis of this *process*, and it is this *knowing* which I have described as a form of access to it. Clearly, however we theorise its 'origins', there is always the issue of its fate and wider effects as these are played out at the macro-level of society and all the institutional and cultural practices relating to it. The Deleuzian philosophy of cinema does not simply annul or displace the ideology critique of, say, Adorno or Althusser as these may be applied to the cinema and its function in society. It does, however, provide the basis for thinking how the theoretical enterprise itself can never claim immunity to the 'effects' of that of which it speaks. The power of film (like that of 'drugs') extends beyond, and is felt outside of, what is literally the 'scope' of individual viewings of a film (or experiences of drug taking) and its effects are not restricted to those which may be claimed to ensue directly from its being 'seen' (after all, what is it to 'see' a film?). Indeed, banned films and prohibited substances both acquire a particular allure and accrue a particular kind of force as a consequence of their proscription. Whilst Deleuze's philosophy of film in many ways emphasises the visible, it is not a purely visual aesthetic theory of spectatorship and, as is evident in Deleuze's serial-associative readings of shots, angles, cuts and so on, the film is not in any way considered a self-contained aesthetic object. The cinema opens up, rather, specific lines of communication across culture and in doing so 'virtualises' the real *differently* than was possible before the cinematic age.

As Barbara Kennedy succinctly puts it, Deleuze re-articulates the figural as 'a concept of an immanent process of forces' and 'sensation operates on a plane of immanence, through the processual and intensity' (Kennedy, 2000: 110). This gives rise to a condition of existence that can exceed what is perceived through language. The viewer engaged by film becomes part of 'cinema' in the form of what Deleuze calls an 'abstract machine': the spectator is incorporated into the totality of all processes constituting cinema as a whole – whose ostensible internal borders are only arbitrarily drawn in terms of the 'actual' machines and machinic parts involved, such as lenses, projectors, celluloid, screens, sound tracks and the bio-machinery of human eyes and ears and so on. After Bergson's discovery of the 'movement-image', the traditional philosophical ground for thinking the image as a representation of what 'consciousness' regards as external to it, is displaced. Film enjoins the spectator with a specific 'cultural formation'; relocating him or her within a specific 'plane of immanence' – a set of interconnected movements within the material continuum; it interconnects him or her with a movement-image which produces 'perception' in the first place. Perception in this sense is impersonal; it is a resonance, a 'vibration' within the 'medium' itself, which, as Bergson says, travels 'in every direction like shivers through an immense body' (Bergson, 1988: 208). The cinema is a zone of empathetic resonance with what we would ordinarily say is external to it and which it represents, but now must think of as immanent to the 'automatic movement' of the cinema(tic whole). The artistic essence of the cinematic image, says Deleuze, is the 'shock to thought' produced by 'communicating vibrations to the cortex, touching the nervous and cerebral system directly' (Deleuze, 2000: 156).

## Heroinised bodies

The 'images' of heroin available in film are a subset of the *ensemble* of all heroin images. It is our inevitably partial connection to this *ensemble* which gives us our shared and our differing senses of heroin and which is real on the 'plane of immanence' and more or less spectacularly embodied. This variable connection to heroin can be expressed as a range of 'heroinised' bodies. Their movements will signal the diverse range of heroin effects, signalling various personal, social, political, juridical and stratified reactions to heroin.

Vondie Curtis Hall's *Gridlock'd* (1997) foregrounds the way that heroin animates, articulates and disarticulates planned courses of action that the characters may attempt to undertake. The two principal junkies, Stretch (Tim Roth) and Spoon (Tupac Shakur), are chased around the city by cops and drug dealers alike whilst constantly seeking to get registered for a methadone rehab programme. Their efforts are repeatedly blocked by the bureaucracy of the MedicAid system and by all the accidental encounters that simultaneously needing heroin and needing to quit it give rise to. The impossibility of their kicking the habit is the explicit narrative theme of the film, which presents the story of the interactions between the addicts, the drug, dealers, the law and the medical welfare system.[9] This subset of the *ensemble* seems to confirm an inescapable connection between heroin, desperation, criminality and death, but the Deleuzian perspective provides a different view, *since no single set of connections within the ensemble is inescapable.* The sense of flux across the whole range of the heroin *ensemble* is rarely summoned up, but is the basis for the understanding that 'narcotic modernity' can also (like 'economic modernity') experience huge change.

At one point in *Gridlock'd* the two protagonists attempt to short-circuit the workings of the 'system' (which seems rigged to thwart their best intentions – and I shall just leave to one side the question of Deleuzian explanations of such regularity). They think that a stab wound to the body (mimicking, as it were, the puncture of a syringe) is the type of wound which will make a fast connection to the medical network and allow them to trick their way through their otherwise blocked route into hospital, via the Emergency Room. Whether it succeeded or failed, this set of interactions would in turn generate further 'images' of heroin; showing, in a routine way, that it is through the image productivity of connecting heroinsed bodies that the becoming-culture, or, the cultural 'virtualisation' of heroin proceeds. Like any cultural symbol, heroin is multiply connected throughout culture and society; its range of affect is extensive and visible in 'extension' in everyday life; in sensation and thought, in social organisation, in art, in politics, in crime, violence and corruption, in the agri-business of poppy production and in the pharmaceutical industry – in short, everywhere the touch of 'heroin' is discernible.

The degree of extension is a measure of the power of heroin and perhaps any other specific cultural symbol. Heroin's power ought not to be understood in the restricted sense given to it by pharmacology. The measure is its *productive force*, its scope from localised effects in the brain to the disseminated forms of its manifestation in the everyday life of society: in the street, the police cell, the hospital, the shooting gallery, through to the various discursive forms of its cultural mythologising and political scapegoating.

## The cinematic fix

Film reproduces the ontological order of sensation and movement. Making connections, getting a fix, is – and this is not a coincidence – the language of heroin use, the language of film production, and the language of contemporary social ontology. Cinematic effects are already connections, already active interpretations, already a fall from the meta-order of movement and sensation down to the fix of a specific connection set on the screen. Cinema is thus a modality of the becoming-virtual of the material universe. Film's presentation to the senses of the material interconnectedness of phenomena is achieved through a panoply of technical devices: editing, montage, flashback, slow motion, colour, sound, music and so on. It is not, however, that the cinematic image, or specifically the heroin film, gives us the cultural phenomenon of heroin in its entirety (first representing and then supplanting the real with the virtual – as does the image for Baudrillard). Rather cinema provides a specific subset of heroin images, and, as Deleuze puts it, makes the world 'unreal'. This de-totalising process is already metaphoric, already comparative, certainly to the point of dramatisation, and probably, as Deleuze suggests, to the point of unreality. However, this does not produce necessarily (nor need it be aimed at) a denial of material significance, nor does it mean that the only consistent position that a film-maker can take is nihilistic. The propriety of the film-maker – in this case of the heroin film – is to 'feel' directly, through the medium of the movement-image itself, the effects of 'heroin'. Whether, dear reader, you take fifteen minutes to find a vein, watch a junkie fixing in an alleyway, or see a heroin film, you are differently, but equally, located within heroin culture. Bearing in mind that cinema abstracts from the totality, one might even say that the heroin film can offer a concentrated dose of that culture.

### Heroin's signature–autograph

Deleuze suggests that one may learn from cinema experientially what one may learn from Bergson philosophically, namely, the *immanence of perception*. In filmic terms, a single frame, shot or sequence can be a 'signature' of the film as a whole. Deleuze famously associates this 'signature' with the visual style of the *auteur*. It would be extraordinary, however, to neglect the last fifty years of theoretical and cultural development – with respect to subject positions, questions of agency, and the decentring of the human – and meekly comply with the *politique des auteurs* assignment of prime authorship to the director. As would by now be expected, the question which arises concerns the cultural signature of heroin itself: heroin as *auteur*. I shall now illustrate this idea with reference to several films in which the signature of heroin may be discerned.

In *Liquid Sky* (Tsukerman, 1984) extraterrestrials descend on Lower East Side New York in search of heroin. From a dinner-plate-sized space craft, the alien (or aliens – it is not clear whether there is one or more than one) snoops on a group of party animal, bohemian fashion industry punks with a penchant for heroin and other illicit substances. The object of desire is absorbed directly through the connection made by looking. The alien vision of the human world takes the form of quasi-psychedelic thermal images in which people and environment are barely distinguishable. With a perceptual disregard for the distinction between humans and anything else, even for the border between the inside and outside of the human body, the alien sees not only the drug but also the effect of the drug in the bodies and brains of its users: an orgiastic pulse emanates from the point where the drug interacts within the brain or where it is injected into the body. This is represented by an initially expanding ball of colour which subsequently implodes till it disappears to a point, after which the screen cuts back to ordinary human vision. Each time this sequence of events takes place, the human heroin user drops dead. The alien also senses – rather than deduces, for it seems to be a creature of immanence and pure sensation – that whenever humans have an orgasm, their brains react in a similar way, and their hunger for the connection to the heroin experience can also be satisfied by connecting with that. It is the orgasmic event itself which most attracts it, and at the point of its irruptive occurrence, translated into explosion-implosion imagery, there is a merging of the alien's experience with what happens in the brain (or body) of its 'victim'.

The alien's interest becomes focused on one woman – the heroin(e) of the film – waiting for her to have sex. Whenever she does, her sex partner is victimised and dies as his neurochemical output is absorbed by the alien. She survives these encounters as she doesn't orgasm. Spying on these events from a neighbouring apartment block are a German scientist and a local resident who, following a chance encounter, and acting on a sexual attraction of her own, has taken him in. Over dinner, the scientist articulates a transcendental perspective on the mysterious and fatal goings-on in the apartment opposite. He explains that research has shown that the human brain has special receptors for opiate molecules and hypothesises that 'if all humans have in their brains some substantial process based on the opiate mechanism of action, why can't there exist somewhere else in the universe some other form of consciousness that would depend on this even more?' The 'pleasure principle' would not be an exclusively human affair but a consequence of the very receptivity of one chemical structure for another. It would be intrinsic to life itself, which we might have to begin to understand as the organisational action and reaction of connecting matter.

When the scientist explains his theory to the neighbour, she sceptically asks: 'What are they doing these opiate receptors in the human brain? Waiting around for someone to come and give them heroin?' It's an anthropomorphic question, demonstrating the tendency to humanise or personify the 'life' of organic structures, and to suppose that when an organism interacts with its environment it must be acting intentionally. Such a perspective, as Ansell-Pearson commenting on Bergson's critique of natural perception says:

> reduces the activity and becoming of life (movement) to a centred
> subject of perception... Not only is the border between the organism

and its environment never clear-cut, being always porous and sympathetic, but so are the boundaries which separate and divide bodies.

and he continues, citing *Matter and Memory*:

the close solidarity which binds all objects of the material universe, the
perpetuality of their reciprocal actions and reactions, is sufficient to
prove that they have not the precise limits which we attribute to them.
(Ansell-Pearson, 1999: 34; Bergson, 1988: 209)

In *Liquid Sky's* orgiastic event shot, form almost disappears, and
in that movement the boundary between what is alien and what is human
dissolves. With that dissolution we see, as it were, sensation itself: impersonal, unattributable, its image coincides with movement itself. *Liquid
Sky*, as directly as any heroin film could, gives us an image of heroin in
its purest form: as *movement*. The recurrent instances of the alien 'heroinised event' image express the sensorial impact Deleuze associates with
the 'affection-image', in which there is, he says, a 'coincidence of subject
and object or the way the subject perceives itself, or rather experiences
itself, or feels itself from the inside' (1997: 65). At such points Tsukerman
dispenses entirely with narrativity: in its place, rasping, synthetic,
pulsating, deep cello-like chords rhythmically beat to dynamic screens
of colour, filling the viewer's vision, closing down the viewer's separation
from the experience itself. The cinematic image effectively gives us at such
points a 'shot' of the drug in a diluted form.

For Bergson matter is an aggregate of 'images', and by image he
meant a certain existence which is 'more than the idealist calls *representation*, but less than that which the realist calls a *thing*' (Bergson, 1988: 9).
Tsukerman provides such an image of heroin. As Deleuze says, effectively
repeating the 'more than but less than' formulation, it *is* the object, but as
'the modulation of the object itself' (2000: 27).[10]

### Heroin close-up

Whilst *Liquid Sky's* alien theme incorporates an affection-image of
heroin as disembodied sensation, much more commonly and typically
in the heroin film the affection-image is expressed by various other – to
borrow a term from Deleuze – *visagéifications* of heroin. Perhaps the most
archetypal of signature affection-images of heroin is that of the close-up
of the face of the user at the point of transformation as the drug takes
effect. Such shots are to be found throughout the genre from early 'drug

hysteria' and 'drugsploitation' movies through to its most recent examples. We see it, for instance, in a close-up of the face of Frankie Machine (Sinatra) in Preminger's *The Man with the Golden Arm* (1955); in Greta's face (Clarkson) with its always half-closed eye in Cholodenko's *High Art* (1998) and in the face of the bad cop (Keitel) in Ferrera's *The Bad Lieutentant* (1992); in Renton's (McGregor) face as he sinks, following his fix, into a plush red carpet and into a coma (and in reverse in his 'cold turkey' scenes) in *Trainspotting* – to list an indicative few. But affect is not expressed only by the image of a character's 'actual' face: Deleuze tells us it is expressed by a face or 'a facial equivalent (a faceified object)' (1997: 97). In the heroin film this is evident in close-ups of injecting and snorting; syringes emptying into arms, powder disappearing off mirrors up rolled-up banknotes, smoke being sucked up tubes over tin foil; solutions being heated on spoons; full screen shots of bloody mixtures in syringes; shots from the perspective of the paraphernalia itself, for instance the view from inside an injecting syringe (*Trainspotting*); hyper-close-ups of needles entering veins, for instance in Aranofsky's *Requiem for a Dream* (1998).

In *Requiem*, as the film's montage-tempo and soundtrack reflects the various degrees of intoxication, disorientation and changing energies of its protagonists, we see again and again rapid-fire, almost subliminal, sequences of such close-ups. One notable shot is that of a full-screen human eye whose pupil rapidly dilates to signal the drug's taking effect. Another shows the close-up face of Mrs Goldfarb (Burstyn), whose amphetamine/barbiturate addiction is played out in the film against her son's heroin addiction, in the top half of a split screen and her daily intake of pills laid on a table in the lower screen. Drug effects, in *Requiem*, propel the narrative forward, organise its changes of pace, pushing the four principals into the world of action and then withdrawing them into their heads. They all progressively lose control of the drugs, their effects and simultaneously their lives. The film parallels the demise of a son, Harry (Leto), his girlfriend Marion (Connelly) and another friend Tyrone (Wayans), on the one hand, and his lonely, widowed mother, Mrs Goldfarb, on the other. The three friends attempt to harness the energies and possibilities of both using and trading in heroin (and cocaine) to realise their dreams of a better life, whilst the mother uses the drugs she's been prescribed, initially and vaguely for depression, to regain the slim figure of her youth for an appearance on a television game show with which she is delusionally obsessed. As the young friends' lives collapse into crime, serious addiction, prostitution, ill-health and depravity, the mother drifts into amphetamine psychosis and hospitalisation. The framing of the face or some other body part, such as the forearm or the vein which receives the needle, the mouth which grimaces and compulsively grinds its teeth, opens, swallows, twitches and so on, forms the basis for the affective reading of the film as whole. This is illustrated poignantly toward the end of the film as Harry and Tyrone, heading south by car, in search of heroin and fleeing drug dealers back home, stop to fix the last of their stash. We see a close-up of Harry's forearm with a gaping, pustulant, purple hole on his vein into which a needle is slowly inserted. The film begins with a shot (from its end) of an amputated Harry on a hospital bed, and we now come to realise how this comes about. It thus gathers the film in its entirety, short-circuiting itself on the injection shot. Close-up shots such as these, especially injection shots, are instances of *visagéification*. They are shots in which narrative structure from the heroin *ensemble* is concentrated into the close-up micro-movements of the more-than-represented-but-less-than-concretised object. In this case – exquisitely – the amputated limb is both there and not there.

## Heroin as icon

Such shots can be said to be 'iconic' of the individual film in which they occur, but not only of the individual film. They are iconic (by definition also) of the whole 'narcotic assemblage'; the whole set of narcotic images. This is iconicity understood in the sense of the materialist-phenomenological semiotics of Peirce rather than the narratological semiotics of Saussure, for whom everything begins and ends with language. In Peirce's thinking what is iconic is 'firstness' or sensation itself – and it is this which is expressed by the affection-image, for instance exemplified in 'faceifying' close-ups. But through a series of displacements, what is given 'first' effectuates 'secondness' – the existential realm of things-happening – which Deleuze says corresponds to and is expressed in the 'action-image'. This is an image relating firstness to its representation as such, in a series of actions or events: for example, the compulsion to repeat played out on various levels, such as in the biological organism or in the anxious attempt to acquire the drug through action in the 'seedy world' of drug dens, drug dealers and cops. This movement outward – from sensation to action – is ultimately determinative of an entire world: the world of meaning. This is 'thirdness' in the Peircean schema; the symbolic order in which 'the story' can unfold as a complete narrative. But as the 'story' writ large *is* the becoming-virtual of the 'world', it can be claimed that cinematic perception gives us a sense of how the world in all its materiality is recognisably orchestrated and opened up by various dominant themes, such as heroin and narcotics in general. It is in this way that narcotic effects ripple outward (as Bergson says, as a 'vibration' in the cultural continuum) into social and political phenomena in the world at large. The injection shot is thus already iconic of heroin 'writ large', not merely because it is a fetishised image in the ordinary sense of the term 'image', but because the image is an image of *the movement itself*, of a crossing over of heroin as 'narcotic substance' into the body of the user. *It is therefore 'iconic' also of the entire process*, of the transmissibility of heroin effects across the permeable borders between 'bodies' in general: between, for instance, the body of the user and the cultural body at large. It is symbolic of the 'becoming-culture' of heroin. How this 'becoming' will pan out – as a particular story, narrative or event – is not predetermined by the thing we call heroin *itself*, for heroin has no *essential nature* as such, but by the arrangement and organisation of the bodies its effects pass into, and how this constellation of bodies reacts to this movement. This zone of total affect, or the whole (*le Tout*), is precisely what cinema, according to Deleuze, gives us a sense of.

## Heroin's redeeming feature (film)

I shall conclude now with a brief and partial reading of the Ferrera's *Bad Lieutentant* showing how the connectivity of heroin to 'the whole' is made perceptible in the context of a particular film, in this case by the connections it makes between addictive-compulsive drive for narcotic pleasure and release and the desire for spiritual redemption.

In *Bad Lieutenant* Ferrera's corrupt junky-cop's everyday life is structured by acquisition and consumption of heroin and the other narcotics he steals from the various criminals his job brings him into contact with. In the course of the film, the solace he takes in narcosis is mapped onto what becomes, eventually, a slowly emerging awareness of the need for spiritual redemption. The affection-image of his transformation through narcotics is exemplified in the scene in which he visits a junky acquaintance who administers to him a fix of heroin. The camera lingers on the injection and the micro-movements of his face as the drug takes effect. This process of transformation is then extended outward to the action of tracking down two young rapists of a nun in church: a crime which, despite his general moral lassitude, he abhors. His pursuit of these criminals now becomes the thing which he is driven to do with the kind of obsessive intensity which structures his 'bad habits', albeit still with what is initially a blind urge for vengeance. His instinct for vengeance is challenged, however, when he goes to the church and meets there the rape victim, who tells him that she is not going to seek prosecution of her attackers because she has forgiven them. Perplexed and almost apoplectic, save for his facial contortions, he manages to say to her: 'Do you have the right to let these boys go free?' She replies: 'Speak to Jesus.' Shortly afterwards, still in the church, Christ appears to him in a vision. He comes to realise that it is he, and only he (as only a bent cop can), who must allow them to leave town *unprosecuted*. Following a clue he is given as to the whereabouts of the rapists, he captures them and, after helping himself to their drugs, escorts them to a bus station, where he tells them to get out of town. His moral lostness is affectively expressed at this point, as in other key moments in the film, in close-ups of his pained facial expressions. This 'moral lostness' is also a 'lostness for words'. In these facial close-ups he grimaces twitches, squeaks, blubbers and cries (Keitel gives a fine exhibition of Artaudian acting). His addiction to heroin is, effectively, also addiction to relieving his moral, but none the less visceral pain, through narcotics. We see in the micro-movements of his anguished face how he becomes increasingly pacified by the drugs, but later comes to understand this as a displacement of the spiritual desire for 'absolution' he later begs in the church scene, kissing the feet of Christ (in a distorted echo of Lenny Bruce's remark about taking heroin cited earlier).

In this film Ferrara uses heroin to articulate catholicity itself – and especially the injunction to forgive. Despite my own use of interpretative language here, this illustrates how it is the affection-image of heroin expressed as and through the bad lieutenant's face (Keitel's facial acting faceifying heroin) which expresses also the 'image' of the entire classical theological conundrum the film poses, of God's action in the world and the possibilities of redemption.

Perhaps it was God who gave us this affinity with narcotics for a purpose!

## Notes

1 I would like to thank the British Academy for the travel grant that enabled me to present a version of this chapter at the 2004 International Association

for Philosophy and Literature 'Virtual Materialities' Conference at Syracuse University, USA.

2 Lenny Bruce: 'I'll die young but it's like kissing God.'

3 For brief synopses of many of the films I refer to here see Stevenson (2000).

4 Deleuze writes 'we must then recognise that difference itself is not simply spatio-temporal, that it is not generic or specific, in a word – difference is not exterior or superior to the thing' (2004: 33). So, reflection on heroin (or any *thing* for that matter) whether it takes the form of narrative philosophical critique or the form of cinema, is essentially the movement of thought along a specific pathway taken through culture (*le Tout*) as a whole. Heroin, therefore, (its only privilege in this respect residing in its material history and differentiated effects), permits a particular set of possibilities for following the connections between distinct phenomena.

5 See, for instance, *Panic in Needle Park* (Schatzberg, 1971).

6 In *Understanding Media: The Extensions of Man* (1964) McLuhan says: 'The Greek myth of Narcissus is directly concerned with a fact of human experience, as the word *Narcissus* indicates. It is from the Greek word *narcosis*, or numbness. The youth Narcissus mistook his own reflection in the water for another person. This extension of himself by mirror numbed his perceptions until he became the servomechanism of his own extended or repeated image. The nymph Echo tried to win his love with fragments of his own speech, but in vain. He was numb. He had adapted to his extension of himself and had become a closed system' (2001: 45).

McLuhan's thought seems close to both Deleuze's Bergsonism and his privileging of cinema art when he says: 'The serious artist is the only person able to encounter technology with impunity, just because he is an expert aware of the changes in sense perception' (2001: 19).

7 A further example of the 'slippage' along this line of 'analogical' connection is evident also in a recent review of Aronofsky's *Requiem for a Dream* (1998) bearing the title 'How heroin can still give Hollywood a hit', and leading with the comment that this 'is the latest release to show film's enduring addiction to the most notorious of drugs'.

8 'It is through the body (and no longer through the intermediary of the body) that cinema forms its alliance with the spirit, with thought' (Deleuze, 2000: 189).

9 At this point one could say that the narrative 'story' exposes the production of the *récit*, as Deleuze understands this, as a specific virtualisation, a 'making-unreal', of the world itself.

10 Whilst Deleuze himself does not discuss narcotic imagery in cinema, he does, in *Difference and Repetition* (1962), associate what he calls 'pharmacodynamic experiences' with the experience of difference *qua* difference: 'that depth in itself or that intensity in itself at the original moment (in which) it is neither qualified nor extended'(1994: 237).

# References

Adorno, Theodor W. 1970. *Über Walter Benjamin*, ed. Rolf Tiedemann (Frankfurt am Main: Suhrkamp Verlag).

Adorno, Theodor W, 1978. *Minima Moralia*, trans. E. F. N. Jephcott (London: Verso).

Amis, Martin. 1975. *Dead Babies* (Harmondsworth: Penguin Books).

Ansell-Pearson, Keith. 1999. *Germinal Life: The Difference and Repetition of Deleuze* (London: Routledge).

Aschenbrandt, Theodor. 1883. 'Die physiologische Wirkung und Bedeutung des Cocains'. *Deutsche Medizinisches Wochenschrift* (Dec. 1883).

Baudrillard, Jean. 1988. 'The Masses: The implosion of the social in the media', in Mark Poster (ed.), *Jean Baudrillard: Selected Writings* (London: Polity), pp. 207–19.

Beauvoir, Simone, de. 1965. *The Prime of Life*, trans. Peter Green (Harmondsworth: Penguin).

Benjamin, Walter. 1972. *Walter Benjamin Über Haschisch*, ed. Tillman Rexoth (Frankfurt am Main: Suhrkamp).

Benjamin, Walter. 1973. *Charles Baudelaire: A Lyric Poet in the Era of High Capitalism*, trans. Harry Zohn (London: NLB).

Benjamin, Walter. 1999. *The Arcades Project*, trans. Howard Eiland and Kevin McLaughlin (Cambridge, MA: Belknap Press).

Benjamin, Walter. 2000. *One Way Street and Other Writings*, trans. Edmund Jephcott and Kingsley Shorter (London: Verso).

Bergson, Henri. 1991. *Matter and Memory*, trans. N. M. Paul and W. S. Palmer (New York: Zone Books).

Boon, Marcus. 2002. *The Road to Excess: A History of Writers on Drugs* (Cambridge, MA: Harvard University Press).

Booth, Martin. 1996. *Opium: A History* (New York: St Martin's Press).

Boothroyd, Dave. 1996. 'Foucault's Alimentary Philosophy: Care of the Self and Responsibility for the Other', *Man and World*, 29:4, 361–8.

Boothroyd, Dave. 2005. '"To Be Hospitable to Madness": Derrida and Foucault *Chez Freud*', *Journal for Cultural Research*, 9:1, 3–21.

Buck-Morss, Susan. 1989. *The Dialectics of Seeing* (Cambridge, MA: MIT Press).

Burroughs, William. 1993. *Naked Lunch* (London: Flamingo).

Byck, Robert (ed.). 1974. *The Cocaine Papers* (New York: Stonehill Press).

Davenport-Hines, Richard. 2001. *The Pursuit of Oblivion: A Social History of Drugs* (London: Weidenfeld and Nicolson).

Debord, Guy. 1977. *The Society of the Spectacle*, trans. Fredy Pelman and John Supak (Detroit: Black & Red).

Deleuze, Gilles. 1988. *Foucault*, trans. Sean Hand (London: Athlone, 1988).

Deleuze, Gilles. 1990. *Logic of Sense*, trans. Mark Lester and Charles Stivale (New York: Columbia University Press).

Deleuze, Gilles. 1994. *Difference and Repetition*, trans. Paul Patton (London: Athlone).

Deleuze, Gilles. 1997. *Cinema 1: The Movement Image*, trans. Hugh Tomlinson and Barbara Habberjam (London: Athlone Press).

Deleuze, Gilles. 1998. *Gilles Deleuze: Essays Critical and Clinical*, trans. Daniel W. Smith and Michael A. Greco (London: Verso).

Deleuze, Gilles. 2000. *Cinema 2: The Time Image*, trans. Hugh Tomlinson and Barbara Habberjam (London: Athlone Press).

Deleuze, Gilles. 2004. 'Bergson's Conception of Difference', trans. Michael Taormina, *Desert Islands and Other Texts 1953–1974*, ed. David Lapoujade (Paris: Semiotext(e)).

Deleuze, Gilles and Guattari, Félix. 1992. *A Thousand Plateaux*, trans. Brian Massumi (London: Athlone).

Derrida, Jacques. 1976. *Of Grammatology*, trans. G. C. Spivak (Baltimore: Johns Hopkins Press).

Derrida, Jacques. 1978. *Writing and Difference* (Baltimore: Johns Hopkins Press).

Derrida, Jacques. 1981a. *Positions*, trans. A. Bass (Chicago: Chicago University Press).

Derrida, Jacques. 1981b. 'Plato's Pharmacy', in *Dissemination*, trans. B. Johnson (Chicago: Chicago University Press), pp. 61–172.

Derrida, Jacques. 1987. *The Postcard: From Socrates to Freud and Beyond*, trans. A. Bass (Chicago: Chicago University Press).

Derrida, Jacques. 1991a. 'Ulysses Gramaphone: Hear Say Yes in Joyce', in *Between the Blinds*, ed. P. Kamuf (Hemel Hempstead: Harvester), pp. 569–98.

Derrida, Jacques. 1991b. 'Eating Well', an interview with J.-L. Nancy in E. Cadava, P. Connor and J.-L. Nancy (eds), *Who Comes After the Subject* (London: Routledge), pp. 96–119.

Derrida, Jacques. 1991c. 'Letter to a Japanese Friend', in *Between the Blinds*, ed. P. Kamuf (Hemel Hempstead: Harvester), pp. 269–78.

Derrida, Jacques. 1992a. 'Passions: "An Oblique Offering"' in *Derrida: A Critical-Reader*, ed. D. Wood (Oxford: Blackwell), pp. 5–35.

Derrida, Jacques. 1992b. 'This Strange Institution Called Literature: An Interview with Jacques Derrida', in D. Attridge (ed.), *Acts of Literature* (London: Routledge), pp. 33–75.

Derrida, Jacques. 1992c. 'Afterw.ds: or, at Least, Less than a Letter About a Letter

Less', trans. Geoff Bennington, in N. Royle (ed.) *Afterwords* (Tampere, Finland: Outside Books), pp. 197–203.

Derrida, Jacques. 1993a. *Aporias*, trans. D. Dutoit (Standford: Standford University Press).

Derrida, Jacques. 1993b. 'Before the Law', in D. Attridge (ed.), *Acts of Literature* (London: Routledge), pp. 181–220.

Derrida, Jacques. 1994. *Spectres of Marx* (London: Routledge).

Derrida, Jacques. 1995. 'The Rhetoric of Drugs', trans. M. Israel in E. Weber (ed.), *Points: Interviews, 1974–1994* (Stanford, CA: Stanford University Press), pp. 228–54.

Derrida, Jacques. 1998. *Resistances of Psychoanalysis*, trans. P. Kamuf, P.-A. Brault and M. Naas (Stanford: Stanford University Press).

Derrida, Jacques. 1999. 'Hospitality, Justice, and Responsibility: Dialogue with Jacques Derrida', in Richard Kearney and Mark Dooley (eds), *Questioning Ethics: Contemporary Debates in Philosophy*, (London: Routledge), pp. 65–83.

Derrida, Jacques and LaBarrierès, Pierre-Jean. 1986. *Altérités* (Paris: Editions Osiris).

Foucault, Michel. 1965. *Madness and Civilisation: A History of Insanity in the Age of Reason*, abridged and trans. R. Howard (New York: Random House).

Foucault, Michel. 1970. *The Order of Things* (New York: Pantheon).

Foucault, Michel. 1977. *Language, Counter-memory, Practice* (Ithaca: Cornell University Press).

Foucault, Michel. 1979. 'My Body, This Paper, This Fire', trans. Geoff Bennington, *Oxford Literary Review*, 4:1, 9–28.

Foucault, Michel. 1985. *History of Sexuality Vol. II: The Uses of Pleasure* (New York: Random House).

Foucault, Michel. 1986. *History of Sexuality Vol. III: The Care of the Self* (New York: Random House).

Foucault, Michel. 1987. *Death and the Labyrinth: The World of Raymond Roussel*, trans. C. Ruas (London: Athlone Press).

Foucault, Michel and Blanchot, Maurice. 1987. *Foucault/Blanchot* (New York: Zone Books).

Frazer, J. G. 1971. *The Golden Bough* (London: Macmillan).

Freud, Sigmund. 1953. *My Views on the Part Played by Sexuality in the Neuroses* (1906), Standard Edition, vol. 7 (London: Hogarth), pp. 271–9.

Freud, Sigmund. 1961. *Civilisation and its Discontents* (1929), Standard Edition, vol. 21 (London: Hogarth), pp. 64–145.

Freud, Sigmund. 1963. *Introductory Lectures on Psychoanalysis* (1917), Standard Edition, vol. 7 (London: Hogarth), pp. 243–448.

Freud, Sigmund. 1966. *Project for a Scientific Psychology* (1895), Standard Edition, vol. 1 (London: Hogarth), pp. 295–387.

Freud, Sigmund. 1991. *The Interpretation of Dreams* (1900) (Harmondsworth: Penguin).

Gasché, Rodolphe. 1986. *The Tain of the Mirror* (Cambridge MA: Harvard University Press).

Gasché, Rodolphe. 1987. 'Infrastructures and Systematicity', in *Deconstruction and Philosophy*, ed. J. Sallis (Chicago: Chicago University Press), pp. 3–20.

Goodman, J., Lovejoy, P. E., and Sherratt, A. 1995. *Consuming Habits: Drugs in History and Anthropology* (London: Routledge).

Hall, Gary. 2002. *Culture in Bits* (London: Athlone).

Hall, Stuart and Jefferson, Tony (eds). 1976. *Resistance Through Rituals* (London: Hutchinson).

Hammond, Michael, Howarth, Jane and Keat, Russell. 1991. *Understanding Phenomenology* (Oxford: Blackwell).

Harvey, Irene. 1992. 'Derrida and the Issue of Exemplarity', in ed. D. Wood, *Derrida: A Critical Reader* (Oxford: Blackwell), pp. 193–217.

Hayter, Alethea. 1968. *Opium and the Romantic Imagination* (London: Faber and Faber).

Heidegger, Martin. 1973. *Being and Time*, trans. John Mcquarrie and Edward Robinson (Oxford: Blackwell).

Hebdige, Dick. 1979. *Subculture and the Meaning of Style* (London: Methuen).

Husserl, Edmund. 1962. *Ideas*, trans. W. R. Boyce Gibson (New York: Collier).

Jay, Mike (ed.). 1999. *Artificial Paradises* (Harmondsworth: Penguin).

Jay, Mike. 2000. *Emperors of Dreams: Drugs in the Nineteenth Century* (Cambridge: Dedalus).

Joel, Ernst and Frankel, Fritz. 1926. 'Der Haschisch-Rausch', *Klinische Wochenschrift* 5, 1707.

Jones, Ernest. 1953. *The Life and Work of Sigmund Freud Vol. 1* (New York: Basic Books).

Kearney, Richard. 1988. *The Wake of the Imagination* (London: Hutchinson).

Kennedy, Barbara. 2000. *Deleuze and Cinema: The Aesthetics of Sensation* (Edinburgh: Edinburgh University Press).

Kristeva, Julia. 1994. 'What Good are Psychoanalysts at a Time of Distress Oblivious to Itself?', in eds S. Shamdasani and M. Munchow, *Speculations after Freud: Psychoanalysis, Philosophy and Culture* (London: Routledge).

Leavis, F. R. 1930. *Mass Civilisation and Minority Culture* (Cambridge: Cambridge University Press).

Lenson, David. 1995. *On Drugs* (Minneapolis: University of Minnesota Press).

Lewin, Louis. 1964. *Phantastica, Narcotic and Stimulating Drugs* (London: Routledge).

McCole, John. 1993. *Walter Benjamin and the Antinomies of Tradition* (Ithaca: Cornell University Press).

McLuhan, Marshall. 2001. *Understanding Media: The Extensions of Man* (London: Routledge).

Masson, J. M. (ed. and trans.) 1985. *The Complete Letters of Sigmund Freud to Wilhelm Fliess, 1887–1904* (Cambridge, MA: Harvard University Press).

Mehlman, Jeffrey. 1993. *Walter Benjamin: An Essay on his Radio Years* (Chicago: Chicago University Press).

Merleau-Ponty, Maurice. 1965. *The Phenomenology of Perception*, trans. Colin Smith (London: Routledge).

Meszaros, Istvan. 1979. *The Work of Sartre: Volume 1, Search for Freedom* (Brighton: Harvester Press).

Michaux, H.1974. *The Major Ordeals of the Mind* (1966), trans. R. Howard (London: Secker and Warburg).

Miller, James. 1994. *The Passion of Michel Foucault* (London: Flamingo).

Nancy, J.-L. 1993. *The Birth to Presence* (Stanford: Stanford University Press).

Nietzsche, Friedrich. 1969. *Ecce Homo*, trans. Walter Kaufmann (New York: Vintage Books).

Nietzsche, Friedrich. 1974. *The Gay Science*, trans. Walter Kaufmann (New York: Vintage Books).

Nietzsche, Friedrich. 1983. 'On the Use and Disadvantages of History for Life', in *Untimely Meditations*, trans. R. J. Hollingdale (Cambridge: Cambridge University Press).

Plato. 1978. *Phaedrus*, trans. Walter Hamilton (Harmondsworth: Penguin).

Plant, Sadie. 1999. *Writing on Drugs* (London: Faber and Faber).

Pribam, K. H. and Gill, M. M. 1976. *Freud's Project Reassessed* (London: Hutchinson).

Rexroth, Tillmann. 1972. *Über Haschisch* (Frankfurt am Main: Suhrkamp Verlag).

Ronell, Avital. 1992. *Crack Wars* (Lincoln: University of Nebraska Press).

Royle, Nicholas. 2003. *Jacques Derrida* (London: Routledge).

Rudgley, Richard. 1993. *The Alchemy of Culture: Intoxicants in Society* (London: British Museum Press).

Rudgley, Richard. 1999. *An Anthology of Wildest Dreams: Drug Related Literature*, (London: Little, Brown and Co.)

Sartre, J.-P. 1957. *The Transcendence of the Ego*, trans. Forest Williams and Robert Kirkpatrick (NewYork: Noonday Press).

Sartre, J.-P. 1960. 'The Room', in *Intimacy*, trans. Lloyd Alexander (St Albans: Panther), pp. 75–109.

Sartre, J.-P. 1962. *Imagination: A Psychological Critique* (Ann Arbor: University of Michigan Press).

Sartre, J.-P. 1965. *Nausea*, trans. Robert Baldwick (Harmondsworth: Penguin).

Sartre, J.-P. 1970.'Intentionality:A Fundamental Idea in Husserl's Phenomenology', trans. J. P. Fell, *The Journal of the British Society for Phenomenology*, 1:2, 4–5.

Sartre, J.-P. 1972. The *Psychology of Imagination* (London: Methuen).

Sartre, J.-P. 1973. *Existentialism and Humanism*, trans. Philp Mairet (London: Methuen).

Schivelbusch, W. 1992. *Tastes of Paradise: A Social History of Spices, Stimulants and Intoxicants*, trans. David Jacobsen (New York: Pantheon).

Scholem, Gershom G. (ed.) 1992. *The Correspondence of Walter Benjamin and Gershom Scholem 1932–1940*, trans. Gary Smith, Andre Lefevere and Ansom Rabinbach (Cambridge, MA: Harvard University Press).

Stevenson, J. 2000 *Addicted: The Myth and Menace of Drugs in Film* (Creationbooks.com).

Strasbaugh, John and Blaise, Donald. 1990. *The Drug User Documents 1840–1960* (New York: Blast Books).

Szasz, Thomas. 1974. *Ceremonial Chemistry: The Ritual Persecution of Drugs, Addicts and Pushers* (New York: Anchor Press).

Thompson, Scott J. 1997. 'Hashish in Berlin: An Introduction to Walter Benjamin's Uncompleted Work on Hashish'. www.wbenjamin.org./benjamin.html.

Vice, S., Campbell, M. and Armstrong, T. (eds) 1994. *Beyond the Pleasure Dome: Writing and Addiction from the Romantics* (Sheffield: Sheffield Academic Press).

Von Scheidt, Jürgen. 1973. 'Sigmund Freud und das Kokain', *Psyche*, 27, 385–429.

Welsh, Irvine. 1993. *Trainspotting* (London: Secker & Warburg).

Welsh, Irvine. 1996. *Ecstasy* (London: Jonathan Cape).

Wettlaufer, Alexandra. 1996. 'Paradise Regained: The *Flâneur*, the *Badaud* and the Aesthetics of Artistic Reception in *Le Poème du haschisch*', *Nineteenth-Century French Studies* 24:3–4: 388–97.

Willis, Paul. 1978. *Profane Culture* (London: Routledge).

Wolin, Richard. 1982. *Walter Benjamin: An Aesthetics of Redemption* (New York: Columbia University Press).

Wood, David. 1990. *Philosophy at the Limit* (London: Unwin Hyman).

Wood, David (ed.). 1992. *Derrida: A Critical Reader* (Oxford: Blackwell).

Young, Jock. 1971. *The Drugtakers* (London: Palladin).

# Index